North Korea's Juche Myth

NORTH KOREA'S
JUCHE MYTH

B. R. MYERS

STHELE PRESS

North Korea's Juche Myth
© 2015 B. R. Myers
All rights reserved

Published by Sthele Press, Busan (ROK)
sthelepress@gmail.com
First Sthele Press printing: August 2015
Second Sthele Press Printing: October 2015

ISBN: 1508799938
ISBN 13: 9781508799931

For Myunghee

CONTENTS

	Acknowledgements	ix
	Introduction	1
Chapter 1	Speaking in Two Tongues: 1945-1955	23
Chapter 2	The Watershed that Wasn't: December 28, 1955	45
Chapter 3	On The Edge of Sloganhood: 1956-1962	63
Chapter 4	The Party's Subject Thought: 1962-1967	85
Chapter 5	Kim Il Sung's Subject Thought: 1967-1971	105
Chapter 6	The Great Charm Offensive: 1972	119
Chapter 7	"The Era of the Subject": 1973-1981	141
Chapter 8	A Father and Son Affair: 1982-1994	161
Chapter 9	The Myth in Decline: 1994-2011	185
Chapter 10	The Myth Under Kim Jong Un	211
	Conclusion	219
Appendix 1	On Eliminating Dogmatism and Formalism and Establishing the Subject in Ideological Work: Speech to Workers in Party Propaganda and Agitation, December 28, 1955	227
Appendix 2	"Subject Thought" (Encyclopedia Entry, "*chuch'e sasang*," 2001)	255
	References	261

Acknowledgements

An earlier version of the second chapter of this book appeared in *Acta Koreana* in 2006. A few other arguments in these pages were made in a second *Acta Koreana* article (2008) and in *Pacific Affairs* (2014).

I would like to thank Pär Cassel, Nick Frisch, Christopher Green, Ichiro Kawabe, Kim Young-hwan, Charles Kraus, Mary Nasr, James F. Person, Alfred Pfabigan, Balazs Szalontai, Fyodor Tertitskiy and Jacco Zwetsloot for answering inquiries or otherwise helping me in the course of my research. I am grateful to John Mclaughlin for reading through part of the manuscript. I would also like to thank Dongseo University for its support.

B.R. Myers, Busan, South Korea, August 2015

Introduction

WITH MINOR VARIATIONS from writer to writer, the Western version of North Korea's ideological history goes like this: In 1955, seven years into his rule, Kim Il Sung proclaimed the nationalist ideology that had been guiding him all along. Instead of mimicking the USSR, he said, Korea had to establish Juche — which is usually translated as self-reliance, but means much more than that. Although Kim did not mention Juche for the next few years, he formalized it in 1965 on a visit to Indonesia. In 1972 its central maxim, "man is the master of all things," was revealed to a delegation of Japanese journalists. But by that time Juche had already replaced Marxism-Leninism as North Korea's official ideology, intensifying the country's obsession with self-reliance. Unfortunately, this only made it more dependent on aid. While pragmatism is now on the rise in Pyongyang, ideologues inside the elite try to reassert their influence by provoking the outside world. A proper grasp of Juche therefore remains necessary if one is to understand the country's behavior. Alas, we foreigners cannot hope to get past its impenetrable, ever-receding name.

It's a tall tale indeed; one needs only an open mind to see the holes and implausibilities. Yet it continues to inform the assumption that in 1955 North Korea's goal changed from the unification of the peninsula to the establishment of Juche above the thirty-eighth parallel. We are therefore told not to take its bellicose rhetoric too seriously; the country really just wants the United States "to keep the South from swallowing it. Sooner or later an American president will come to understand this, the crisis will end, embassies will be exchanged," etc.[1] Whatever the North Koreans may understand by self-reliance, then, their commitment to it is in itself quite harmless. The problem lies in the counter-productive excitability with which they react to perceived encroachments on their quasi-religious mission. Nuclear armament, periodic attacks on South Korean troops, talk of a "holy war" of unification: such things are but the Juche state's way of asking for peace and respect.[2]

Although this foreign consensus served the dictatorship well for decades, the country has finally grown powerful enough to want to be feared — particularly by South Korea, which, rationally enough, it would rather bully into submission than have to fight. Now as in 1950, its goal, though no longer a short-term one, is unification on its own terms.[3] The world's underestimation of the regime's seriousness only results in more dramatic demonstrations of it. The Juche fallacy is therefore more than just a cautionary example of academic groupthink. It induces so gross a misunderstanding of this rising nuclear state as to be downright dangerous. In the following pages I will try to lay it to rest.

The state of research need not detain us long. Bruce Cumings, who is by my count the authority cited most often, has for decades asserted that "the closer one gets to [Juche's] meaning, the more it slips away."[4] Authors of ostensibly comprehensive tomes on the country get around the topic by claiming it has been researched enough already: "There have been many books written by political scientists about this bizarre ideology."[5] South Korean books, certainly; our own political scientists have yet to come up with one. The occasional scholar who promises to supply the deficiency can be counted on to deal with the DPRK's foreign policy instead, or some other presumed example of Juche in action. Journalists looking for answers about the doctrine *per se* end up with lists of ingredients: humanism, Christianity, Confucianism, even shamanism.[6]

If the convention is to stress Juche's ideological centrality while dodging explanation of the thing itself, I aim in this book to do the opposite, namely, to demonstrate its peripherality to North Korean ideology by tracing its history in detail and explaining its content as thoroughly as necessary. I do not deny that the Juche *myth* — the myth of a guiding ideology or philosophy conceived by Kim Il Sung — has done great service for the personality cult. My point is that the content of the thing in question has never played a significant role in policy-making or even domestic propaganda. It exists to be praised and not studied, let alone implemented.

The Juche myth's other main function has been to decoy the world's attention away from the *de facto* ideology of radical race-nationalism.[7] This is not the only state compelled by foreign-policy considerations to dissimulate its unifying obsessions; Saudi Arabia and Iran come to mind at once. More relevant to North Korea, however, are historical examples of secular *taqiyya*. Mussolini espoused his thuggish fascism to the Italian masses while presenting a more sophisticated, ethically-minded doctrine to intellectuals abroad, with no small success. Even Hannah Arendt took the "ideology for export," as Dante Germino called it, for the real one.[8] In comparable fashion the Nazi propaganda apparatus whipped up xenophobia and anti-Semitism on the home front while Hitler reassured Europe with his *Friedensreden*.[9] The pretense of being guided by something high-minded or abstruse may enhance a dictator's standing even with his own people, and inhibit them from judging the discrepancy between official intentions and performance. The key is that the "front-stage" message — to borrow a term from Cas Mudde's discussion of right-wing parties in pluralist societies — must never be espoused urgently enough to interfere with the "back-stage" one.[10]

It is harder than ever these days to keep a national mission secret, but invoking it only in the indigenous language while making cant available in English (and online, if possible) tends to keep the world's attention where one wants it. Being in on the game, the man on the street knows what to say around foreigners. Should the regime be called to account for its back-stage propaganda, it can always speak of errors down the line of command, or the need to address the masses in their own crude terms. Such excuses are accepted more readily than one might think. Whenever an exotic government or movement professes two contradictory ideologies at once, the urbane Westerner will assure himself that the more moderate one is operative.

Granted, the communist states of old were no models of transparency either. China's Red Guards used to rough up foreign visitors caught reading wall-poster criticisms of top officials.[11] But what they sought to hide was the disparity between ideology and reality, not the ideology itself. The Moscow Olympics of 1980 were meant to convey much the same message to everyone: the USSR was the only peace-loving superpower, its system the best for helping man fulfill his potential, and so on. The Berlin Olympics of 1936, in contrast, saw Germans unite in an elaborate effort to hide core Nazi values.[12]

Although North Korea is no Nazi Germany, it too is a far-right state, by which I mean one that derives support mainly from the public's perception of its strength, resolve, and commitment to enhancing the stature of the race. A communist state on the other hand, be it ever so nationalist or well-armed, asks to be judged by its performance on the socio-economic front. Political scientists who lump the DPRK in with Ceauşescu's Romania and Hoxha's Albania, perhaps under the clunky term "national Stalinist,"[13] are overlooking the very reason why only this regime — the one with the worst economic record of all — is still going strong. They also fail to understand how different nationalism in the literal and North Korean sense is from mere loyalty to a multi-ethnic state.[14] I am not wedded to the terms *far left* and *far right* for their own sake. We can say "square" and "round" for all I care, so long as we understand how different the two kinds of state are, and how differently they must therefore be dealt with. The one cannot yield on matters which to the other are only of secondary importance.

In 2004, when I wrote of North Korea in this vein in *The Atlantic*, liberal readers thought I just wanted to paint the regime in the worst possible colors. By printing my article, Chalmers Johnson wrote, the magazine had itself moved closer to fascism.[15] I suspect that what bothered these people most was the inference to be drawn from the piece, namely, that one cannot reason with a dictator whose legitimacy derives from a pose of implacable hostility to a race enemy. To grasp North Korea as

INTRODUCTION

a far-right state is to admit the futility of engagement, something many remain reluctant to do. Even the Stalinist label is thought preferable, despite its evocation of a far more murderous regime, because it holds out hope for a thaw.

The last ten years have confirmed my assessment, however, just as Kim Jong Il's successor has so far fulfilled the prediction I made at the end of *The Cleanest Race* (2009) — which was drowned out at the time by cheerier talk — that he would stay on the Military-First road, regardless of what happened in the economic sphere. Judged by the percentage of citizens in uniform, North Korea is now a more highly-militarized society than Italy and Nazi Germany were in the 1930s. The more its economy resembles the rival state's, the more it *must* show its superiority on far-right grounds. (Those who keep calling on the DPRK to take the "pragmatic" road to reform are yet to explain how a poor man's version of South Korea could hope to maintain public support.)[16] Already Kim Jong Un has had more belligerent and racist notes struck in exoteric propaganda than were heard during his father's rule. Take, for example, the description of President Obama recently published by the Korean Central News Agency: "That blackish mug, the vacant, ash-colored eyes, the gaping nostrils: the more I study all this, the more he appears the spitting image of a monkey in an African jungle."[17]

But much of this book deals with the Kim Il Sung era, when the regime tried to keep its worldview under wraps in order to maintain the communist camp's support and protection. The extremes of left and right being neighbors on a circular spectrum, dissimulation was not as hard as all that. The language barrier helped enormously. But Kim soon realized that if he was to succeed in marginalizing Seoul, his republic had to be seen as the better Korea by non-aligned countries too. Thus did the front-stage ideology change in the early 1970s from bloc-conform Marxism-Leninism into the people-first uplift of Juche, the relationship of which to communism had to be kept uninterpretable.[18]

A former South Korean dissident has dismissed Juche as being on the intellectual level of "if you raise a lot of chickens, you will get a lot of eggs."[19] I couldn't agree more, but I see no reason to dwell on its triteness. As Henry David Aiken summed up Lenin's insight, ideology is a form of thought "meant to focus, guide, and energize the minds of men in society. . . . [It] is the role, not the content, which determines whether a theory or doctrine is working ideologically."[20] Before I am accused of ignoring the compromises and dilutions every ideology must put up with, let me make clear that I have judged Juche by the loosest possible definitions of focusing, guiding and energizing minds. Even so, I have had to conclude that it was never *meant* to work ideologically.

Others figured this out long before I did. Communist states' refusal to criticize Juche — an attitude the former East German ambassador says he found "astonishing"[21]— suggests that they knew it was not being preached in earnest. In 1978, the West German Sinologist Helmut Martin stated that "Kim's writings are not invoked . . . as a means of legitimation," and that his "biography has the central function in the canon."[22] (*Voilà tout*.) In 1986, Alfred Pfabigan, an Austrian professor who studied the doctrine at the official Juche Institute, pointedly noted "the randomness of its formulae."[23] After defecting to South Korea, Hwang Jang Yop, who served for many years as Party Secretary for Juche, made clear that it was conceived to enhance the DPRK's reputation abroad.[24] The leader of South Korea's own Juche movement, Kim Young-hwan, finally met Kim Il Sung in 1991, only to find him ignorant of the doctrine and uninterested in discussing it. Now a critic of Pyongyang, the ex-dissident repeatedly asserts, "Juche and North Korean ideology are two different things."[25]

I have argued that last point on and off for the past ten years, to little avail.[26] One still comes across sentences such as: "There is no dispute that [Juche] has over the decades become the dominant leitmotiv that shapes the ways in which the North's political, social and economic activities are organized."[27] Judging from citations I read here and there, I have at least made headway against the myth that Kim Il Sung's speech to propagandists in 1955 marked a watershed in the republic's history. The unfortunate result is that Juche's emergence is often projected back to an even earlier time.

INTRODUCTION

I concentrate in this book on the West's Juche fallacy, because debunking the version current in the ROK (where I live) would entail emphasizing very different things. South Korean scholars at least know the relevant primary materials well enough to discuss Juche at length. Depending on their own politics, they either chew solemnly over assertions that man is the master of all things, born with creativity, and so on, or have a field day mocking their claim to profundity. Either way they regard the doctrine as the basis of North Korean life.[28]

In contrast, Western observers reduce Juche to an ideology of self-reliance before boiling it down further to Korean nationalism. It means "putting Korea first in everything," it is "a passionate and unrestrained *cri de coeur* against centuries of perceived incursion," and so on.[29] If this were a mere matter of applying the wrong name to a properly-understood nationalism, I would not complain. After all, average citizens of the DPRK have long used the term to denote the *de facto* ideology, not Juche doctrine, about which they know almost as little as our Pyongyang watchers do. A woman who had taught high school near the border to China once told my students in Busan how she had had to interrupt her mathematics classes for excursions into *chuch'e sasang*. I asked for specifics. "Well, I would praise Kim Il Sung, or condemn the Yankees' crimes." Thus is the name of the leader's doctrine applied to the ultra-nationalist personality cult that preceded it by a quarter of a century. The latter is so forceful and appealing an affair that truisms like "man is the master of all things" scarcely register beside it.

The problem is that foreigners insist on viewing North Korean nationalism through Juche's cosmetic haze.[30] Instead of realizing that the republic's mission has always been the unification of the race, they take its nationalism for an inward-directed kind. Here too we are dealing with that exasperating Western confusion of nationalism with loyalty to a state.[31] Yes, North Koreans are loyal to their state; but their nationalism — like their state's — entails a commitment to the entire peninsula, not just the part the Yankees pushed them back up on.

Last year a researcher asked me rather testily why I want to debunk something the field has tacitly abandoned. It is true that Juche is not referred to as often as it used to be, but isn't that because the conventional wisdom has become so familiar? The Kim Il Sung era is still looked back upon as a broadening of Juche from precedent to precedent.[32] The *New York Times* and other newspapers still refer to the country's "ideology of 'juche' — or self-reliance."[33] Even the current *Sŏn'gun* or Military-First doctrine is derived from Juche, and denatured accordingly.[34] That's not the worst part. Because today's North Korea is equally uninterested in communism and self-reliance, more and more observers, mistaking this for a new development, assume that ideology has dwindled down to a "residual" role in the country, which they call a "reactive" state.[35] According to two journalists' recent book, ideology "no longer matters" there.[36] The old Juche myth thus inspires a new misperception from which the regime can benefit.

The consensus that Juche is central to North Korean ideology (if not necessarily to the state as a whole) has always accommodated a range of varying opinions. Conservatives have demonized the doctrine as a cynical rationale for one-man rule. The softliners who dominate academia, on the other hand, tend to take even its claim to humanism seriously. Some people use the word Juche as a name for the personality cult.[37] Others apply it to the entirety of Kim Il Sung's discourse, or to all political discussion under his rule after 1955. A few imagine it as a written canon consulted before big decisions, but most talk in broader terms of an all-pervading commitment to self-reliance. That last word — which has no direct Korean equivalent[38]— is itself subjected to different interpretations. Some Pyongyang watchers think in terms of literal self-sufficiency.[39] Others thin it out to independence, autonomy, or a hankering after more respect; this allows them to concede the DPRK's chronic dependence on aid while still granting it points for self-reliance.

It is telling that these differences of opinion are not considered worth resolving. But whether or not the fallacy has become a matter of mere lip service, it must still be ruthlessly cleared away. Only then can we come

INTRODUCTION

to terms with the regime's true ideology, and the dangerous role it still plays.

Each chapter of this book refutes one or more elements of the overarching fallacy: that Kim began showing his feisty autarkic spirit during the 1940s, that he proclaimed a new ideology in 1955, which supplanted Marxism-Leninism in the 1960s, and so on. Why a chronological approach? Because this is a classic case, to borrow what Nietzsche said about another myth, of "the historical refutation as the final one."[40] Not for nothing are our traditionalists so desperate to date the advent of the Juche era back to 1955, when much of Pyongyang was still in ruins. Only then can the doctrine plausibly be said to have shaped the DPRK. Date it to 1967 or 1972, and there is no dodging the question of which ideology prevailed in the country's formative years, and what (if any) assignable changes Juche wrought thereafter. I will also analyze the main doctrinal texts, which contain much the sort of thing one would expect from something issued during a charm offensive. Later chapters will show how the Juche myth has influenced Western perceptions of North Korea's nuclear program, its economic woes and its attacks on the rival state, usually to the dictatorship's benefit.

In the course of this book I will make frequent reference to North Korea's multi-track discourse. There are more tracks and track-internal gradations than I need to deal with here. It is enough if the reader keeps in mind a distinction between a) the *inner track*, by which I mean propaganda intended for North Koreans only, b) the *outer track*, which is propaganda written for domestic consumption in the constraining awareness of outside monitors, and c) the *export track*, or propaganda for outsiders. This last, which includes statements made in negotiations, can in turn be divided into the kind aimed at South Koreans and the kind aimed at foreigners. The man on the street knows that the inner track is where the ideological action is. This is not to imply that he ignores or disbelieves the outer one. (The existence of an export track does not appear to be widely known.) We are not so different; we nod in approval when spokesmen for our in-groups tone down our views for out-group consumption. In any case, the North Korean gets more of an inner-track message from the outer track than most Pyongyang watchers do, because he knows how to read it in context.

He knows, for example, that the formal commitment to "peaceful unification" reflects the hope that the DPRK need not fight the South Korean *masses* again; the inner track acknowledges the likely need for a preliminary South Korean uprising, and vows revenge on the Yankee enemy no matter what. It also raises the possibility of a straightforward war of unification.[41]

Although I cannot assert the currency of a fallacy without citing examples, too exclusive a focus on the top spreaders of the Juche myth will make readers think I am carrying out a vendetta. On the other hand, if I give equal attention to researchers of economics, culture, etc, who have merely followed those authorities' lead, I will be accused of making things too easy for myself. I have therefore opted for a middle course, which will no doubt result in my being criticized on both counts. It should go without saying, however, that disagreeing with people about a certain point, even one as important as this, is not the same as dismissing their research as a whole. Of the many scholars I cite critically in this book, there are only a few from whom I have not learned much of value. I approach no one's work from a presumed position of infallibility, having made enough mistakes of my own — not least in regard to Juche, which I too used to take at its orthodox valuation. Like every book this one will have its errors. I am confident that they will not nullify my argument.

Before going on, I would like to discuss the keyword *juche* (주체), or *chuch'e* as it is written according to the McCune-Reischauer system. Standard Western practice is to repeat and at the same time disparage the translation of it as self-reliance, while hinting at a world of additional meaning one lacks the space to go into. *Chuch'e* is "often rendered as

INTRODUCTION

self-reliance, but such a translation is woefully inadequate"; it "is usually described in shorthand as self-reliance, but there is much more to it than that,"[42] and so on. It is also common for writers to dilate on the ancient meanings of the constituent characters 主 (main) and 體 (body), leaving readers to assume that the compound, "unique to Korea," sprang out of deep indigenous soil.[43] One scholar claims it "has been in use as long as the [Korean] language itself."[44] Others assert or imply that it was an obscure or archaic word until Kim Il Sung breathed new life into it; still others seem to regard it as his invention.[45]

In fact *chuch'e* comes from the Sino-Japanese compound *shutai* (主體), which first appeared in 1887 in a book entitled *The Basics of Philosophy* (*Tetsugaku yōryō*).[46] The author, Inoue Enryō, used the word to translate the German word *Subjekt*, i.e., the entity perceiving or acting upon an object or environment. By 1903 Chinese residents of Japan were using it in their own discussions of Kant, in which the relevant compound was pronounced *zhuti*.[47] The word found its way into Korean at about the same time. The nationalist-anarchist Sin Ch'ae-ho used it a few times in 1908 in a polemical text, under the apparent assumption that readers either knew it already or would grasp its meaning from the self-explanatory ideograms.[48] Such Japanese loanwords are very common in modern Korean and Chinese.[49]

J. Victor Koschmann has explained how the philosopher Nishida Kitarō employed the words *shukan* (主觀) and *shutai* in the early 1900s to distinguish between the passive and active senses of *Subjekt*. While the older word *shukan* "took on the connotations of contemplative consciousness . . . *shutai* referred to the ethical, practical subject theorized by Kierkegaard and Marx."[50] This distinction too was adopted by the Koreans.

The above may confuse speakers of Western languages. English and French complicate matters by using the word *subject / sujet* more often in the sense of an entity under another's control. The anti-monarchist slogan "Citizens, not subjects," which I saw recently on a pop star's guitar, shows how far from the average Anglophone's mind the other sense of the word is. We also refer to the *subject* of an article or sentence. Few of us, therefore, would immediately grasp the statement "The proletariat is the subject of history" to mean, "The proletariat is the central force of history."

Even philosophy majors would have a moment's trouble with "Progress in science demands a subjective attitude," so accustomed are we to use the adjective to mean "emanating from a person's prejudices or partiality." But if it is rendered into the right one of the two Korean words for *subjective* (namely *chuch'ejŏk* and not *chugwanjŏk*), any teenager on the street in Seoul will readily understand that we must take the initiative as the protagonists of scientific progress. In short, the ambiguity lies not in the Korean word, as so many outsiders seem to think, but in its English equivalent. (Andy Warhol: "My mind always drifts when I hear words like 'subjective'. . . . I never know what people are talking about.")[51]

The words *shutai* and *chuch'e* were used by bilingual Koreans throughout the colonial period in a variety of contexts. Those who read Marx in Japanese encountered the compound in a few of his works.[52] (Kim Jong Il or his ghostwriter acknowledged its appearances in "antecedent classics" of socialism.)[53] When Yŏ Un-hyŏng accepted the transfer of power from Japanese authorities in August 1945, it was under the condition that Korea "subjectively" (*chuch'ejŏgŭro*) manage its own security.[54] The following year he said publicly, "Because we are Koreans to the end, we are the masters of Korea and the subject [*chuch'e*] of Korean politics."[55]

INTRODUCTION

A former member of the Seoul-based Workers' Party has said that it used the word after liberation in a vain effort to assert indigenous communists' primacy over Koreans arriving from China and the USSR.[56] Early North Korean editions of Marx used the word too. All this being so, it was too current for Kim Il Sung's belated mentions of it in 1955 to make it his own, especially since he did not recur to it for years.

Until the mid-1960s use of the word *chuch'e* and its cognates *chuch'ejŏk* (subjective) and *chuch'esŏng* (subjectivity) was more of a South Korean thing. Cho Pong-am ran for president in 1956 on a platform advocating development of the country's "subjective capabilities."[57] Calls for "national subjectivity" were common among intellectuals during the turbulent term

of the premier Chang Myŏn (1960-1961).[58] Park Chung Hee spoke of *chuch'esŏng* more often in his first three years in power (1961-1964) than Kim Il Sung had done in his first fifteen.[59] If the West failed to notice, it was because Park's translators put his words into plain English: "We must grasp the subjectivity of the Korean nation."[60] When he created a rubber-stamp electoral college in 1972, he called it *T'ongil chuch'e kungmin hoeŭi*, which literally means Unification Subject Citizens' Assembly. The word *chuch'e* thus made it into the South Korean constitution first. It featured during the memorial service for Park in 1979, when a taped excerpt from one of his speeches boomed out from loudspeakers: "The spirit of autonomy means the awareness that we are the masters of this country and the subject [*chuch'e*] that creates history."[61]

The word's popularity in the DPRK has never been held against it by the South Korean right. During the ROK presidential campaign in 2012, both candidates referred to the country's "main economic actors" or *kyŏngje chuch'e*. All this is in contrast to foreigners' assumption that if North Korea did not create the word, it effectively took it over.⁶²

Not wanting us to trust our instincts when reading its propaganda, the regime in Pyongyang has left the word *chuch'e* untranslated in foreign-language texts: from 1961-1964 as Jooche, then as Juche.⁶³ In this way the reader is given an impression of Kim-trademarked abstruseness quite unlike the impression Koreans get. Western scholars and translators should stop following that practice when rendering North Korean texts into English. It is also high time that the pan-Korean word *chuch'esŏng* were translated as "subjectivity" or "agency" instead of "Juche-ness."⁶⁴ To avoid confusion, I make sure in the rest of this book to use the English words *subject, subjective* and *subjectivity* only in the sense corresponding to *chuch'e, chuch'ejŏk* and *chuch'esŏng*.

Let us turn now to *sasang* (思想), the word with which *chuch'e* is so often linked in the DPRK. Of the two this poses more difficulty for the translator, because it can refer either to an idea or a body of thought. Official use of the phrase *chuch'e sasang* or "subject(ive) thought" in the 1960s shows that it was understood much as the Chinese understood *Mao Zedong sixiang*, i.e., to mean guidelines for the country-specific application of Marxism-Leninism.⁶⁵ It made no claim to being a stand-alone ideology. The Workers' Party treated it as its collective product until Kim's purge of top officials in 1967. From then on, *chuch'e sasang* was touted as his personal conception. In English-language propaganda it was referred to, with uncharacteristic modesty, as "the Juche idea," so that foreigners could praise it without appearing to betray their own creeds.

Not being bound by official conventions, I can translate *chuch'e sasang* as I like. Unfortunately no English equivalent fits the bill entirely. I have decided to translate its use inside quotes and excerpts as "Subject Thought" — "subject(ive) thought" in texts written before its exclusive attribution to Kim — so as to convey the un-exotic and dry feel the words convey to native speakers. I reluctantly use the realia *chuch'e sasang* in order to distinguish the prop in the domestic personality cult from the

INTRODUCTION

"Juche idea" exported for public-diplomatic purposes. Instead of talking of a pseudo-ideology or pseudo-anything I will be referring to a doctrine, this word being applicable to any body of teaching, regardless of its content, scope, function, originality or sincerity.

I use the McCune-Reischauer system of transliteration with the customary exception of Korean words and names (Kim Il Sung, Pyongyang) better known under other spellings. Unfortunately there are various ways to write the one I use the most often: namely *juche* and, in more academic texts, *chuch'e*, each one appearing with and without a capital letter, in plain and italic script. Inexplicably, *juch'e* and *Juché* have also been introduced. I trust I can replicate various spellings in quotations of secondary literature without confusing the reader.

List of Abbreviations

CC	Central Committee
CCP	Chinese Communist Party
CPSU	Communist Party of the Soviet Union
DA/WWC	Digital Archive, Woodrow Wilson Center
DMZ	Demilitarized Zone
DPRK	Democratic People's Republic of Korea
KCNA	Korean Central News Agency
KPA	Korean People's Army
MIA	Marxists Internet Archive
NAM	Non-Aligned Movement
ROK	Republic of Korea
WP	(Korean) Workers' Party

1. Bruce Cumings, *North Korea: Another Country* (New York, 2004), x. Although rarely expressed quite so guilelessly, this is a common view.
2. The only worry? North Korea might sell atomic material to a less harmless country: "The danger is not that they're going to attack us or our allies, but that they're going to sell enriched uranium to bad actors." Bill Richardson, "Obama Administration Policy on North Korea Is Not Working," *TIME*, 8 May 2015. Note the absence of the word "again" after "allies"; the events of 2010 are already ancient history.
3. It is an ambitious goal, but still more modest than the one so often attributed to this mountainous yet populous state. Most observers reason that the commitment to unification must have been abandoned, because war would mean the end of the regime, which isn't suicidal, etc. But there is more than one way to unify a peninsula, as Kim Il Sung recognized. (See Appendix 1.) An invasion-inviting South Korean uprising of the kind he tried so long to bring about now appears unlikely ever to happen. That still leaves the strategy of intimidating the ROK into ever-greater sacrifices of dignity, autonomy and territorial integrity. The question is not whether it is viable, but whether the regime thinks it is.
4. "Corporatism in North Korea," *The Journal of Korean Studies* 4 (1982-1983), 289. Renewals of the assertion can be found in *Origins of the Korean War* 2 (Princeton, 1990), 313; "The Corporate State in North Korea," in *State and Society in Contemporary Korea*, ed. Hagen Koo (Ithaca, 1994), 214; *North Korea: Another Country*, 159 and *Korea's Place in the Sun* (updated edition, New York, 2005), 414.
5. Victor Cha, *The Impossible State* (New York, 2012), 39.
6. See for example Philip Gourevitch, "Letter from North Korea," *The New Yorker*, 8 September 2003.
7. My last book, *The Cleanest Race* (New York, 2009), is devoted to the myths that make up this nationalism.
8. "Der italienische Faschismus in vergleichender Perspektive," *Theorien über den Faschismus*, ed. Ernst Nolte (Cologne, 1973), 436.

9. Relevant in this context are also Hitler's efforts to persuade Arabs that Nazism had nothing against the Semitic race, but merely against the Jewish "character." Thomas J. Kehoe, "Fighting for our mutual benefit," *Journal of Genocide Research*, Vol. 14 (June 2012), 146-147.
10. *The Ideology of the Extreme Right* (Manchester, 2003), 20-21.
11. See Harold C. Hinton, *An Introduction to Chinese Politics* (New York, 1973), 232.
12. David Clay Large, *Nazi Games* (New York, 2007), 179-189.
13. Cheng Chen and Ji-Yong Lee, "Making sense of North Korea: 'National Stalinism' in comparative-historical perspective," *Communist and Post-Communist Studies*, Vol. 40 (2007), 459-475. Stalinism condoned nationalism everywhere so long as it stopped short of racial supremacism or "zoological nationalism." It was also supportive of economic autarky. The term *national Stalinism* is therefore either a tautology or an oxymoron, depending on how the first word is meant.
14. For a discussion of the difference between the two: Walker Connor, *Ethnonationalism* (Princeton, 1994), 41.
15. "Letters to the Editor," *The Atlantic*, 1 November 2004.
16. Stephan Haggard and Marcus Noland put the problem in a nutshell: "If North Korea embraces the path toward a market economy that would ultimately resemble the South, why have a separate regime at all?" See "Book Review Roundtable," *Asia Policy* 5 (2008), 217.
17. "Sesang e hana pakk e ŏmnŭn pullyanga Obama ege ch'ŏnbŏl ŭl," KCNA, 5 May 2014.
18. I borrow this adjective from Enoch Powell, who said this was how the relationship between India and the rest of the Commonwealth was formulated to be. Quoted in Simon Heffer, *Like the Roman* (London, 1998), 184.
19. Ryu Kŭn-il, Hong Chin-p'yo, *Chisŏng kwa pan chisŏng*, 219. The words are Ryu's.
20. Bell, Aiken, "Ideology – A Debate," in *The End of Ideology Debate*, ed. Chaim I. Waxman (New York, 1968), 273.

21. Maretzki, *Kim-ismus in Nordkorea* (Böblingen, 1991), 69.
22. Martin, *Cult and Canon* (Armonk, NY, 1982), 157-158. German edition 1978.
23. Pfabigan, *Schlaflos in Pjöngjang* (Vienna, 1986), 247.
24. Hwang, *Pukhan ŭi chinsil kwa hŏwi* (Seoul, 1998), 69; *Hoegorok* (Seoul, 2006), 215-216, 227.
25. Kim Yŏng-hwan (Kim Young-hwan), *Sidae chŏngsin ŭl mal hada* (Seoul, 2012), 157. See also "Na rŭl 'paesinja' kŭgu kkolt'ong ŭro pogido hajiman," *Chosŏn Ilbo*, 21 July 2014.
26. Myers, "Mother of all Mothers," *The Atlantic*, September 2004. I could go into a long explanation of the difficulty of challenging an academic orthodoxy, but the relevant pages on primatologists in Shirley C. Strum's *Almost Human* (New York, 1990, 158-163) are hard to improve upon. I thank the friend who sent me the book.
27. Jae-Jung Suh, "Making Sense of North Korea," in *Origins of North Korea's Juche* (Plymouth, UK, 2013), 8. The evasive word *leitmotiv* is not uncommon in this context. See also Cumings, *North Korea*, 119.
28. Song Tu-yul takes the myth at face value in "Chuch'e sasang e issŏsŏ hyŏngmyŏng kwa yŏksa," in *Pukhan ŭi chŏngch'i i'nyŏm chuch'e sasang* (Seoul, 1990), 239-265. A harshly critical treatment is Sin Il-ch'ŏl, *Pukhan 'chuch'e ch'ŏrhak' ŭi pip'anj'ŏk punsŏk* (Seoul, 1987).
29. Bruce Cumings, "North Korea's Dynastic Succession," *Le Monde diplomatique*, 7 February 2012; Carter Eckert, *Korea Old and New* (Seoul, 1991) 145.
30. Naturally they prefer to think in terms of a sharpening "Lens of Juche," to quote the title of an article by Allan Kang in *Review of International Affairs*, Vol. 3, Issue 1 (Autumn 2003), 41-63.
31. Connor, *Ethnonationalism*, 41.
32. Charles Armstrong's *Tyranny of the Weak* (Ithaca, 2013), the most Juche-centric history of the DPRK to appear in years, received good reviews and a book prize; no one can now claim it represents an obsolete school of thought. I have therefore drawn especially often from it for examples of the orthodoxy.
33. Choe Sang-hun, "North Korea Plans to Indict Two Americans," *New York Times*, 29 June 2014. See also the reference to the "North's hardline ideology

of self-reliance," in "No sign of Kim Jong Un as North Korea welcomes home Asian Games athletes," *The Guardian*, 6 October 2014.
34. Armstrong, "The Role and Influence of Ideology," 12.
35. Patrick McEachern, *Inside the Red Box* (New York, 2010), 228, 233. See also "North Korea's Foreign Policy is Reactive, Lacks Strategy" (Interview with Gordon Flake), *NK News*, 26 November 2013. Jim Maceda quotes John Delury to that same effect in "North Korea blinked in missile standoff, but will threaten again," *NBC News*, 23 April 2013.
36. Daniel Tudor, James Pearson, *North Korea Confidential* (Tokyo, 2015), 45.
37. See for example Thomas J. Belke, *Juche: A Christian Study of North Korea's Religion* (Bartlesville, OK, 1999), 4.
38. In South Korea the title of Emerson's famous essay is rendered into more sociable-sounding words like *chasin'gam* (confidence), *chagi sirwoe* (self-trust), *chagi sinnyŏm* (believing in oneself), etc. The term *charyŏk kaengsaeng*, literally "revitalization through one's own strength," does not connote, as our *self-reliance* does, the principled eschewal of outside help. The Korean for literal self-sufficiency, *chagŭp chajok*, never became the object of *bona fide* sloganization.
39. Andrew S. Natsios, *The Great North Korean Famine* (Washington, DC, 2001), 6.
40. *Morgenröte* (Cologne, 2011), 81.
41. Pak Yun's propaganda novel *Mount Osŏng*, which is set around the turn of the millennium, contains a cameo by a youthful Kim Jong Un. Vice Marshal Jo Myong Rok smilingly remarks, "In the future, he is going to lead the holy war of homeland unification." (*Osŏngsan*, Pyongyang, 2012, 400-401.) The real-life Jo visited the White House in 2000. In military-internal propaganda, unification by force is described as a necessity, and in October 2013 South Korean intelligence reported that Kim Jong Un had promised a military audience that unification would be achieved within three years. See Lee Jong-heon, "North Korea's Kim predicting unification by force within 3 years," *World Tribune*, 24 October 2013. See also Yi Sŏk-chong, "Pukhan'gun ŭi chŏnjaenggwan kwa t'ongilgwan," *Pukhan*, July 2015, 121-125. The importance of this propaganda should not be overestimated, but to go on ignoring it, as the Western world does, would be more foolish.

42. Eckert, *Korea: Old and New*, 145; and Oberdorfer, *The Two Koreas*, 16.
43. See for example Kenneth Quinones, "Juche's Role in North Korea's Foreign Policy," International Symposium on Communism in Asia, 7 June 2008; Eckert, *Korea: Old and New*, 145. The "unique to Korea" bit is from Armstrong, *The Koreas* (New York, 2007), 40.
44. Han S. Park, *North Korea: The Politics of Unconventional Wisdom* (Boulder, CO, 2002), 17.
45. Andrei Lankov refers to Kim as having "coined" the word "in the later North Korean sense." *Crisis in North Korea*, 5. Hwang Jang Yop gave readers to understand that it did not exist before the DPRK's founding. *Ŏdum ŭi p'yŏn i toen haetbyŏt' ŭn ŏdum ŭl palkhil su ŏpta* (Seoul, 2001), 34. Cumings writes that Kim Il Sung "took the ch'e character [from chŏngch'e, or "correct basis"] into his Juche doctrine, and the chŏng character into his eldest son's name." *Korea's Place in the Sun* (New York, 2005), 52. In other texts, however, he seems aware that it was not Kim's creation.
46. From Michael Burtscher's "Facing 'the West' on Philosophical Grounds: A View from the Pavilion of Subjectivity on Meiji Japan," *Comparative Studies of South Asia, Africa and the Middle East*, 2006, as cited in Toshiaki Kobayashi, *'Shutai' no yukue* (Tokyo, 2010), 66.
47. Ibid. Yet the word *zhuti* does not seem to have become all that popular. Mao, like most of his propagandists, used the word *zhuguan* even when conveying the sense of an active subject. For one of his few references to *zhuti* see *Mao Zedong zhe xue pi zhu ji* (Beijing, 1988), 17. I thank Charles Kraus for finding this for me.
48. The Juche myth has so colored Western researchers' understanding of the word that they read it even in colonial contexts as a nationalist, DPRK-prefiguring concept in its own right. See for example, Michael Robinson, "National Identity and the Thought of Sin Ch'aeho," *The Journal of Korean Studies* 5 (1984), 123-124.
49. Wong Siu-lun says it has been estimated that half the loanwords in Chinese are of Japanese origin. *Sociology and Socialism in Contemporary China* (Abingdon, UK, 2005), 5.
50. *Revolution and Subjectivity in Postwar Japan* (Chicago, 1996), 2.

INTRODUCTION

51. *The Philosophy of Andy Warhol: From A to B and Back Again* (New York, 1977), 184.
52. Kobayashi notes that *shutai* was used in 1930 in two separate translations of Marx's work. *'Shutai' no yukue*, 96-97.
53. Kim Jong Il, "Chuch'e sasang ŭn illyu ŭi chinbojŏk sasang ŭl kyesŭng hago paltchŏn sik'in sasangida," *Kim Chŏng-il sŏnjip* 8 (Pyongyang, 1998), 439.
54. I initially assumed that the point must have been made in Japanese, but Professor Jung Byung Joon, an expert on the man's life, informs me that although Yŏ was fluent in Japanese, he issued his conditions in Korean.
55. From an article in *Chosŏn Inminbo*, 6 April 1946, quoted in Yang Tong-an, "Minjokchuŭi – pan'gong seryŏk i Taehanmin'guk ŭl kŏnsŏl hetta" in *Taehan min'guk ŭi 3 dae nonjaeng* (Seoul, 2005), 24.
56. Pak Kap-dong, cited in Kim Yŏn-gak, "Chuch'e sasang," in *Kim Chŏng-il sidae ŭi Pukhan* (Seoul, 1997), 194-195.
57. "Cho Pong-am ŭi chinbodang sŏn'ŏnmun (1956)."
58. A prominent user of the word in the early 1960s was Pak Chong-hong, a philosophy professor at Seoul National University. See Kim Hyung-A, "The Eve of Park's Military Rule," *East Asian History*, Number 25/26 (June/December 2003), 121.
59. See Pak Chŏng-hŭi (Park Chung Hee), *Chungdan hanŭn cha nŭn sŭngni haji mot handa* (Seoul, 1968), an anthology of speeches, especially 19, 70, 85, 166, 168, 269.
60. Park Chung Hee, *Our Nation's Path* (Seoul, 1970), 119.
61. Cho Kap-che, *Pak Chŏnghŭi ŭi kyŏljŏngjŏk sun'gandŭl* (Seoul, 2009), 799.
62. It is also assumed that "autonomy" (*chaju*) was another distinctly North Korean concern, although Park spoke more often of that too. The agreement to pursue an "autonomous" drive to unification that was reached in the 1972 North-South Communique has thus been described as a show of South Korean respect for the North's principles. (Quinones, "Juche's Role in North Korea's Foreign Policy," 4-5.) In fact, the DPRK's representative at the talks praised the ROK leadership for promoting mistrust of "powerful states."
63. *Chosŏn rodongdang che 4 ch'a taehoe chuyo munhŏnjip* (Pyongyang, 1961), 103. It gives the Japanese their word back to them in *katakana* script, to

comparable exotic effect. Many Japanese, in my experience, refer to it as *shutai shisō* anyway.
64. Armstrong writes of "Juche-ness" in *Tyranny of the Weak*, 110.
65. Franz Schurmann, *Ideology and Organization in Communist China* (Berkeley, 1971), 58-68.

1

Speaking in Two Tongues: 1945-1955

From the start Pyongyang watchers have sought out the middle ground between American or South Korean propaganda on the one hand, and the North Korean kind on the other. Unfortunately this well-intentioned centrism has tended to incline them toward the side with fewer compunctions about lying outright. In the 1960s and 1970s, North Korea's improbable economic statistics were interpreted as an indication that at least a highly respectable growth was being achieved. The rise of tendentious or "revisionist" scholarship in the 1980s brought with it assaults on parts of the conventional wisdom deemed still too hard on the DPRK. Bruce Cumings wrote a much-praised book in which he challenged the assumption that Kim Il Sung had, with Soviet backing, planned and initiated the Korean War.[1] The book has survived the refutation of its main thrust remarkably well; its interstitial paragraphs on North Korea remain a much-cited source. Sympathy for the regime has declined since its highpoint during the North-South summit of 2000, but this trend has been offset in recent years by an increase in visa-minded self-censorship. The more a scholar's work requires research *in situ*, the more diplomatic he or she is likely to be.

Whether sincere or affected, the apologism usually reflects (as befits its object) Korean-nationalist and not left-wing values. Nothing is downplayed more vigorously than the Japanese influence on North Korea. Most of the country's distinguishing characteristics, like its resilience, and even the undistinguishing ones, like its attention to hierarchy, tend to be derived from Confucianism instead. Scholars tracing the DPRK's cultural roots usually limit themselves to Korean-penned contributions to that ancient tradition, while zeroing in on the progressive-seeming strains inside *them*, as opposed to seeing Korean Confucianism in the greater Sinophone context in which it saw itself. And so one finds, say, a direct line drawn from the DPRK's constitution back to Chosŏn Dynasty scholars.[2]

Why the ethos of the doomed *yangban* class should have provided just the prole-pleasing, longevity-ensuring element that Korean communism needed is a question no one deigns to answer. Nor does anyone explain how the Japanese- and Soviet-educated men who founded the DPRK became so steeped in pre-colonial thought. Of few nations can it be said with more truth that the past is a foreign country. In contrast to ancestor worship and respect for the elderly, the peninsula's intellectual heritage was not something young people in the 1920s and 1930s could just pick up around the house. The relevant texts, most of which were in classical Chinese, had to be studied or at least read, an activity which the young were no more inclined to pursue in that forward-looking age than they are today. The average Korean alive in 1945 was to a far greater degree the product of Japanese rule than of the Chosŏn Dynasty, which is not to deny the latter's influence altogether.

A line of apologetics more to Pyongyang's own liking runs through Western discussion of Kim Il Sung's younger years. His mindset in the 1930s, of which there is no record, is reconstructed in the spirit of the personality cult. We are told he was "obsessed with national independence and distrusted superpowers."[3] This of an able-bodied young man who then spent almost five years in the neutral USSR, while Japan tightened the screws on his homeland. We are to imagine him as having somehow remained a guerrilla during that time.[4] Another assault on common sense and the English language is the now standard claim that he went on to lead a revolution under Soviet military rule.⁵

There would be no need for a book like this one if the puffery did not extend to his intellectual attainments. Stylistic evidence that many of his speeches were not penned by a colonially-bred Korean was enough for the field to conclude that Kim wrote them himself.⁶ Some scholars even treat as authentic the talks he purportedly gave in the 1930s, none of which was "discovered" until his old age.⁷ His so-called memoirs, thick instalments of which continued appearing years after his death, are regarded with a sort of willed gullibility as his own work — even as the definitive word on problems that have long puzzled historians.⁸ As for the fable of his teenage conception of Juche Thought, it is told in such tones as to suggest that after all this time we might as well accept it. Some American scholars outdo the personality cult itself: "Kim Il Sung, as the 'creator' of *Juche*, used the concept extensively from the mid-1920s."⁹ He was about thirteen at the time in question.

The first step towards rolling back the Juche fallacy, therefore, is to state that Kim engaged in no known writing or speech-making before October 14, 1945, when he spoke at a Soviet-organized rally in Pyongyang.¹⁰ Whether Russian sources are right about his having been "utterly ignorant" of Marxism-Leninism at the time, he was so lacking in political sense as to think that wearing a Soviet medal would recommend him to the locals.¹¹ However ruthlessly he may have later consolidated his power, his role in rising to it was passive. Having been installed as head of the North Korean Provisional People's Committee in February 1946, he frequently expressed the wish to return to military life. A Red Army veteran who knew him recalled, "He was very frustrated and told me: "I want

[to command] a regiment and then — a division. What is this for? I don't understand anything and don't want to do this."[12]

Kim showed little interest in ideological discussion even after the DPRK's founding in 1948. Most of his speeches, as we now know from various sources, were written for him by officials who had either grown up in the USSR or spent years in China.[13] Hagiographers preferred not to dwell on his intellect. Instead he was presented as a jovial, spontaneous warrior whose best ideas came to him while fishing or asleep.[14] The reputation he now enjoys among Western scholars, some of whom talk of the regime as having propagated "Kimism" from the start,[15] would have puzzled most top officials well into the 1960s.[16] Kim himself later stated that for the first eight years of his rule he did not lead ideological discussion.[17]

The tendency to misperceive him as a kind of Korean Mao appears to derive from the assumption that a nation broken by colonial rule could not have found its way to nationalism without a leader's guidance. In fact it was the Japanese who first taught urban Koreans to see the world in racial terms. (The very word for "nation" came from Japan.)[18] They were encouraged to pride themselves on their Koreanness, so long as they grasped themselves as part of the Japanese race.[19] Norman Jacobs has made the crucial but overlooked point that for average people, this was "the first time any authority had ever tried to involve them . . . in politically generated social action."[20] It was also a time when material conditions improved greatly for all classes except the *yangban* or Confucian literati.[21] Most city-dwellers had little difficulty reconciling pride in Korea with support for a world-conquering Japan. (To understand such an attitude, it may be helpful to consider those equally proud of being Scottish and British.) None of this is to deny the cruel injustices perpetrated by the colonial administration in these years. But John Lie's description of educated Koreans in Tokyo and Osaka also fits their counterparts back home: "Japanization was very much the rule. . . . To stress their 'lack of assimilation' . . . is anachronistic, a decidedly postwar, postcolonial misrecognition."[22] As a former leftist dissident in South Korea has put it, "Those who didn't experience the colonial period as adults get much more worked up about it than those who did."[23]

SPEAKING IN TWO TONGUES: 1945-1955

Hirohito's surrender speech of August 15, 1945 occasioned little of the immediate jubilation one reads about in history books published on and outside the peninsula.[24] The consternation with which the Korean working class greeted the news was noted at the time.[25] The defeat of the Axis did not end admiration for Hitler, or the feeling that although Japanese were not Koreans, they were not quite *oegugin* (foreigners) either.[26] But ethnic pride could finally be expressed in race-national terms. It was already on the rise when Kim Il Sung turned up on the peninsula in mid-September 1945, a full month after liberation.[27]

During the 1930s, communists in Japan and Korea had converted to fascism with special alacrity. As the historian Saburo Ienaga has written,

> [Marxism] had much in common with the ideology of the emperor system, a rote submission to authority. In one sense Marxism was simply the reverse coin of a *banzai*-shouting, emperor-worshipping statism. That partially explains why those committed communists reversed themselves so much more quickly and totally than moderate dissidents.[28]

Should we be surprised that after Japan's defeat the attraction worked in the opposite direction, drawing many of Korea's former *banzai*-shouters to what passed itself off as communism? Some stayed south of the thirty-eighth parallel, Park Chung Hee being only the most famous example. But the North, with its personality cult, its passion for regimentation and industrialization, and its hostility to the West, evinced a more obvious continuity with the fascist order.[29] Contrary to a common myth, it was *more* hospitable to former intellectual collaborators than the South. Kim Il Sung condemned only Koreans who had served in the police or played a leading role in government or business. In this way he absolved his own brother, who had assisted Japanese troops in Manchuria.[30] Such plum posts were given to veterans of the emperor's propaganda machine that one can only conclude their experience worked in their favor.[31]

In short, the DPRK was far from the romantic "guerrilla state" of academic legend.³² Few of Kim's former comrades-in-arms were literate enough to be of use outside the military.³³ Whether for this reason or due to pressure from Moscow, many top posts (including ministerial ones) were filled with Soviet Koreans, who retained their foreign citizenship. These Marxist-Leninists managed the showcase culture — the party organ, monthly journals, etc — while colonially-bred intellectuals prevailed in propaganda aimed at the bulk of citizens still learning to read.³⁴ As a result two different if not yet obviously incompatible worldviews were preached: a bloc-conform communism in the one track and a Japanese-influenced race-nationalism in the other.

The former appears to have set the tone at first.³⁵ Even the personality cult existed in a separate Marxist-Leninist version for a few years.

(One prize-winning epic poem portrayed Kim as an avid reader of Soviet history.)³⁶ By 1950, however, the dominant cult was the inner-track one that glorified Kim, as Hirohito had been glorified, as the embodiment of racial virtues. Naturally our scholars prefer to derive the cult from indigenous tradition instead: "this is how Korean kings also instituted their rule," etc.³⁷ In fact, most people living under the Chosŏn Dynasty did not know who their king was. What Pär Cassel has written of old China goes for old Korea too: "Only civil and military officials were expected to be loyal to the [monarch] and render active service to the state . . . 'patriotism' was the realm of officialdom."³⁸ In any case the symbolism of the Kim cult is itself un-Confucian, as I pointed out in my last book.³⁹ The only monarchy of which it would have reminded North Koreans was the Japanese one.

The fascist-bred propagandists may not have known the Soviet orthodoxy well enough to realize they were violating it. Like those northern-German Nazis who admired Lenin in the 1920s, they appear to have regarded their own worldview as the natural adaptation of a multi-ethnic state's communism to mono-ethnic conditions.[40] The literary scene was startled by Soviet objections to an ethnocentric story about how a saintly local boy redeems a drunken Red Army brawler.[41]

Yet the USSR was all in favor of populist, culturally-oriented nationalism in its new dependencies, so long as it was channeled in support of the international cause. Why else would Moscow have given the North Koreans a leader who had *only* anti-Japanese credentials to his name? Ruling parties throughout the communist camp were told to deny all intention of imposing Soviet models. Klement Gottwald promised a march to socialism on the "Czechoslovak road."[42] In Budapest it was pledged that Marxism-Leninism would be applied "according to Hungarian conditions."[43] The regime in East Berlin appealed to "patriotic Germans," spoke of how the "German *Volk* must go its own way," called for independence and "self-help," and so on.[44] All this was naturally balanced out with praise for the USSR and declarations of fraternity with its people. Only in this way was it possible to forge broad coalitions supportive of the new dispensation.

It is time Kim's outer-track references to Korean independence were read in this context. The following is from October 18, 1945:

> We who were liberated by Soviet military power must do all we can to strengthen our friendship with the USSR. The Red Army not only liberated us with its blood, but it now resides in our country in order to help our struggle to build a democratic, autonomous and independent state. Let us not make too much work for these righteous friends, but instead strengthen our unity and erect a new government as fast as possible by our own efforts.[45]

For comparison's sake, let us remember that below the thirty-eighth parallel, Syngman Rhee was then making statements like this: "Be it the

USSR or the United States, if [a country] obstructs our country's autonomy and independence, we too will have no choice but to fight against it."[46]

The Juche myth has long induced Western scholars to interpret Kim's first references to an independent economy as early evidence of his commitment to self-reliance.[47] (The fact that he was then trying to secure massive foreign support for an invasion of the South is thought beside the point.) But Stalin himself had encouraged the states in the Soviet sphere of influence to develop autarkic economies. As Erik Van Ree has written, "'socialism in one country' turned from a necessity into an ideal of self-reliant economic development."[48] This went also for signatories to the Comecon (1949), North Korea's refusal to join which has always been made so much of.

Just as bloc-conform were Kim's calls for his countrymen to "inherit our magnificent cultural heritage."[49] Lenin himself had called for proper inheritance of tradition, and the socialist realist aesthetic stressed *narodnost'* (roughly translatable as "folksiness") as a means of making propaganda more accessible.[50] In any case, Kim's uninformed nods at tradition were outnumbered by his fawning references to "advanced" foreign cultures. Even during the war, writers and artists were urged to

> absorb large quantities of the world's advanced culture, especially the cultures of each of the people's democracies, starting with the great Soviet Union. . . . [O]nly by learning the Soviet Union's advanced culture and art can we build a brilliant national culture. . . . In our literature and art the Soviet Union, that bastion of peace in the world; the Soviet Union, that liberator of our country; the Soviet Union, that eternal friend of our masses, has still not been magnificently depicted.[51]

Western scholars' approach to this sort of thing is to overlook it, or to rely on editions of Kim's speeches that conveniently do the overlooking for them. Others shrug it off as not reflecting the leader's true sentiments, his nationalism having supposedly been proven for all time by his

Manchurian exploits — for which, as for our own young men's decision to join the US Army, more than one motivation can be imagined. It is indeed unlikely that Kim penned such tributes himself, but he was free to reject or amend them. They are not the only evidence of his deference to Moscow. Conquered Seoul was festooned with posters describing him as the loyal "General" to Stalin's "Great Marshal."[52] In 1952 the party newspaper devoted 70 editorials to praising the USSR, far more than the 40 devoted to Kim. A mere 22 were in praise of the country saving the DPRK from annihilation.[53]

Pro-Soviet rhetoric did not preclude calls for proper consideration of Korea's special conditions. At a Central Committee plenum in December 1952 Kim Il Sung said:

> Marxist-Leninist instruction does not mean blindly reading thousands or ten thousands of works of Marx, Engels, Lenin and Stalin. It means . . . instilling in cadres the methods of a Marxist-Leninist standpoint, and the rich knowledge and experiences gained by advanced revolutionary parties in revolutionary practice, so that they learn how to apply it in accordance with our country's conditions.[54]

Such remarks are often taken in the West for deviations from Soviet orthodoxy, but it wasn't called dialectical materialism for nothing.[55] Marx made clear that the historical situation is always being modified by what it conditions. Engels had only contempt for those who treated his friend's theory as "something which has got to be learnt off by heart . . . as a dogma and not a guide to action."[56] Lenin made much of this point:

> "Our theory is not a dogma, but a guide to action," Marx and Engels always said, rightly ridiculing the mere memorizing and repetition of "formulas," that at best are capable only of marking out general tasks, which are necessarily modifiable by the concrete economic and political conditions of each particular period of the historical process.[57]

Stalin professed to rule in the same spirit. "Marxism does not recognize invariable conclusions and formulas, obligatory for all epochs and periods. Marxism is the enemy of all dogmatism."[58] No one spoke as often on this topic as Mao, whose declared goal since the 1930s had been the "Sinification of Marxism."[59] But the need for creative or original approaches was obviously no secret to the North Koreans either. In his novel *The Descendants of Cain* (*K'ain ŭi huye*, 1954), which dealt with the land reform of 1946, the defector Hwang Sun-wŏn made a running gag out of one cadre's stress on the need for "creativity in all areas."[60] Kim's later talk of adapting communism to national conditions was therefore not a deviation from orthodoxy but the orthodoxy itself. The local press praised him for following *Stalin's* opposition to the "mechanical" application of Bolshevik experience to other countries.[61]

Upon his death in March 1953, the Soviet leader was mourned in the DPRK as the eternal "father of Korea," its "liberator," its "*suryŏng*" (leader), whose "loyal pupil" Kim would remain.[62] The North would win the war "while holding high Stalin's invincible banner."[63] As it happened, of course, the war ended in a truce on July 27. (This is now remembered as an unconditional Yankee surrender, a fact which would complicate that peace treaty the regime sometimes claims to want.) At a rally the day after the truce, Kim appeared under a large portrait of himself. Portraits of Lenin and Stalin were hung higher, albeit below the republic's seal.[64]

Westerners have long taken it for granted that the devastation caused by American bombs put Kim off war forever; henceforth he would focus on self-reliance instead. No great signs of such an obsession were noted abroad until 1965, when everyone was suddenly able to trace its origins back twenty years. But I do not claim that North Korea never exhibited autarkic tendencies. During the 1950s Kim Il Sung did indeed aspire to establish or at least simulate a comprehensive range of production facilities. Every so often the country took a stab at building its own machinery.[65] Foreigners footed the bill, both for the shoddy production itself and the machines Pyongyang then had to import. Especially valued were machines from East Germany, which, taking import substitution far more seriously, ended up producing everything from apple sauce to microchips.

There is ample reason to believe the testimony of the North Korean cadre who told some Hungarians in 1962 that his leader's "theoretical and economic learning was very scanty."[66] But Kim was surely clever enough to know that development would take longer than his impatience for unification would allow. He seems always to have believed a South Korean uprising likely in the short-to-middle term, though he later concluded he would have to kill his Blue House rival first. The important thing for him, as he made clear in party-internal speeches (like the one in December 1955), was to convey to the southern masses the best impression of the DPRK as quickly as possible.

Occasionally his reluctance to provide goods to his patron-states is regarded by Westerners as self-reliance too, but it was common practice across the East Bloc to buy low from socialist countries and sell high to capitalist ones. If the North Koreans stuck out, it was because their allies expected to see more of a return for their aid. No other country, after all, imported so much without paying for it.

Let us return from economic matters to ideological ones. After the war the WP continued urging the "creative application" of communism to local conditions.[67] Increasingly often, this message was voiced in opposition to the Soviet Koreans in the elite, who (naturally enough) insisted on close adherence to the CPSU trends they were uniquely qualified to interpret. According to a Soviet Korean who later defected to the ROK, one Kim Ch'ang-man took the lead in criticizing the faction, becoming in the process "the first in Pyongyang to use the word *chuch'e*."⁶⁸ The assertion is backed up by a Soviet embassy report (1960) according to which this top official — who since 1945 had occupied various posts in propaganda and party instruction — was known to have authored the "thesis" of *chuch'e*.⁶⁹ Since the word is no thesis in itself, we can safely conclude that he had initiated the call for Korea to establish its subjectivity in revolutionary work instead of blindly following Soviet practices.

Moscow would not have minded such talk. After Stalin's death the USSR was, as Donald S. Zagoria has written, readier than ever to acknowledge "that all bloc countries must find a way to socialism in accordance with their own peculiar and historic circumstances. . . . [The] peculiar domestic problems of each country were taken into consideration." Moscow's primary need was not for imitation, after all, but for "the maintenance of Russia's dominating position in the world."⁷⁰ Allies were indeed strong-armed, but in order to dissuade them from ramming through industrialization and collectivization. "Little Stalins" across Eastern Europe had to scrap their personality cults or step down altogether. One can well imagine where Kim stood in regard to these tendencies. Not only had he made himself the object of a lavish cult, but his brutal collectivization of agriculture resulted in 1955 in famine, just as Eastern European embassies had warned it would.⁷¹

Even after purging a prominent Soviet Korean in 1953, the dictator resisted calls for a crackdown on the entire faction. He did, however, work to reduce contacts between foreigners and his own people. The East Bloc legation was more isolated in Pyongyang than in Western capitals.⁷² By the end of 1955, the Korean Society for International Cultural Exchange, a front for the dissemination of Soviet culture, had effectively ceased to function.⁷³ Such measures were probably motivated less by nationalism — which, as the South Korean kind demonstrates, is reconcilable with the absorption of foreign culture — than by the need to isolate the republic from the Soviet thaw.⁷⁴

At a party plenum in April 1955, Kim again complained about cadres "swallowing Marxism-Leninism whole," and reminded them that "things of our own constitute living Marxism correctly applied to Korean reality."[75] A resolution calling for proper study of local conditions reverberated in the press for months.[76] The point was made again in October 1955 in an issue of the journal *Kŭlloja*. Too many in the party were taking a dogmatic or "sutraist" approach; for the sake of national unification and independence one needed a deep understanding not only of Soviet but also of Korean revolutionary history, and of Kim Il Sung's works.[77]

The leader's complaints about dogmatism have long been taken at face value in the West. Yet he was the one who, contrary to Moscow's own recommendations, had been brutally ramming through old Soviet-style measures; he was the one ignoring warnings that over-hasty collectivization would make the North less attractive to the southern masses. Even this, I suppose, is independent-mindedness of a sort, but Kim did not want his patrons regarding it as such. Scarcely a month went by in which he did not publicly thank the "great Soviet Union" for something. Lenin's eighty-fifth birthday in April 1955 saw Kim praise the "leader of the whole world's workers" for having shown "the only correct road to victory."[78] The phrase puts into proper perspective the WP's talk of applying Marxism-Leninism to local conditions. The tenth anniversary of liberation occasioned still more "deep thanks to our liberator and benefactor, our closest friend, the great Soviet people, the Soviet Communist Party, the Soviet government, and the Soviet army."[79]

I have no interest in reviving the Dullesian canard of a docile Far Eastern satellite, an Asian Bulgaria. My goal in this chapter has been to correct the myth that replaced it: the myth of a Kim who, "once in power . . . adopted a freewheeling nationalist posture."[80] Until about 1960 the regime hewed to an obsequiously pro-Soviet line in the outer track while espousing a moralizing, Kim-centric blood-nationalism in the inner one. The Russians should have seen all this coming when they put a minor ex-guerrilla in power with instructions to keep his years in the Red Army a secret. Had propaganda monolithically credited the USSR with liberating the homeland, Kim would neither have been able to secure mass support for his rule, nor been able to safeguard it against challenges from the superior minds around him. Nor could he have competed for South Korean public opinion against a rival leader who enjoyed more freedom to strike populist notes.

It will not do, however, to apply the name Kimism only to the Korean nationalist line, as if Kim Il Sung's speechifying in almost exclusive service of the other were beneath notice. In any case, the fascist-bred intellectuals running the personality cult hardly needed his guidance in order to see the world in racial terms. Considering his record of assimilation in two foreign armies, and his trust in ex-collaborators and Soviet passport-holders, it seems safe to conclude that on the march toward a bolder nationalism, he was more led than leading.

1. No one who was not in Korean studies in the early 1990s can imagine what the *Origins* cult was like. To differ with the book's author at all, let alone in the tone in which he criticized others, was to be asked in the editorial process if one didn't want to reword things. I speak from experience.
2. Jiyoung Song, *Human Rights Discourse in North Korea: Post-Colonial, Marxist and Confucian Perspectives* (New York, 2011), 63-68. The subtitle says it all; no effort is made to consider a Japanese influence on North Korea's human rights discourse. Scholars' urge to indigenize is such that even North Korean talk of the proper *sŏnbae-hubae* relationship — a Japanese-Confucian institution — is said to reflect the "deeply traditional" sentiments of Korean Confucianism (Armstrong, "The Role and Influence of Ideology," 10).
3. Gi-wook Shin, *Ethnic Nationalism in Korea* (Stanford, 2006), 86.
4. He "spent his entire youth until the age of thirty-three as an anti-Japanese guerrilla fighter, only the last three or four years of that period in the USSR." Armstrong, *Tyranny of the Weak,* 92. Note also the fudging of the time involved. Kim entered the USSR in December 1940 and left in September 1945. Lankov, *From Stalin to Kim Il Sung,* 57.
5. See for example Suzy Kim, *Everyday Life in the North Korean Revolution, 1945-1950* (Ithaca, NY, 2013). Like Auden, I believe in the OED, the shorter version of which (2007) defines *revolution* as: "The complete overthrow of an established government or social order by those previously subject to it."
6. Dae Sook-Suh, *Korean Communism, 1945-1980* (Honolulu, 1981), 12-13.
7. Shin, *Ethnic Nationalism in Korea,* 258. He concedes only that the text might have been edited.
8. Kim Il Sung, *Segi wa tŏburŏ* (Pyongyang, 1992-1998). See for example Hongkoo Han's "The Minsaengdan Incident of the 1930s," in *Origins of North Korea's Juche,* 33-62. Hwang Jang Yop says that before his defection he fretted that the posthumous continuation of Kim's "memoirs" would make the DPRK a laughing stock. (*Hoegorok,* 296.) He gave the West a little too much credit.

9. Han S. Park, *North Korea: The Politics of Unconventional Wisdom*, 20. The cult has Kim espousing Juche from 1930. According to the dictator's private testimony, he did not begin any revolutionary activity until 1928. "Memorandum on the Conversation between Kim Il Sung and Todor Zhivkov," 30 October 1973, translated by Donna Kovacheva, DA/WWC.
10. Suh, *Korean Communism, 1945-1980*, 1; Lankov, *From Stalin to Kim Il Sung*, 19.
11. Quote and information from the English translation of an interview in 1984 with Nikolai Lebedev. See Fyodor Tertitskiy, "Soviet Officer Reveals Secrets of Mangyongdae," 2 January 2014, dailynk.com.
12. V.V. Kovyzhenko in a 1991 interview with Lankov, quoted in *From Stalin to Kim Il Sung*, 59.
13. "Letter from Ri Sang-jo to the Central Committee of the Korean Workers Party, 5 October 1956," translated by Gary Goldberg, DA/WWC; Cumings, "Corporatism in North Korea," 285; Hwang, *Hoegorok*, 136.
14. Myers, *Han Sŏrya and North Korean Literature*, 135-142.
15. See for example Adrian Buzo, *The Guerrilla Dynasty* (London, 1999), 22.
16. See for example I.F. Kurdyukov, "Memorandum of a Conversation with DPRK Ambassador to the USSR Ri Sang-jo, 16 June 1956," translated by Gary Goldberg, DA/WWC; and Károly Fendler, "Report, Embassy of Hungary in North Korea to the Hungarian Foreign Ministry, August 1962," translated by Balazs Szalontai, DA/WWC.
17. "Tangsaŏp ŭl kaesŏn hamyŏ tang taep'yojahoe kyŏljŏng ŭl kwanch'al halde taehayŏ," *Kim Il-sŏng chŏjakchip* 21 (Pyongyang, 1983), 136-137. That the regime did not bother deleting these words is another indication of the peripherality of Kim's speeches to his biography, which depicts him as having led ideological discussion from the start.
18. Yi Yŏng-hun, *Taehan min'guk yŏksa*, 29.
19. Japanese ethnicity was then still considered "eclectic and hybrid." John Lie, *Zainichi* (Berkeley, 2008), 16. But Western scholars are unlikely to stop asserting that the Japanese sought to "eradicate all vestiges of Korean culture." Mitchell Lerner, "'Mostly Propaganda in Nature,'" NKIDP Working Paper #3 (December, 2010), 14.

20. Norman Jacobs, *The Korean Road to Modernization and Development* (Urbana, IL, 1985), 71.
21. Everett Taylor Atkins, *Primitive Selves* (Berkeley, 2010), 27.
22. Lie, *Zainichi*, 10-11.
23. Ryu Kŭn-il, Hong Chin-p'yo, *Chisŏng kwa pan chisŏng* (Seoul, 2005), 167. The remark is Ryu's.
24. "The Koreans greeted their liberators in 1945 with uncommon enthusiasm." Dae-Sook Suh, *Kim Il Sung* (New York, 1988), 55.
25. Kim Il-yŏng et al, "Haebang chŏnhusa ŭi saeroun chip'yŏng," in: *Haebang chŏnhusa ŭi chaeinsik 2*, ed. Pak Chi-hyang (Seoul, 2006), 625. See also Yi T'ae-jun's autobiographical short story "Haebang chŏnhu," (1946), which describes bus passengers' subdued response to the news. Tatiana Gabroussenko discusses the story in *Soldiers on the Cultural Front* (Honolulu, 2010), 115-116.
26. In the speeches of the man who became the ROK's first prime minister, anti-Japanese sentiment went hand in hand with praise for Hitler. Yi Pŏm-sŏk, *Minjok kwa ch'ŏngnyŏn* (Seoul, 1948), 30. Korean bookstores, incidentally, still divide novels into "Korean," "Japanese" and "foreign."
27. Lankov, *From Stalin to Kim Il Sung*, 58.
28. Ienaga, *Pacific War, 1931-1945* (New York, 1979), 122. Goebbels said that the backbone of the Nazi movement were Germans who had come "mostly out of Marxism." See Markus März, *Nationale Sozialisten in der NSDAP* (Graz, 2010), 415.
29. Neo-Nazis and other far-right extremists now abound among the Kim dynasty's Western admirers. See "Jubel von ganz links und ganz rechts: Kim und seine deutschen Freunde," *Die Tageszeitung*, 14 April 2013.
30. See the speech "Tang saŏp pangbŏp e taehayŏ," *Chosŏn chung'ang nyŏn'gam* (Pyongyang, 1960), 38. See also Kim's speech of 27 March 1961, quoted by Szalontai in *Kim Il Sung in the Khrushchev Era* (Washington, DC, 2006), 168-169. Thousands of officers went directly from the Japanese armed forces into the DPRK's. Hong Chin-p'yo: "The belief that North Korea conducted a thorough purge of pro-Japanese elements is definitely a fiction." *Chisŏng kwa pan chisŏng*, 166-167. This should not surprise anyone, considering how many SS veterans joined

East Germany's military. Heiner Emde, "Aus Braun Mach Rot," *Focus*, 3 March 1997.
31. Myers, *Han Sŏrya and North Korean Literature*, 38-39. Kim urged a distinction between intellectuals who had served Japan out of a treasonous instinct and those who had done so "out of necessity." (Former policemen, who had come from much poorer backgrounds, were not treated so leniently.) "Tang saŏp pangbŏp e taehayŏ," 38. This in contrast to the not uncommon notion that "the Kimilsungists [sic] . . . labeled anyone who remained in Korea . . . as collaborators and tried to purge them." McEachern, *Inside the Red Box*, 53-54.
32. See for example Wada Haruki, *Kita Chōsen: yūgekitai kokka no genzai* (Tokyo, 1998) and Heonik Kwon and Byung-Ho Chung's *North Korea: Beyond Charismatic Politics* (Lanham, MD, 2012). Cuba, China and Vietnam were truer guerrilla / partisan states, yet Pyongyang watchers use such terms the most; Kim's behavior, especially his duplicity, is routinely derived from his Manchurian experiences, to glamorizing or at least apologetic effect.
33. Hwang Jang Yop bemoaned the ex-partisans' ignorance even while admiring their heroism. *Hoegorok*, 143. Kim Il Sung told a foreign delegation they "did not know how to build institutions." Mark Barry, "Meeting Kim Il Sung in his Last Weeks," *NK News*, 15 April 2012.
34. Myers, *Han Sŏrya*, 49-51.
35. Hwang Sun-wŏn's *The Descendants of Cain* (*K'ain ŭi huye*, 1954) draws from his own life before defecting to the South. In one scene a cadre berates the protagonist for teaching young people about Tan'gun, the legendary progenitor of the race. Today the DPRK even claims to have excavated Tan'gun's tomb.
36. For a discussion of the Soviet Korean poet Cho Ki-ch'ŏn's work, see Gabroussenko, *Soldiers on the Cultural Front*, 55-63; compare with Han's depiction of Kim Il Sung, discussed in my book *Han Sŏrya*, 135-142.
37. Cumings, "Corporatism in North Korea," 285.
38. *Grounds of Judgment* (Oxford, 2012), 16. Cassel also makes the point that Confucius, far from putting the state above everything, praised fathers and sons who covered up each other's crimes. Park Chung Hee blamed the

Confucian tradition for Koreans' extreme family-egoism, one of the things he railed against most often. To think that Kim could simply co-opt that tradition by likening himself to a parent is to take a very shallow view of culture. The *yangban* were over-represented among people fleeing to the South; they knew an anti-Confucian dispensation when they saw one.

39. See *The Cleanest Race*, 94, 105-107. On this as on so many points, I must fight the common assumption that what North Koreans say to the White Man trumps what they say to each other. Felix Abt tries to counter the textual evidence of matricentricity I adduced in my book (Kim Jong Il as "our great mother," "mother of all mothers," etc) by stressing that the locals talk in English only of the Father Leader. *A Capitalist in North Korea* (Tokyo, 2014), 62-63. I was also told by a Korean American in an Ivy League audience that comparing the leader to a mother is a *very* Confucian thing, because the mother calls the shots in a Korean home. Alas, the assumption that Koreans all know their Confucianism remains as common in the West as the notion that everyone born in the East Bloc knows his Marxism-Leninism.

40. Otto-Ernst Schüddekopf, *Linke Leute von rechts* (Stuttgart, 1960), 178. Goebbels originally faulted Hitler for not being pro-Soviet enough.

41. Myers, *Han Sŏrya*, 46. I want to re-assert a point I made in an otherwise laudatory review of Gabroussenko's *Soldiers on the Cultural Front*. In *Han Sŏrya* I argue that the Soviet aesthetic of socialist realism struggled from the start in North Korea and ceased to be a force by the end of the 1950s. (The bulk of prose fiction has generally been a medium for inner-track propaganda.) Gabroussenko attempts to refute this by applying the looser standards of socialist realism introduced in the USSR in the 1960s. This is a bit like saying it was perfectly Catholic to use the vernacular in mass in the 1950s, because Rome later authorized it. In any case North Korean literature fails to reflect a Marxist-Leninist worldview, and therefore violates the Soviet aesthetic even in the latter's liberalized form.

42. Otto Ulc, "Czechoslovakia," in *Communism in Eastern Europe*, ed. Teresa Rakowska-Harmstone (New York, 1979), 117.

43. László Borhi, *Hungary in the Cold War, 1945-1956* (Budapest, 2004), 129.

44. Dietrich Staritz, *Die Gründung der DDR* (Munich, 1995), 18, 25, 34, 72, 167-168, 176, 183, 201-202.
45. "Sae minjujuŭi kukka kŏnsŏl ŭl wihan uri ŭi kwaŏp," in *Kim Il-sŏng sŏnjip* 1 (Pyongyang, 1960), 13.
46. Quoted in Yang Tong-an, "Minjokchuŭi," 9.
47. This tradition seems to go back to Koh, "North Korea and its Quest for Autonomy," 295. Cumings puts his thumb on the scale by translating *chajusŏng*, which means autonomy or independence, as "self-reliance." *The Origins of the Korean War*, Vol. 2, 313.
48. *The Political Thought of Joseph Stalin* (Plymouth, UK, 2003), 95.
49. "Munhwaindŭl ŭn munhwa chŏnsŏn ŭi t'usa ro toeŏya handa," *Kim Il-sŏng sŏnjip* 1 (Pyongyang, 1960), 100.
50. Frank J. Miller, *Folklore for Stalin* (New York, 1990), ix-x.
51. "Chŏnch'e chakka yesulgadŭl ege," *Kim Il-sŏng sŏnjip* 3 (Pyongyang, 1953), 300.
52. Sin Il-ch'ŏl, *Pukhan chuch'e sasang ŭi hyŏngsŏng kwa soet'oe* (Seoul, 2004), 79.
53. Scalapino and Lee, *Communism in Korea,* 1:415.
54. "Chosŏn rodongdang chungang wiwŏnhoe che 5-ch'a chŏnwŏn hoeŭi esŏ chinsul han pogo," *Chosŏn chung'ang nyŏn'gam* (Pyongyang, 1953), 70.
55. Chong-sik Lee lapses into thrilled italics when quoting Kim's call to "study the theory and principles of Marxism-Leninism *by linking them with the specific realities of Korea.*" See *The Korean Workers' Party* (Stanford, 1978), 90-92. For a lively discussion of communism's oft-overlooked flexibility, see Boris Groys' *Das kommunistische Postskriptum* (Frankfurt am Main, 2006).
56. "Letter to Friedrich Adolphe Sorge in Hoboken," 29 November 1886, MIA.
57. "Letters on Tactics," 8-13 April 1917, MIA.
58. "To Comrade A. Kholopov, 28 July 1950," MIA.
59. Quoted in Stuart R. Schram, *The Political Thought of Mao Tse-tung* (New York, 1963), 57.
60. *K'ain ŭi huye* (1954, repr. Seoul, 2014), 115, 118.

61. Pak T'ae-hwa, "Yi. Bŭ. Ssŭttallin e ŭihan maksŭ-reninjuŭi chŏllyak chŏnsul ŭi paltchŏn," *Cho-Sso Ch'insŏn*, April 1953, 12-13.
62. Ri (Yi) Ki-yŏng, "Widaehan Ssŭttallin ŭn inmin ŭi simjang sok e yŏngwŏnhi sara issŭl gŏsida," *Cho-Sso Ch'insŏn*, April 1953, 14-19.
63. Ki Sŏk-pok, "Renin, Ssŭttallin ŭi kyosi nŭn uri rŭl sŭngni ero komu handa," *Cho-Sso Ch'insŏn*, April 1953, 6.
64. For the full official photograph, of which this is a small part, see Chris Springer, *North Korea Caught in Time* (Reading, 2010), 66. The book has other relevant ones too.
65. Szalontai, "You Have No Political Line of Your Own," 89-90.
66. "Report, Embassy of Hungary in North Korea to the Hungarian Foreign Ministry, August 1962," translated by the Balazs Szalontai, DA/WWC.
67. In July 1954 universities were told to teach how the party had "guaranteed all victories of the Korean masses by creatively applying to the Korean reality both the theory of revolutionary Marxism-Leninism and the revolutionary experiences of the great Communist Party of the Soviet Union and other advanced parties." Paek, *Pukhan kwŏllyŏk ŭi yŏksa* (Seoul, 2010), 262.
68. Im Ŭn, *Kim Il-sŏng chŏngjŏn*, 311, 313.
69. "From the Diary of Torbenkov N.E. Top secret, No. 2, 13 June 1960," translated by Gary Goldberg, DA/WWC. I thank Fyodor Tertitskiy for bringing this report to my attention.
70. "Some Comparisons between the Russian and Chinese Models," in *Communist Strategies in Asia*, ed. A. Doak Barnett (London, 1963), 11-12.
71. Over thirty years after Scalapino and Lee mentioned this food crisis, Cumings was still asserting that no one had gone hungry in "Kimilsungland" until the 1990s (*North Korea*, 150). The first scholar to discuss the starvation deaths at any length was Balazs Szalontai, in 2004 and 2006. See "You Have No Political Line of Your Own," 90; *Kim Il Sung in the Khrushchev Era*, 64-65.
72. Szalontai, *Kim Il Sung*, 54.
73. Lankov, *Crisis in North Korea*, 58.
74. Strengthening this assumption is the fact that publishers continued putting out pre-thaw Soviet and Russian works: *Yi.We. Ssŭttalin chŏjakchip* 7

(Pyongyang, 1957); *Mayakkobŭssŭkki sŏnjip* [Selected Works of Mayakovsky] (Pyongyang, 1957) *Ssalttŭikkobŭ-Swedŭrin sŏnjip* [Selected Works of Saltykov-Shchedrin] (Pyongyang, 1957), We. Yi. Renin (V.I. Lenin), *Munhak e kwanhayŏ* [On Literature] (Pyongyang, 1958), etc.

75. The quotes are from "Tangwŏndŭl sok esŏ kyegŭp kyoyang saŏp ŭl tŏuk kanghwa halte taehayŏ," in *Kim Il-sŏng chŏjak sŏnjip* 1 (Pyongyang, 1967), 511-512; and "Sahoejuŭi hyŏngmyŏng ŭi hyŏn tangye e issŏsŏ tang mit' kukka saŏp ŭi myŏt kaji munje dŭl e taehayŏ," *Kim Il-sŏng chŏjak sŏnjip*, 1:537-538. These were speeches on different days at the same plenum.
76. Paek, *Pukhan kwŏllyŏk ŭi yŏksa*, 264. See for example Ri Chŏng-gu, "Uri simunhak ŭi che munje," *Chosŏn Munhak*, August 1955, 128.
77. "Maksŭ-reninjuŭi riron ŭi ch'angjojŏk sŭpdŭk ŭl wihayŏ," *Kŭlloja*, October 1955, 5, 7-10. "Sutraist" (*tokkyŏngjŏk*) was North Korean translators' equivalent of Stalin's term Talmudist.
78. "Renin ŭi haksŏl ŭn uri ŭi chich'im ida," in *Kim Il-sŏng sŏnjip* 4 (1960), 287.
79. Kim Il-sŏng, "Widaehan ssobet'ŭ kundae e ŭihan 8.15 haebang 10-chu'nyŏn kyŏngch'uk taehoe esŏ han pogo, 1955-nyŏn 8-wŏl 14-il," in *Kim Il-sŏng sŏnjip* 4 (1960), 300-301.
80. Selig Harrison, *Korean Endgame* (Princeton, 2009), 12.

2

THE WATERSHED THAT WASN'T: DECEMBER 28, 1955[1]

NIETZSCHE WROTE THAT the biblical exegesis of his day put him in a state "between anger and laughter," so obvious was the effort to shoehorn each text into the prevailing orthodoxy. I feel the same way whenever I read how Kim Il Sung supposedly "launched North Korea's 'Juche' ideology" on December 28, 1955.[2] Before approaching the relevant speech, let us recall that his main concern at the time was how to deal with two hostile or at least critical factions in the ruling elite. One consisted of officials who had lived as exiles at Mao Zedong's base in Yan'an; the other was made up of some of the Soviet Koreans I have already discussed.[3] Background did not necessarily dictate allegiance; Kim Il Sung had Yan'an veterans and Soviet Koreans in his own inner circle. (For example, Pak Chŏng-ae, who led women's affairs under various titles, had grown up in the USSR.) Nor is it clear whether either faction wanted him removed

from power.⁴ What is certain is that top-ranking Soviet Koreans supported greater prioritization of light-industry development and consumer goods production, in opposition to Kim, who favored development of heavy industry and the rapid collectivization of agriculture.⁵

For years he had resisted his followers' calls to limit the influence of these factions, or even to force their members to relinquish foreign citizenship. Only after his gross mismanagement of the economy had made him more vulnerable to criticism did he decide to move against them, the Soviet Koreans in particular. His first target was their informal leader Pak Ch'angok, then chairman of the State Planning Commission and thus the republic's leading economic strategist.⁶ After Kim faulted his work in November 1955, he made allegations of disloyalty and bourgeois beliefs against Pak and other Soviet Koreans at two party gatherings in December.⁷

Kim criticized these officials again in a speech to propagandists on December 28, 1955, although on that occasion, as we shall see, their errors were made to sound much less grave. A photograph in one of his biographies shows him in a beautiful suit and tie, smiling Buddha-like as he pens something at a desk, but there is no reason to believe the caption's claim that it was this very speech.⁸ Discussion of culture was not the man's forte and he knew it. Kim Ch'ang-man had already supplied him with a few speeches on such matters. The official's relevant background in managing propaganda and party instruction makes it all the more likely that he wrote this one too, or at least supplied what would today be called "talking points." This would explain the frequent mentions in it of the word *chuch'e*, which Kim Il Sung had not used before in three and a half volumes' worth of speeches.⁹

According to the subtitle, the audience consisted of "officials working in party propaganda and agitation." So far, Western scholars have assumed that these words are inaccurate or incomplete: Kim must

have given the speech at a Central Committee gathering that same week. I grant there is some evidence to support this theory, but such an event is still too small-scale to be reconciled with the myth of an ideological watershed.[10] Until we get more information, in any case, we must give the editors of Kim's works the benefit of the doubt; they had no reason to make the event seem less important.

The title under which the speech was published: "On eliminating dogmatism and formalism and establishing the subject [*chuch'e*] in ideological work."[11] It is a clumsy choice of words; the subject can only be the establishing body and not the thing established. Whether Kim Ch'angman had been using this phrase is unclear, although, having spent twenty-some years in China, his Korean was perhaps none too smooth either. A colonially-bred man would have spoken — as Park Chung Hee later did so often — of a need to establish subjectivity or agency (*chuch'esŏng*, from the Japanese *shutaisei*).[12] In any case, the audience would have been familiar enough with the word *chuch'e* to understand what was meant.[13] It might have been more stirring to call for the Koreanization of communism, just as Mao had called for its Sinification,[14] but the last thing Kim Il Sung wanted was for Moscow to think him chauvinist. "Establish the subject" was a fittingly unobjectionable way of asking for less imitation of foreign models.[15]

The other two keywords in the title are exact equivalents of terms long current in China. Mao had inveighed against "dogmatism," or the rigid application of Soviet theory and custom, during his so-called rectification campaign in the early 1940s.[16] In the 1950s the pejorative was popular across Eastern Europe.[17] North Korea's own press had been railing against dogmatism for months, as I wrote in the last chapter. As for "formalism," Mao had made heavy use of the term to mean adherence to revolutionary forms at the expense of substantive change.[18] Most of those forms, naturally enough, were Soviet in origin, but he had called for more study of local conditions without criticizing the USSR itself.[19] Moscow shared Mao's hostility to the tendency described.[20] The communist world's antidote to both problems was the same: apply Marxism-Leninism creatively. Kim Il

Sung could hardly have dreamed that Americans would one day think him bold for having swum with this bloc-wide current.

Although the speech runs to 25 pages in the 1960 edition, only the first half, which can be read aloud in half an hour, covers the topics mentioned in the title. The second half (which makes no mention of *chuch'e*) deals with the need for the North to project the proper image to the ROK, so as to encourage an uprising there. I have included a full translation of the 1960 version in the appendix of this book, not only to forestall charges of having cherry-picked excerpts, but also to discourage the standard practice of relying on bowdlerized editions. The reader might find it helpful to read through Appendix 1 now before proceeding with my interpretation of the main passages.

Kim started by saying, "Today I would like to express a few opinions to you comrades on the shortcomings of our party's ideological work and on how to eliminate them in the future."[21] After reminding his audience of errors uncovered on the literary front the day before, he moved on to the topic at hand.

> Obviously, then, our propaganda work cannot have gone well either. Unfortunately it has lapsed into dogmatism and formalism in many respects. The most fundamental shortcoming of ideological work is the failure to delve deeply into all matters and the absence of a subject. It may not be correct to say that there is no subject, but the truth is that it has not yet been firmly established. This is a serious matter.[22]

We see here that Kim uses *propaganda work* and *ideological work* as interchangeable terms, an important point in itself. Note that I am translating the keyword *chuch'e* in the sense then current; we need not concern ourselves with translations conceived at home and abroad in later years. Note also the insecurity with which the speaker immediately qualifies his remark about "the absence of the subject." Use of the word *subjectivity* would have precluded this confusion.

THE WATERSHED THAT WASN'T: DECEMBER 28, 1955

He goes on:

What is the subject in our party's ideological work? What are we doing? We are engaged in Korea's revolution and not some other country's. Precisely this Korean revolution is the subject of our party's ideological work, all of which must therefore be made to serve its interests. Whether we research the history of the Communist Party of the Soviet Union, the history of the Chinese revolution, or the general principles of Marxism-Leninism, it is all in order to carry out our own revolution correctly.[23]

Western scholars like to isolate this part from the rest of the speech, the better to play up its boldness. Read in context, however, it expresses mere "domesticism" of the usual toothless sort.
Kim continues:

To carry out a revolution in Korea, we must know Korean history and geography as well as the customs of the Korean people. . . . Only when we educate our people in the history and tradition of their own struggle can we stimulate their national pride and rouse the broad mass of people to revolutionary struggle.[24]

The words *nation* and *national* (*minjok, minjokchŏk*) are to be understood throughout as referring to Koreans on both sides of the DMZ. Keeping this in mind makes for a very different reading from the conventional one. Kim went on to complain that many cadres were ignorant of Korean history and tradition.

Those mistakes too which have recently been made by Pak Ch'ang-ok and others are due to their negation of the history of the Korean literary movement. The struggle waged by the fine writers of the . . . Korean Proletarian Literature League, and the

— 49 —

fine works of progressive scholars and writers like Pak Yŏn-am and Chŏng Ta-san are not in their field of vision.[25]

Thus did Kim open yet another attack on the Soviet Koreans, who had little involvement in literary matters at this time anyway.[26] The mistake in question was hardly endemic to the party. Only months earlier, the thirtieth anniversary of the Proletarian Literature League's founding had occasioned a lavish public ceremony as well as commemorative articles. Most of the praise had centered on Han Sŏrya and Yi Ki-yŏng, former members who had gone on to become the DPRK's most famous novelists.[27] As for Pak Yŏn-am (1737-1805) and Chŏng Ta-san (1762-1836), two Confucian scholars of a pragmatic stamp, the press had already begun glorifying them.[28]

Kim went on to criticize the Soviet Koreans for failing to memorialize events in the anti-Japanese struggle, specifically the Kwangju student uprising of November 3, 1929, which the rival state had begun commemorating with an annual Student's Day:

> It played a huge part in instilling anti-Japanese spirit in broad sections of Korean youth. Accordingly, we should publicize this movement widely, and educate our students and other young people in the brave fighting spirit displayed by their forerunners. While our propaganda cadres fail to do this, Syngman Rhee has been making use of this movement in his propaganda. In this way Communists have ended up looking like disregarders of national traditions. How dangerous a thing this is! We will never win over the south Korean youth in this manner.[29]

This paragraph foreshadows the main thrust of the speech, i.e., that the WP had to do a better job of propaganda in order to win over the South Korean public.

We should keep in mind that in the mid-1950s, as the Soviet ambassador reported to Moscow, the two Koreas were not yet "hermetically sealed" off from each other. There were informal contacts between the regimes (usually via Tokyo) and industrial supplies went back and forth

THE WATERSHED THAT WASN'T: DECEMBER 28, 1955

across the DMZ — as of course did radio broadcasts.[30] Each side had a better understanding of the other's economic and political conditions than we tend to assume today. This was one reason why the embassies in Pyongyang were so opposed to Kim's insistence on rapid collectivization, which probably derived more from his desire to maximize internal regimentation than anything else. We should not assume that he understood the ROK populace better than the Soviet Koreans did. His personality cult has always been a greater blight on the DPRK's reputation in the South — and a bigger boon to Seoul's counter-propaganda — than any of the problems he mentioned in the speech.

To return to which: Kim took education officials to task for neglecting Korean history and hanging portraits of Pushkin *et al* in classrooms.[31] "The result of this forgetting of the subject is that much harm has been done to party work."[32] At about this point the speech takes on a rambling quality which suggests that Kim either began speaking off the cuff or had been referring all along to very rudimentary notes.[33] I will focus on points relevant to the thrust of this book.

Kim went on to criticize Pak Yŏng-bin, who had become the head of the Central Committee's Department of Propaganda and Agitation in February 1955.[34] The Soviet Korean had apparently returned from the USSR to recommend that Pyongyang follow Moscow's lead in toning down its anti-American propaganda. Kim:

> It is utterly ridiculous to think that our people's struggle against the US imperialists conflicts with the efforts of the Soviet people to ease international tension. Our people's condemnation of and struggle against the US imperialists' policy of aggression against Korea do not undermine but rather conduce to the struggle of people around the world to lessen international tension and defend peace.[35]

Note that Kim was not asking his audience to ignore Moscow's guidance, but to ignore this official's interpretation of it, the result not of misplaced loyalty but of foolishness.

He then criticized propagandists who "swallow Marxism-Leninism whole" instead of assimilating it with Korean realities and traditions. "Otherwise our people will lose faith in their own ability and become effete people who only try to copy from others."[36] There followed a dig at those who squabbled about whether to do things "Soviet-style" or "Chinese-style."[37] This is a more accurate translation of *ssoryŏn-sik, chungguk-sik*, than the bolder phrases "the Soviet way," "the Chinese way," which our academics prefer.[38] (Let us remember Kim's statement the previous April that the USSR had already shown the "only correct road" to revolution.)[39]

> There can be no principle that we must do things Soviet-style.... [Is] it not high time we made our own style?... So, while continuing to learn consistently from the Soviet Union, we must put stress not on the form but on the essence of its experience.[40]

Kim made clear what he opposed by citing the party newspaper's word-for-word imitation of *Pravda* headlines, something that would have elicited a chuckle from Soviet observers as well.[41] (At another point he mentioned the "ridiculous" example of tables of contents being printed in the back of books, Soviet-style.)[42]

Kim then moved on to what many foreigners regard as an especially interesting part of the speech:[43]

> Marxism-Leninism is not a dogma, it is a guide to action and a creative theory. So only when it is applied creatively to suit the specific conditions of each country can it display its indestructible vitality.[44]

In fact this was well-worn East Bloc rhetoric, especially that unacknowledged Lenin quote (itself adapted from Engels) in the first sentence. Nonetheless, the leader thought it necessary to ask again that his remarks be understood in an internationalist context.

THE WATERSHED THAT WASN'T: DECEMBER 28, 1955

> Loving Korea is the same as loving the Soviet Union and the socialist camp and, likewise, loving the Soviet Union and the socialist camp means loving Korea. It's a complete whole. This is because there are no borders in the great cause of the working class. ... For the victory of the Korean revolution, for the great cause of the international working class, we must strengthen our solidarity with the people of the Soviet Union, our liberator and benefactor. ... This is our sacred internationalist duty. ... A true patriot is an internationalist and vice versa.[45]

To emphasize that he and the USSR were in perfect agreement, Kim invoked the advice of the Red Army commander whose troops had liberated the peninsula: "Korean people! ... Happiness is in your hands. ... The Korean people must become creators of their own happiness."[46] (What kind of nationalist, one wonders, would invoke a foreign authority in such a context?) Kim warned that if the party failed to heed this message, "we may lose the broader public."[47] Again, people on both sides of the DMZ were meant. On that note, the first and more famous half of the speech was over; Kim made no more mention of *chuch'e*.

There followed a long appeal for better "political work directed towards the South."[48] I lack the space to go into this second half of the speech in detail, but encourage the reader to read it in the appendix. Suffice to say here that Syngman Rhee was right in claiming that the North remained committed to the destruction of the ROK.

Hanging incongruously over the speech is a distinctly Chinese "smell," as Koreans would put it. The WP's Sinophiles get off much more lightly than the Soviet Koreans, and in stretches the text reads like a simplified version of Mao's criticism of Wang Ming.[49] (There is also a Mao-like comparison of the masses to an ocean in which the revolutionary must swim.) Some in the audience must have smiled inwardly when, minutes after deprecating advocates of doing things Chinese-style, the speaker said, "We too need to carry out a rectification, like the Chinese party."[50] This also

— 53 —

points to the speech's having been written by the former Yan'an resident Kim Ch'ang-man.

As the second half meanders on, the first feels even less like a proclamation of anything. Finally, after some criticism of the former foreign minister Pak Hŏn-yŏng (who had been purged on trumped-up spy charges), the leader wraps everything up in fittingly un-programmatic fashion, by complaining that the republic's newspapers each lack a specific character.

The conclusion:

> Today I have spoken about some problems in our party's ideological work. I hope you comrades will take them into consideration, eliminate the shortcomings that have become apparent so far, and strive to raise our party's ideological work to a higher level.[51]

And there we have it: a speech which, far from launching a new ideology, did not even hint at the existence of one. Nowhere in it did Kim suggest changing any part of Marxism-Leninism as it was then espoused from the Elbe River to the Bering Strait. Nor, as we have seen, was his message new to his own people, even if it did need reiterating. Perhaps most importantly: There is no mention of self-reliance in the speech. In evidence is little more than an innocuous pride in indigenous tradition, something then standard across the East Bloc.

Kim's opposition to minority dissent conformed even to post-Stalinist norms in the USSR.[52] The Soviet Koreans' espousal of a Khrushchevian line therefore won them no support from the embassy that their passports allowed them to visit at will. One diplomat there, S. Filatov, later described Kim's criticism of Pak Ch'ang-ok *et al* as a just response to their arrogance.[53] In conversation with a Polish diplomat in 1957, another of Moscow's emissaries recalled the faction's comeuppance with equal approval.[54] As the Pole put it: "In Pimenov's opinion, and this is what is being said at the Soviet embassy, the DPRK's party policies . . . are correct."[55]

THE WATERSHED THAT WASN'T: DECEMBER 28, 1955

In 1972 the American political scientists Robert Scalapino and Chong-sik Lee wrote of the speech, after quoting the livelier parts ("We are not engaged in another country's revolution," etc): "None of this was particularly unorthodox when viewed against current trends in the international Communist movement . . . the Soviet Union would have found the passages quoted entirely acceptable."[56] The East Bloc archives show how correct this assumption was. But the further the USSR recedes from memory, the more rigidity and meddlesomeness people ascribe to it. As a result the speech is regarded not just as the foundation of a new ideology, but as an "anti-Soviet" or "radically nationalistic" text, even as "a declaration of independence from Soviet control."[57] In 2011 I opened a journal to see it treated as an effort to restore a Chosŏn Dynasty school of Neo-Confucianism:

> The political message Kim was sending to the WP was clear: Korean ideology was more important than Russian ideology. *Sirhak* was more important than Marxism-Leninism.[58]

It is as if discussion of Juche came with the license to float above primary materials entirely. But of all that more later.

1. This chapter draws substantially from (while correcting errors in) my article of the same name: "The Watershed that Wasn't," *Acta Koreana*, 9, No. 1 (2006), 89-115.
2. Armstrong, *Tyranny of the Weak*, 81.
3. The best source of information on these factions is Lankov, *Crisis in North Korea*, 7-25.
4. James F. Person, "New Evidence on North Korea in 1956," Cold War International History Project Bulletin, Issue 16 (Washington DC, 2007), 447.
5. Ibid., 455.
6. Lankov, *Crisis in North Korea*, 29.
7. Ibid., 44.
8. Paek Pong, *Minjok ŭi t'aeyang Kim Il-sŏng changgun* 2, 349.
9. At the plenum in April 1955 he had used the word *chugwanjŏk* in a phrase ("subjective capability") which cried out for *chuch'ejŏk* instead. "Sahoejuŭi hyŏngmyŏng ŭi hyŏn tangye e issŏsŏ tang mit' kukka saŏp ŭi myŏt kaji munje dŭl e taehayŏ," *Kim Il-sŏng sŏnjip* 4 (Pyongyang, 1960), 258. This was of course in line with Mao's practice of saying *zhuguan* in such contexts instead of *zhuti*. The reference was corrected to *chuch'ejŏk* in later editions.
10. It is advanced by Lankov, *Crisis in North Korea*, 40-41 and Szalontai, *Kim Il Sung*, 78-79. In the December 28 speech (as published), Kim said, "As you comrades have learned through yesterday's conference, there have been big ideological errors on the literary front" ("Sasang saŏp," 325). Kim also referred to Han Sŏrya's having spoken on the previous day (ibid., 329). This would seem to suggest that the December 28 speech was indeed held at a CC event that week, of which we know that it began with Han's report on literature. On the other hand, the editors of Kim's works had no plausible reason to describe such a function as a mere gathering of propagandists. Another problem is that our sources of information about that week's events are contradictory. Foreign Minister Nam Il reported to the Soviet embassy on December 29, 1955 that a conference of the CC's Standing Committee, extended to accommodate workers from the *literary* front, had been held from December 26-27. ("Dnevnik za period c 20 Dek. 1955 – 19 Jan. 1956,"

in Soviet archives accessed at the Woodrow Wilson Center, March 2014.) But the following March, Pak Ch'ang-ok told the embassy that the CC had held an extended *plenum* from December 27-29. (Filatov, "Memorandum of Conversation with the DPRK Vice Minister of the Cabinet of Ministers and Member of the KWP CC Presidium, Pak Ch'ang-ok, 12 March, 1956.") In any case, Kim's speech of December 28 seems to fit into neither the two-day event described by Nam, which had already ended the day before, nor the three-day event described by Pak, which, he said, Kim had concluded with a speech on December 29. Besides, the published speech of December 28 is quite different in tone and content from the harangues which Pak reported to the Soviet diplomat. These had imputed to him and his associates such grave offenses as believing in "bourgeois ideology." It is hard to believe the dictator took the floor at such an event to criticize such things as the printing of tables of contents at the back of books! We also have it on Pak's testimony that Kim's speech at the late-December event was even harder on him than a polemic delivered earlier that month, and that it mentioned fifteen followers of Hŏ Ka-i. This description does not tally with the speech to propagandists. Was a harsh original version of the text circulated in 1956, only to be softened for publication in 1960? I doubt it. This was still quite a truthful time in the party's management of its own discourse. Besides, the maundering speech published bears little sign of significant editing. Even a reference to "Comrade" Pak Yŏng-bin was left in, suggesting that the original might have been softer in tone ("Sasang saŏp," 333).

11. Kim Il Sung, "Sasang saŏp esŏ kyojojuŭi wa hyŏngsikchuŭi rŭl toech'i hago chuch'e rŭl hwangnip halde taehayŏ," in *Kim Il-sŏng sŏnjip* 4 (Pyongyang, 1960), 325-354.

12. My (South) Korean-Korean dictionary lists the standard phrase as *chuch'esŏng ŭl hwangnip hada*, i.e. establish subjectivity. *Minjung essensŭ kug'ŏ sajŏn* (Seoul, 2001), 2117.

13. The word had done service in the latest editions of Marx's work. K'a. Maksŭ (K. Marx), "P'oierŭbaha e kwanhan t'eje," in *Maksŭ, Engelsŭ chŏjak sŏnjip 2* (Pyongyang, 1955), 136; K'al Maksŭ, *Chabonron* (Pyongyang, 1955), 217. None of the South Korean university students I have asked could remember

having heard the term "establish the subject" before, but almost all guessed correctly at its meaning.
14. Nick Knight, "The Form of Mao Zedong's 'Sinification' of Communism," *The Australian Journal of Chinese Affairs* 9 (January 1983), 18.
15. Even among Japanese fascists, use of *shutai* had been largely restricted to theoretical discussion.
16. See for example, Mao Zedong's "Rectify the Party's Style of Work," 1 February 1942, in MIA.
17. See, for example, "Die Entlarvung des Dogmatismus als einer Waffe der Parteifeinde," *Neues Deutschland*, 8 August 1953.
18. Brian Kai Hin Tsui, "China's Forgotten Revolution: Radical Conservatism in Action, 1927-1949," Ph.D. thesis, Columbia University, 2013, 65.
19. Suzanne Pepper, *Radicalism and Education Reform in Twentieth-Century China* (Cambridge, 1996), 139.
20. The Russians, however, used the word formalism (*formalizm*) much more often in a different sense, namely to denote deviations from the socialist realist aesthetic. Robert V. Daniels, *Trotsky, Stalin and Socialism* (Boulder, 1991), 143-144. Incidentally, throughout late 1955 the North Korean education press had been calling on teachers to "eliminate formalism," using the pejorative mainly to mean going through the motions, not teaching thoroughly enough, etc. See for example Paek Kyu-hwan, "Kyosu saŏp esŏ ŭi hyŏngsikchuŭi t'oech'i haja!", *Kyowŏn Sinmun*, 24 September 1955.
21. "Sasang saŏp," 325.
22. Ibid.
23. Ibid., 326.
24. Ibid., 326-327.
25. Ibid., 327.
26. Lankov, *Crisis in North Korea*, 36. Since October the faction had evidently been subjected to criticism even in regional party meetings. Filatov, "Memorandum of Conversation with the DPRK Vice Premier," translated by James F. Person, DA/WWC.
27. Myers, *Han Sŏrya*, 92.

28. Pak Chong-sik, "Pak Yŏn-am ŭi sasiljuŭi munhak," *Chosŏn Munhak*, December 1955, 140-58. The man's memory was honored with two more articles in the January 1956 issue, both of which had to have been written before Kim's speech. Han Sŏrya, "Yŏn-am Pak Chi-wŏn ŭi saengae wa hwaldong," *Chosŏn Munhak*, January 1956, 137-156; Sin Ku-hyŏn, "Yŏn-am Pak Chi-wŏn e taehayŏ," *Chosŏn Munhak*, January 1956, 177-183.
29. "Sasang saŏp," 327-328.
30. Szalontai, "You Have No Political Line of Your Own," 89.
31. Lankov, *From Stalin to Kim Il Sung*, 125.
32. Ibid., 331.
33. For what it's worth, the 1980 edition of the speech includes a photograph of what is purportedly a page from Kim's handwritten notes; they are jottings of phrases and keywords, studded with Chinese characters so as to appear more authentic. "Sasang saŏp," *Kim Il-sŏng chŏnjip* 9 (Pyongyang, 1980), 473.
34. Lankov, *Crisis in North Korea*, 32.
35. "Sasang saŏp" (1960 edition), 333-334. Szalontai writes that in August 1955, a North Korean official informed the USSR that it would not tone down its anti-US propaganda. *Kim Il Sung*, 75-76.
36. "Sasang saŏp," 334-335.
37. Ibid.
38. Typical: Armstrong, *Tyranny of the Weak*, 91.
39. Kim Il Sung, "Renin ŭi haksŏl," 287. Not that it would necessarily have been radical or anti-Soviet to talk of a Korean road, as witness East German talk of an *eigenen Weg*.
40. "Sasang saŏp," 336.
41. Ibid.
42. This example was cited earlier on in the speech. Ibid., 330-331.
43. See for example James F. Person, "We Need Help From Outside," Cold War International History Project, Working Paper #52, 17.
44. "Sasang saŏp," 337.
45. Ibid., 338.

46. Ibid.
47. Ibid.
48. Ibid., 340.
49. See "On Practice," in *Mao Tse-tung: An Anthology of His Writings*, edited by Anne Fremantle (New York, 1962), 200-213.
50. "Sasang saŏp," 346.
51. Ibid., 354. Kim would go on to repeat his criticism of newspapers' uniformity at the 3rd Party Congress in August 1956. His words at the event are quoted in the anonymous article, "Chapchi <Ryŏksa kwahak> ŭi chil ŭl tŏuk nop'ija," *Kŭlloja*, February 15, 1960, 60.
52. Lenin had banned "factionalism" — read: all minority agitation against majority decisions — and so had every Leninist party since. The Czechoslovaks' effort to lift the ban in 1968 was one reason for the Red Army's invasion. Harold C. Hinton, *An Introduction to Chinese Politics* (London, 1973), 169.
53. Paek, 310. Filatov disagreed only with the charges of anti-party scheming raised in January 1956. "Memorandum of Conversation with the DPRK Vice Premier of the Cabinet of Ministers and Member of the KWP CC Presidium, Pak Ch'ang-ok, 12 March 1956," translated by James F. Person, DA/WWC.
54. Pimenov disparaged Chŏng Yul, the (Soviet Korean) vice minister of culture, for having promoted the idea that "everything that is Soviet is good and right." Henryk Brzeziński, "From a conversation with the First Secretary of the Embassy of the USSR, Comr. Pimenov of 26-27-28-29.III.1957," in: *New Evidence on North Korea's Chollima Movement and Five-Year Plan (1957-1961)*, ed. James Person (Washington, DC, 2009), 10.
55. Brzeziński, "From a conversation with comr. Pimenov 1st Secretary of the Embassy of the USSR on 15.10.1957," in *New Evidence on North Korea's Chollima Movement and Five-Year Plan*, 16. There is thus no truth to Gwang-Oon Kim's assertion that the re-election of Kim Il Sung as KWP chairman in April 1956 constituted defiance of Moscow. "The Making of the Juche State in Post-Colonial North Korea," in *Origins of North Korea's Juche*, 78.
56. Scalapino and Lee, *Communism in Korea*, 1:502.
57. Suh, *Kim Il Sung*, 145; McEachern, *Inside the Red Box*, 56; Armstrong, *Tyranny of the Weak*, 90.

58. Alzo David-West, "Between Confucianism and Marxism-Leninism," *Korean Studies* 35, No. 1 (2011), 93, 95-96. This little try-on rests on the claim that the speech makes no mention of Marx or Lenin. Either the peer reviewers agreed that fourteen glowing references to Marxism-Leninism do not count, or they had not bothered to read the speech.

3

ON THE EDGE OF SLOGANHOOD: 1956-1962

U NLIKE CAR PROTOTYPES, ruling ideologies are not flashed teasingly in public only to be tinkered with in secret for a few more years. A study of the aftermath of the presumed Juche-launch is therefore just as destructive of the conventional wisdom as a reading of the speech itself. In his New Year's address (1956), Kim Il Sung gave no sign of having just put his country on a new footing. Instead he went out of his way to thank the "great Soviet Union" for all the aid it had given, and the Chinese for so "reassuringly" guarding the DPRK.[1]

A few months later the party contacted the Soviet embassy with a draft of its new statutes, asking to be told which ones needed correcting.[2] In April 1956, Kim forbore to mention *chuch'e* in his long report to the Third Party Congress. It was left to Kim Ch'ang-man, the originator of this so-called thesis, to ask everyone to "eliminate dogmatism, regain the subject, study and creatively apply Marxism-Leninism." The final resolution included a call for these measures to be applied in all ideological work in order to "rectify" the subject.[3] In June Kim Il Sung departed on an aid-begging trip around the East Bloc which lasted no less than seven weeks, and included two separate visits to the USSR.[4] Fulsome internationalist rhetoric ensued as the North Korean press covered each stage of the journey.

This does not mean there was no more talk of what the leader (and others before him) had criticized. The media reported on provincial party criticism of dogmatism and formalism.[5] The *Rodong Sinmun* inveighed against these tendencies on March 26, 1956.[6] More celebration of premodern "reformists" ensued in the following few years, but this trend, which had begun shortly before Kim's speech, merely brought the DPRK in line with other Soviet dependencies, where indigenous revolutionary traditions were projected even further into the past.[7] From a Marxist-Leninist perspective, it was only proper that the DPRK should make up ground lost due to the Soviet Koreans' "national nihilism," to use an old Stalinist pejorative.[8] The ground, however, was never really made up; the WP's blood-nationalists were scarcely more interested in indigenous cultural tradition than the Soviet Koreans had been. What little progress was made in this regard was reversed in the late 1960s, when the Chosŏn Dynasty was reduced to a dark prelude to the Great Leader's coming.[9] To this day the average person in the DPRK is profoundly ignorant of his cultural heritage.[10]

Kim Ch'ang-man had probably settled on the dry phrase "establish the subject" precisely because it did not sound chauvinist. But having originated in a pluralist culture, it allowed more room for interpretation than did other official catchwords, most of which, from "socialist patriotism" to "mass line," had been imported in codified form. The very fact that the keyword *chuch'e* looked homegrown (despite having come from the Japanese) may well have made some cadres think that the task of "establishing the subject" lay outside the Marxist-Leninist framework. The result, it seems, was a confusion Kim Il Sung could ill afford.

On July 21, 1956, therefore, the *Rodong Sinmun* carried an article by one Kim Chin-t'aek bearing the title "For the Proper Understanding of 'the Subject.'"[11] Not a few people, the writer said, lacked proper understanding of that word; some interpreted it "in an unreasonably 'philosophical' manner" while other — doubtless more numerous — cadres grasped it in "exclusionist" (read nationalist) terms.[12] After describing the problem of "establishing the subject" as "a model example of how Marxist-Leninist theory . . . has been creatively applied by Comrade Kim Il Sung," the writer reminded cadres that countries could achieve revolution only if their working classes supported each other. Those in the WP who failed to consider both their national *and* international responsibilities were bound to lapse into the error of nationalism (*minjokchuŭi*), while those who failed to study modern Korean history would be unable to carry out the revolution well.[13]

Outside the official news media, however, nationalism was finding more strident expression. Its central text was Kim's biographical legend, which took on more extravagance in 1956 even as newspapers expressed token criticism of personality cults in general. The Museum of the Korean People's Revolutionary Struggle dealt almost exclusively with the dictator's alleged exploits.[14] Plays and operas strengthened the myth that it was he who had defeated Japan; one showed imprisoned patriots being freed by his partisans. A disapproving cadre reported this to the Soviet embassy.[15]

Meanwhile the regime kept reducing exchanges between natives and foreigners. For the first time in years there was no "Month of Soviet-Korean Friendship" in 1956. Performances of Soviet drama and music were cut back. Russian ceased to be taught to university juniors and seniors, and an institute devoted to teaching it was closed.[16] Thanks to Kim's speech of December 28, 1955, these measures could now be dressed up as a matter of "establishing the subject" and "fighting dogmatism." Indeed, this is precisely how the head of the Department of Propaganda and Agitation defended the decision to stop transmitting Soviet radio broadcasts in 1956.[17]

The leader's own rhetoric remained as tame as ever. Again and again he praised the "great Red Army" for liberating the peninsula. Entire speeches were devoted to thanking Moscow and Beijing for their aid.[18] But nothing gives the lie to the Juche myth quite like his reluctance to return to the keyword. If the 1960 edition of his *Selected Works* is anything to go by, and it is certainly much less corrupt than the editions that followed, the speech of December 1955 marked his only public mentions of *chuch'e* in the 1950s. Particularly conspicuous was the word's absence from a speech he gave in 1958 to mark the DPRK's tenth birthday.[19]

There was no sign of its sloganization in the rest of the print culture either. A dictionary of political terms published in 1957 carried no entry for *chuch'e*.[20] In 1959 the first book-length history of the DPRK's literature appeared. Although it consistently exaggerated the leader's role in cultural affairs, it made no mention of the 1955 speech or of "establishing the subject."[21] This is all outer-track stuff, of course, but according to one Soviet Korean's testimony at the Soviet embassy, the word *chuch'e* virtually disappeared even from party-internal discussion in the late 1950s.[22]

None of this prevents outside scholars from now holding up Kim's every complaint about dogmatism in these years as a bold espousal of his very own "Juche line."[23] While they are right not to focus exclusively on mentions of the word, there was nothing distinctive about the stance in question. In 1957, representatives of the ruling parties of the USSR, China, Albania, Bulgaria, Czechoslovakia, East Germany, Hungary, Mongolia, Poland, Romania, North Vietnam and North Korea signed a declaration stating, *inter alia*, that,

> Marxism-Leninism calls for a creative application of the general principles of the Socialist revolution and Socialist construction depending on the concrete conditions of each country, and rejects mechanical imitation of the policies and tactics of the Communist parties of other countries.[24]

If one subtracts this bloc-wide consensus from the so-called "Juche line" of the 1950s, what is left?[25]

It was only in October 1959 — according to the Soviet Korean official I have just mentioned — that the word *chuch'e* made a comeback: Kim To-man, the chairman of the WP's agitprop department, spoke of it at length before an audience of top officials in Pyongyang. From then on Korea's originality, and the superiority of native things to foreign ones, were stressed "in reports and lectures in restricted audiences," i.e. in the inner track. Especially interesting is the Soviet Korean's remark that senior officials knew the "author of the promotion of the thesis" to be Kim Ch'ang-man, "who is proud of this."[26]

Far from being a crony of the leader's, the propaganda official who revived talk of *chuch'e* was a member of the only remaining faction that still stood between Kim Il Sung and untrammeled power. Headed by Pak Kŭmch'ŏl, the vice-chairman of the Central Committee's Standing Committee, and at least loosely allied with Kim Ch'ang-man, this so-called Kapsan faction consisted of veterans of a resistance group which in the 1930s had operated out of the peninsula's northeast. They now sought to exaggerate the importance of their anti-Japanese activities, which they were careful to attribute to Kim Il Sung's guidance. If anything, this enhanced his stature in the short term. Yet the apparent goal was to strengthen Pak Kŭmch'ŏl's chances of becoming the next leader of the country.[27]

Whether his faction's talk of *chuch'e* is to be understood only in this context is unclear. Like Kim Il Sung's use of the word in 1955, it may well have been inspired by the need to appeal to the masses across the DMZ. In 1959, the Rhee dictatorship's growing unpopularity strengthened hopes that the ROK would collapse. A high-ranking army officer in Pyongyang told a Hungarian diplomat to expect unification in the following year.[28]

Whatever the reason, Kim Il Sung publicly mentioned *chuch'e* on

쓰딸린 거리

February 23, 1960, for the first time since 1955. "Great advances" had been made, he said, "in eradicating dogmatism and formalism and establishing the subject," and the WP was now proceeding "in conformity with . . . the specific conditions of our country."[29] Yet this was but one passing mention in a long speech studded with the true slogans of the day, of which

"*Ch'ŏllima*" (the name of the ongoing industrialization campaign) was paramount. Shortly thereafter the fourth volume of Kim's *Selected Works* appeared, covering the years from 1953 to 1956. Among the seven titles listed in unchronological order in advertisements for the volume, the speech of December 1955 came last.[30] All the same, the publication of the *Selected Works* in an edition of 300,000 must have boosted use of the word *chuch'e*.

Meanwhile, East Bloc diplomats were lamenting the burgeoning of the personality cult as well as the rise in chauvinism among cadres. The trends were connected; the more Kim's achievements were played up, the more the bloc's contributions to the DPRK had to be played down. "If the Korean comrades borrow some experience from the fraternal countries," a Soviet diplomat observed in 1959, "they are loth to speak about it."[31] News of China's great famine, and of Syngman Rhee's flight into exile in April 1960, made the regime all the more pleased with itself. In the company of foreign diplomats, some officials claimed that Kim Il Sung had improved on Marxism-Leninism. One boasted to a Hungarian, "It won't be long before the Europeans come here to learn from us."[32] If they were saying such things to their allies, one can well imagine what they were saying to each other.

Demonstrating that ideology in the DPRK is carried in talk *about* the leader, not in talk by him, Kim Il Sung continued preaching pro-Soviet internationalism in his speeches.[33] But this lip service was becoming harder to sustain. Kim could not go on forever thanking the USSR for liberating the peninsula while his people were lionizing him for the very same thing. Nor could he stay on good terms with both the Russians and the Chinese while paying far more verbal tribute to the former.

Last but not least, the rival Korea's growing instability made it all the more necessary for the North to project a sovereign appearance.[34] Under Chang Myŏn's ill-fated premiership (1960-1961), the ROK had relaxed restrictions on speech and assembly. Leftist parties had sprung up — at least one of which was funded by Pyongyang — and calls for the legalization of communism were going unpunished.[35] Although the leftists formally distanced themselves from Kim Il Sung, they shared a platform very close to what he had long called on the "Yankee colony" to implement: the start of inter-Korean dialogue, the phased withdrawal of US troops, and the introduction of socialism or social democracy.[36] Unfortunately for Kim, these opposition groups failed to appeal to the electorate at large, which remained fearful of the North and contemptuous of its perceived subservience to foreign powers.

It was more than just an excess of smugness, then, or psychological compensation for a reliance on foreign aid, that inspired a rise in North Korean chest-thumping in the latter half of 1960. No sooner had Moscow and Beijing agreed to cancel much of the DPRK's debt than Kim Il Sung, in August 1960, proclaimed the republic free of it altogether. He also asked the East European press to stop covering his aid-mooching trips.[37] The radio station broadcasting into the ROK stopped playing non-Korean music, and the number of foreign works appearing in print dropped sharply. These changes were accompanied by the publication of a brochure on the need to "establish the subject." Although the Hungarian embassy approved of the contents, it appears to have realized that there was more to this "*juche* principle," which had taken a "central position in the cultural and ideological life of the DPRK," than merely the country-specific application of Marxism-Leninism.[38]

In February 1961, the literary monthly printed an article on "the establishment of the subject in our literature."[39] For Pak Chong-sik, the writer, this was a matter of bringing "lofty national characteristics" into proper relief.[40] He recalled a WP resolution from 1947 that had called for the same thing, and quoted Kim Il Sung as having said in 1951 that writers must "reflect national characteristics" without being limited by them.[41] His speech of December 1955 was also quoted; excerpted were the lines in which the Korean revolution is called the subject of ideological work.[42] Such talk was orthodox enough, but Pak went on to imply that the Korean people were all the purer for their society's historical lack of a middle class.[43] Kim Il Sung, he wrote, exemplified the "high intellectual world, the lofty moral character of Korean communists."[44]

The Moscow Declaration of 1960 had made clear that the communist camp would tolerate no "undue emphasis" on national peculiarities.[45] Here was a case of undue emphasis if ever there was one, even if Pak made sure to define the Korean nation in terms of language and culture, not blood.[46] Having suspected that the regime was preaching excessive nationalism in the inner track, East European diplomats (starting with the Romanians) were quick to complain upon seeing evidence of it in the outer one. The guerrilla state of Western legend would have told them to mind their own business. Instead the leadership blamed these "excesses" on the editor of the literary monthly, as well as on local and provincial officials. It was claimed that the propaganda chief Kim To-man — the very man who had revived talk of *chuch'e* in 1959 — had scolded the offenders.[47]

The foreigners were not as naïve as all that. The East German embassy noted in March 1961 that outside the official news media, the personality cult was growing ever more extravagant:

> Everything the Party and the Korean people earn is attributed to [Kim]. There is no room, no classroom, no public building in which a photo of [him] cannot be found. The Museum of the War of National Liberation is designed entirely around the role of Kim Il Sung. . . . The decisive role of the Soviet Union in the liberation of Korea is completely downplayed. . . . Party propaganda is not oriented toward the study of Marxism-Leninism.[48]

That last point is a constatation of the huge gap between the ideology praised in the outer track and the one actually propagated in the inner one. Such remarks were common in the reports of East Bloc embassies.[49] The East German report also lamented a party lecture at which it had been claimed, "We as Korean comrades have always . . . pursued our own standpoint against that of others."

That is naturally a vulgar and false interpretation of the battle against dogmatism. . . . It is frequently stated that only a people like the Korean people is capable of such feats and heroism. All successes . . . are portrayed as their own successes. Great feats that were accomplished by the Soviet Union, the CSSR, Poland, and the GDR are portrayed as accomplishments of the Korean workers "without foreign" assistance. . . . These nationalist tendencies are particularly prevalent in films, in the theater and performances, and in lectures.[50]

In the inner track, in other words; and there they remained prevalent. The embassies' complaints about the journal article merely induced the WP in March 1961 to ensure that the outer track did more to feign internationalism. The literary press went back to publishing the occasional foreigner, and praise of Korea's heritage was again balanced with reminders of the need to learn from abroad.[51] The Ministry of Culture defined "the establishment of the subject" to visiting diplomats as "the combination of the creative application of Marxism-Leninism, the cultivation of progressive traditions, and the study of foreign achievements."[52]

Meanwhile things below the DMZ were looking ever better for the North. The Chang Myŏn government having failed on both the political and economic fronts, the left-wing opposition was rapidly gaining strength.[53] Kim sought to boost it by proposing an inter-Korean confederation that would leave each of the two political systems in place.[54] In later years he admitted to his Bulgarian counterpart that the proposal was meant to soften up the South for a takeover. He must have felt gratified on May 13, 1961, when young Seoulites staged a rally at which they called for a mass meeting at Panmunjŏm on the DMZ, shouting "Let's go north!" and "You [North Koreans] come south!"[55]

To conservatives such trends signified a dangerous collapse of law and order. A mere three days after the rally, the South Korean military deposed Chang in a coup. Newspapers carried the putschists' declaration of an "anti-communist revolution" which, among other things, would establish an "autonomous economy" (*chaju kyŏngje*),[56] i.e., one not dependent on any trade partner in particular. In the hope that it could work with the putschists, who included the former communist Park Chung Hee, the Kim regime delivered to embassies a formal declaration of support. It soon realized its error.[57] After emerging as the leader of the new government, Park announced that the country would cease relying on foreign powers.

Whether in response to these developments or not, the DPRK's literary press issued another burst of chauvinism in June 1961. Entitled "Thoughts on the Subject" (*chuch'e*), the article praised the peninsula's contributions to world civilization — an early planetarium, the first armored ships — before condemning the pre-modern elite for "serve-the-great-power-ism" or *sadaejuŭi*.[58] In the 1930s this pejorative had been leveled against Korean communists for their subservience to the Comintern; before that, pro-Japanese elements had used it to disparage the Chosŏn Dynasty. Neither the writer Sŏk In-hae nor his editors could have been ignorant of the word's anti-Chinese and anti-Soviet connotations.

Praise was lavished on the savior of the race:

> The establishment of our nation's subject can be said to have matured only with the anti-Japanese struggle led by Marshal Kim Il Sung in the 1930s. . . . The thorough hostility to Japanese rule, the liberation of the homeland, all the statesmanship that brought about prosperity for the future of the race, for ten thousand

generations of descendants — all this was nothing other than a struggle for the establishment of the subject.[59]

The implicit downplaying of the Red Army's role in Korea's liberation may have been what made the post office reclaim this issue of the journal from foreign embassies.[60] The regime was having difficulty keeping its propaganda tracks apart.

At the WP's fourth congress in September 1961 Kim again used the word *chuch'e*. The party, he said, had "established the subject more strongly in all fields of work."[61] This was but one lone mention in a 140-page speech. (My reader can guess which speaker discussed subject-establishing at more length, though even he devoted to it only the tail end of a sixteen-page report.)[62] Interestingly, the English-language version of the congress documents rendered Kim Il Sung's mention of the word as "the Party has established Jooche."[63] Perhaps translators were unaware that a direct English equivalent existed. An asterisk, however, led to the innocuous explanation that, "By 'Jooche' we mean that in carrying out revolution and construction we should creatively apply the general truth of Marxism-Leninism to the specific realities of our own country."[64]

In October 1961, at the CPSU congress in Moscow, Khrushchev sharply criticized Albania's personality cult. A North Korean official told the Hungarian embassy that Kim Il Sung worried the USSR would turn on him next. This may be why he stressed the need for "revitalization through one's own strength" (*charyŏk kaengsaeng*) at a Central Committee plenum the following December.[65] The term had been used since the 1930s in China and Korea — as in Japan, whence it came — to encourage citizens to make do with what is at hand instead of waiting for help.[66] This in contrast to our *self-reliance*, which implies the principled eschewal of available aid or assistance from without.

A few months later, near the end of a speech in March 1962, Kim called for "an unrelenting, resolute struggle to oppose serve-the-great-ism and dogmatism and to establish the subject," for only then would cadres be able to motivate workers to exercise "revitalization through [their] own strength."⁶⁷ Kim called for the latter only in order to "prepare for the contingency that the Soviet Union will cast us aside in the same way as happened to Albania."⁶⁸ This rather plaintive remark was kept out of the published version of the speech, which treated *charyŏk kaengsaeng* as a revolutionary virtue in itself, while watering the concept down to near meaninglessness. So often did Kim reconcile it with the acceptance of aid that one suspects (as Pyongyang-based diplomats did) he was only angling for more of the stuff, on the grounds that it would not be needed much longer. To quote the published version:

> We are not people who oppose aid from others. We welcome aid from fraternal countries. There is no one who would turn down aid that is being given. . . . [But by] conducting agricultural work well, we reduce the burden on fraternal allies: how good a thing this is! I think precisely this is internationalism.⁶⁹

And if a certain foreign country didn't like it, he hinted, it could always revert to its old largesse: "How is one to understand people who don't even provide aid, yet complain that it is nationalist to call for revitalization by one's own strength?"⁷⁰ What the Russians and other East Europeans were in fact calling nationalist was the regime's talk of having already rebuilt the country on its own, as if allies had stinted on necessary support.

It is common for militarizing states of limited means to encourage public austerity by stressing the need for autarky, which has a nicer ring to it. Nazi Germany and imperial Japan had done the same thing.⁷¹ North Vietnam was doing it at the very time in question. But Kim had an added incentive to present his republic as almost literally self-sufficient. Had the local masses known how much aid it had received and was continuing to get, they would have been less content with the meager improvement in their standard of living.

In June 1962 the press carried an article on the need to teach high-school and university students how to apply Marxism-Leninism to Korea.

ON THE EDGE OF SLOGANHOOD: 1956-1962

Textbook writers were to ensure "subjectivity" by assimilating the DPRK's own scientific advances as well as the scholarly tradition embodied by Pak Yŏn-am (1737-1805). At the same time they were to filter out foreign findings irrelevant to Korea.[72]

The article may well have inspired the Soviet ambassador to take a closer look at new textbooks, where he found nationalism in excess of East Bloc norms. In August 1962 he told a Czechoslovakian diplomat of how he had broached the matter with the Minister of Higher Education:

> Comrade Moskovskii said that [North Korean] students were recalled from the Soviet Union.... The DPRK Minister of Higher Education said that ... Marxism-Leninism is being taught as well in the DPRK as anywhere else and even better. In response to that, Comrade Moskovskii said that there actually are some differences in teaching Marxism-Leninism and pointed out that in some Korean university textbooks "juche" can be found.[73]

Obviously even the expatriate community had begun employing the word as a synecdoche for Korean chauvinism.

In the outer track, however, it remained a relatively unimportant word. The fat dictionary of the Korean language published in 1962 listed four entries for words written *chuch'e*. The first was for a lowly homonym meaning "manage, get under control" (as in, to quote the example sentence given, "He could not keep his sweat from pouring like rain"). *Chuch'e* as "subject" was but the second-placed entry, and even there the apolitical definition of it came first. Only in the second definition was it explained as the "ideological [or practical-thought, or ideational: *sasangjŏk*] viewpoint and work attitude of keeping one's own conviction, one appropriate to the task or actual situation, in the perception and evaluation of a thing or phenomenon and in all activities." A South Korean would have thought this a definition more appropriate to *chuch'esŏng* (subjectivity). It was followed by a quote from Kim's 1955 speech that clearly did not accord with it: "Precisely the Korean revolution is the subject of our party's ideological work."[74]

This was very much an outer-track definition of the word, which apparently continued to be used in chauvinist contexts in less public discussion. It was about to become a much more prominent part of the official culture as a whole.

ON THE EDGE OF SLOGANHOOD: 1956-1962

1. "Sinnyŏn ch'ukha yŏnsŏksang esŏ hasin Kim Il-sŏng wŏnsu ŭi yŏnsŏl," *Kyoyuk Sinmun*, 3 January 1956.
2. Paek, *Pukhan kwŏllyŏk ŭi yŏksa*, 226.
3. "Paro chapta" was the expression used. See "Chosŏn rodongdang chungang wiwŏnhoe saŏp ch'onggyŏl pogo e taehan Chosŏn rodongdang che-3 ch'a taehoe ŭi kyŏljŏngsŏ," *Chosŏn chung'ang nyŏn'gam* (Pyongyang, 1957), 14.
4. Szalontai, *Kim Il Sung*, 91. Lankov, *Crisis in North Korea*, 76.
5. Chang U-jong, "Tang haksŭp esŏ hyŏngsikchuŭi wa kyojojuŭi rŭl kŭnjŏl haja," *Rodong Sinmun*, 29 January 1956.
6. The article is quoted in Yi Chong-sŏk, *Chosŏn rodongdang yŏn'gu* (Seoul, 1995), 72.
7. I therefore disagree with Leonid Petrov's characterization of such research as "ultra-nationalist." See "Turning Scholars into Party Bureaucrats," *East Asian History* 31 (June 2006), 101-124. Across the Soviet sphere, heroes of the past were touted as proto-revolutionaries or reformers, usually by instancing their humanism or love of the people. Walter Ulbricht: "If you want to know the road ahead, read Goethe's *Faust* and Marx's *Communist Manifesto!*" Quoted by Evelyn Finger in "Vorwärts zu Goethe," *Die Zeit*, 27 March 2008. See also Boris Groys, *Gesamtkunstwerk Stalin* (Munich, 1996), 53-54.
8. In 1954 a Hungarian diplomat had bemoaned the DPRK's neglect of its cultural and artistic heritage. Szalontai, *Kim Il Sung*, 79.
9. Hwang, *Ŏdum ŭi p'yŏn i toen haetbyŏt'*, 42-43. This in contrast to the stubborn Western assumption that North Korea is downright Confucian in its reverence for tradition. See for example Lerner, "'Mostly Propaganda in Nature,'" 15.
10. The regime may impress foreigners with the occasional curving roof, or with the faux-traditional brush painting shown in museums, but North Koreans evince a strong tendency to equate the old with backwardness and inferiority – as every tourist knows who has tried to get his driver and minder to stop at a thatch-roofed house. Even Kim Il Sung's allegedly century-old childhood home is kept looking brand-new, right down to the spotless utensils in the kitchen. It cannot function as the ultimate symbol of racial purity unless kept

innocent of the disgraceful patina of time. One is reminded of the ahistoricity of ancient Greece as described so vividly by Oswald Spengler. (*Untergang des Abendlandes*, 328-330.) But no more than in South Korea does this mindset preclude obsession with a highly mythologized recent past. C.S. Lewis: "The unhistorical are usually, without knowing it, enslaved to a fairly recent past." *Selected Literary Essays*, 12.

11. "'Chuch'e' e taehan olbarŭn rihae rŭl wihaeyŏ," *Rodong Sinmun*, 21 July 1956. I thank Mary Nasr for bringing this article to my attention. Note that the quotation marks around *chuch'e* appear in the original.

12. Ibid.

13. Nothing was said here that had not been said more clearly on December 28, 1955. The fact that the newspaper felt compelled to run this article indicates the speech had not even been circulated inside the WP. Although the writer credited Kim Il Sung with raising the importance of the "subject," the only lengthy quote was from his report at the third WP congress in April 1956, namely the part in which (sans mention of *chuch'e*) he had called for the study of party history. None of the other quotes came from the December speech. For example, Kim was quoted as saying, "Subjugating everything to the successful carrying out of our country's revolution; precisely this is what it means to establish the subject." Though in the spirit of the December speech, that sentence appears nowhere in it. The closest equivalent: "Precisely this, the Korean revolution, is the subject of our ideological work. Therefore all ideological work without exception must be subjugated to the interests of the Korean revolution. Researching the history of the Soviet Party, or of the Chinese revolution, researching the basic principles of Marxism-Leninism: all this is in order to carry out our own revolution correctly." ("Sasang saŏp esŏ," 326.) The writer also refers, sans quotation marks this time, to Kim's having called for establishment of the subject "at every stage and in all work," a point made nowhere in the December speech. Most likely, therefore, these comments had either been recorded at another event or events, or been misremembered from the December speech.

14. Report by N.T. Federenko on a Meeting with DPRK Ambassador to the USSR Ri Sang-jo, 29 May 1956," translated by Gary Goldberg, DA/WWC.

15. A.M. Petrov, "Memorandum of a Conversation with the Head of the Department of Construction Materials under the DPRK Cabinet of Ministers, Li Pil-gyu, 20 July 1956," translated by James F. Person, DA/WWC.
16. Lankov, *Crisis in North Korea*, 58-59.
17. Paek, *Pukhan kwŏllyŏk ŭi yŏksa*, 376.
18. See for example, Kim Il Sung, "Ssoryŏn inmin kwa ŭi ch'insŏn kwa ryŏndaesŏng ŭn uri ŭi sŭngni ŭi hwakko han tambo ida," *Kŭlloja*, 15 April 1959, 30-33. In a talk to China's party organ in September 1959, Kim talked of his people's debt to the "great USSR" that had liberated them from the Japanese yoke, supported them through the war, and given "massive aid." "Cho-Jung ryangguk inmin ŭi chŏnt'ujŏk uŭi," *Kim Il-sŏng sŏnjip* 4 (1960), 441-442.
19. Kim Il Sung, "Chosŏn minjujuŭi inmin konghwaguk ch'anggŏn 10-chu'nyŏn ki'nyŏm kyŏngch'uk taehoe esŏ han pogo," *Kŭlloja*, 15 September 1958, 3-23.
20. Kim Sang-hyŏn, *Taejung chongch'i yong'ŏ sajŏn* (Pyongyang, 1957).
21. *Chosŏn Munhakt'ongsa* 2 (Pyongyang, 1959).
22. "From the Journal of N.E. Torbenkov, Record of a Conversation with DPRK MFA Counselor Pak Deok-hwan, June 01, 1960," translated by Gary Goldberg, DA/WWC.
23. See for example, Paek Hak-sun's attribution of an "emphasis on the *chuch'e* line" to a speech that neither mentions *chuch'e* nor diverges from the bloc line. *Pukhan kwŏllyŏk ŭi yŏksa*, 363.
24. *Complete Text of the Declaration of the Twelve Communist and Workers Parties, Meeting in Moscow, USSR, Nov. 14-16, 1957* (New York, 1957). Khrushchev said at the CPSU congress in 1959, "Marxism-Leninism demands the ability to apply the theory of scientific communism to the concrete conditions of each individual country in the various stages of its development." Quoted in Schlette, *Sowjethumanismus* (Munich, 1960), 62.
25. As it had always done, the WP's press kept referring to Marxism-Leninism as *inherently* creative. (Wŏn Hyŏng-guk, "Tang ŭi kunjung rosŏn ŭi kwanch'ŏl kwa il'gun'dŭl ŭi kunjung kwanjŏm," *Kŭlloja*, 1 February 1958, 38.) The next Moscow Declaration (1960) made the same points again, with more

signatories. See "Statement of 81 Communist and Workers Parties Meeting in Moscow, USSR, 1960" (New York, 1961). It was apparently issued on December 5, 1960.

26. "From the Journal of N.E. Torbenkov, Record of a Conversation with DPRK MFA Counselor Pak Deok-hwan, June 01, 1960," translated by Gary Goldberg, DA/WWC. The translation and attendant commentary evince a certain presentism. First, the Russian original's tentative-looking phonetic transliteration "Чу че" (with a space in the middle), is twice rendered as "Juche." Second, the Russian word *avtor* is watered down into the English *sponsor*, as if to preserve the notion of a thesis authored by you-know-who. The commentary turns the "thesis" into a "philosophy." Kim To-man's affiliation with a faction critical of Kim Il Sung goes unmentioned.

27. A typical Kapsan-mythmaking article of the kind appearing at that time: Kim Ŭl-ch'ŏn, "Changbaek kŭn'gŏji e issŏsŏ choguk kwangbokhoe chojik ŭi hwaktaehwa wa kŭ ŭi yŏkhal," *Kŭlloja*, June 1960, 51-56.

28. Szalontai, "You Have No Political Line of Your Own," 95.

29. "Kangsŏgun tang saŏp chido esŏ ŏdŭn kyohun e taehayŏ," *Kim Il-sŏng chŏjak sŏnjip* 2 (Pyongyang, 1968), 509.

30. See the back page of the May and August 1960 issues of *Kŭlloja*.

31. Quoted in Szalontai, *Kim Il Sung*, 128.

32. Ibid., 158.

33. We know from a Hungarian diplomat's report that in a few never-published talks in 1960 Kim complained about the translation of unsuitable textbooks such as a Hungarian one on horse-breeding. He also complained that North Korean medical science had neglected the anatomical differences (in height, etc) between local patients and the Europeans talked of in foreign textbooks. Szalontai treats this as evidence of a drive against Soviet influence (*Kim Il Sung*, 162-163), but Moscow would have agreed with Kim on the point on the question.

34. Szalontai, "You Have No Political Line of Your Own," 96.

35. Kim Hakjoon, *The Domestic Politics of Korean Unification* (Seoul, 2010), 74. The Soviet Union was informed of Pyongyang's financing of the Socialist

Mass Party. Bernd Schäfer, "Weathering the Sino-Soviet Conflict," Cold War International History Project Bulletin (2003/2004), 28.
36. Kim Hakjoon, op. cit., 78. Only the then-trendy proposal for Austrian-style neutralization of the peninsula differed fundamentally from Pyongyang's line. Advocates of neutrality called on the race to establish *chuch'esŏng* in the peninsula's affairs. Kim Sŏn-mi, "4.19 chŏnhu han sigi t'ongil undong ŭi hŭrŭm" (Seoul, 2007), 55.
37. Szalontai, *Kim Il Sung*, 165.
38. Pál Mátrai, "Embassy of Hungary in North Korea to the Hungarian Foreign Ministry, Report, 31 July 1961," translation by Balazs Szalontai, whom I thank for bringing this report to my attention. It leads one to expect more on *chuch'e* in the *Munhak Sinmun* of early 1961 than one actually ends up finding. To be sure, there were articles in which this or that branch of the cultural apparatus pledged to "establish the subject" (see for example "Chosŏn yŏn'gŭg'in tongmaeng kyŏlsŏng," on January 20, 1961), but the periodical's editors were obviously still mindful of foreign eyes. A great fuss was made in April over Yuri Gagarin's orbit of the earth. See for example Han Yun-ho's panegyric poem, "Kagarin sojwa ege," *Munhak Sinmun*, 14 April 1961.
39. Pak Chong-sik, "Uri munhak esŏ chuch'e ŭi hwangnip kwa minjokchŏk t'ŭksŏng," *Chosŏn Munhak*, February 1961, 97-111.
40. Ibid., 97.
41. Ibid.
42. Ibid., 100.
43. Ibid., 104-105.
44. Ibid., 108.
45. "Statement of 81 Communist and Workers Parties Meeting in Moscow, USSR, 1960."
46. Pak Chong-sik, op.cit., 98.
47. Mátrai, "Embassy of Hungary in North Korea, 31 July 1961."
48. "Report, Embassy of the GDR in the DPRK to the Foreign Policy and International Department of the Socialist Unity Party, GDR, 14 March 1961," translated by Grace Leonard, DA/WWC.

49. A Soviet source had in 1960 already noted that "the poor study of the classic works of Marxist-Leninism remains a significant shortcoming" of the WP ("The Economic and Political Situation of the DPRK, 12 June 1960," translated by Gary Goldberg, DA/WWC). A Czechoslovak diplomat talked of the "low theoretical level of cadres" ("1967: Information about development of politics of the DPRK and of Czechoslovak-Korean Relations," translated by Adolf Kotlik, DA/WWC). The context is the diplomat's effort to explain the WP's shift to China in the early 1960s.
50. "Report, Embassy of the GDR in the DPRK to the Foreign Policy and International Department of the Socialist Unity Party, GDR, 14 March 1961," translated by Grace Leonard, DA/WWC.
51. In the April 7, 1961 issue of *Munhak Sinmun*, several long articles appeared under the headline "The Ch'ŏllima Era and Foreign Literature." They surveyed the important foreign literary works published in the DPRK.
52. Mátrai, "Embassy of Hungary in North Korea, 31 July 1961."
53. A detailed report on these developments by the Chinese embassy in Pyongyang reflects how excitedly the host government was following them. See [PRC Embassy in the DPRK] "New Developments in the South Korean People's Struggle," 27 February 1961, translated by Anna Beth Keim, DA/WWC.
54. Kim Hakjoon, *The Domestic Politics of Korean Unification*, 84. "
55. Ibid., 96. For a photograph of a banner with these slogans see Kim Il-yŏng, *Kŏn'guk kwa puguk* (Seoul, 2004), 295. For the discussion with Bulgaria's leader, see "30 October, 1973 Memorandum on the Conversation between Kim Il Sung and Todor Zhivkov," translated by Donna Kovacheva, DA/WWC. Yet the North's confederation proposal continues to be taken at face value by softline observers in South Korea and the West.
56. "Onŭl mimyŏng kunbu-sŏ pan'gong hyŏngmyŏng," *Donga Ilbo*, 16 May 1961.
57. József Kovács, "Embassy of Hungary in North Korea to the Hungarian Foreign Ministry, Report, 24 September 1961," translated by Balazs Szalontai, and [Embassy of the GDR] "Some Problems of North Korea," 11 August 1961, translated by Bernd Schaefer; both sources DA/WWC.

58. Sŏk In-hae, "Chuch'e e taehan saenggak" [Thoughts on the subject], *Chosŏn Munhak*, June 1961, 79. This loanword had been used by Japanese and pro-Japanese Korean reformists in the late 19th century to denigrate supporters of the waning Chosŏn Dynasty, a vassal state of China. Atkins, *Primitive Selves*, 47, 94.
59. "Chuch'e e taehan saenggak," 79-80.
60. Mátrai, "Embassy of Hungary in North Korea, 31 July 1961." The Hungarian embassy heard that the actual reason was Sŏk's mentions of the word *sadaejuŭi*, which writers had been instructed not to use in official media, i.e. in the outer track. Sober heads in the regime must have realized that talk of Korea's self-liberation in 1945 was more problematic.
61. "Chosŏn rodongdang che 4-ch'a taehoe-esŏ han chung'ang wiwŏnhoe saŏp ch'onghwa pogo," *Kim Il-sŏng chŏjak sŏnjip* 3 (Pyongyang, 1968), 154.
62. Although (or because) Kim Ch'ang-man was known to foreign diplomats as an anti-Soviet element ("Journal of Soviet ambassador to the DPRK A. M. Puzanov for 31 July 1960," translated by Gary Goldberg, DA/WWC), he took pains to define the catchphrase in Marxist-Leninist terms while quoting Lenin's call to "investigate, study, seek, divine, grasp that which is unique to a nation." ("Kim Ch'ang-man tongji ŭi t'oron," in *Chosŏn nodongdang taehoe charyojip* 2, Seoul [sic], 1980, 196.) This quotation, which had turned up in July 1956 in the *Rodong Sinmun*'s clarification of the term *chuch'e*, is from "'Left-Wing' Communism, an Infantile Disorder" in which Lenin had written: "Investigate, study, seek, divine, grasp that which is peculiarly national, specifically national in the *concrete manner* in which each country approaches the fulfilment of the *single* international task, in which it approaches the victory over opportunism and "Left" doctrinairism within the working-class movement, the overthrow of the bourgeoisie, and the establishment of a Soviet republic and a proletarian dictatorship — such is the main task of the historical period through which all the advanced countries (and not only the advanced countries) are now passing." In this of all sections of his report, Kim Ch'ang-man saw no reason even to mention his boss. Cadres were evidently right in telling the Soviet embassy that he still prided himself on having originated the "thesis" of *chuch'e*.

63. *Documents of the Fourth Congress of the Workers' Party of Korea* (Pyongyang, 1961), 103.
64. Ibid.
65. Károly Fendler, "Report, Embassy of Hungary in North Korea to the Hungarian Foreign Ministry, August 1962," translated by Balazs Szalontai, DA/WWC.
66. *Kōsei* (kor. *kaengsaeng*) and *jiriki kōsei* (kor. *charyŏk kaengsaeng*) were sloganized in Japan and thus also on the peninsula in the 1930s. The colonial government started its own "rural revitalization plan" (*nongga kaengseng kyehoek*) in March 1933. Mao often used the Chinese equivalent term *zili gengsheng*. See Sandra Wilson, *The Manchurian Crisis and Japanese Society, 1931-33* (London, 2004), 91, 138; Bill Brugger, *China: Liberation and Transformation, 1942-1962* (Lanham, MD, 1981) 176. The term was also a great favorite of Park Chung Hee's.
67. "Tang chojik saŏp kwa sasang saŏp ŭl kaesŏn kanghwa halde taehayŏ," in *Kim Il-sŏng chŏjak sŏnjip* 3 (Pyongyang, 1968), 329-330.
68. Fendler, "Report, Embassy of Hungary in North Korea to the Hungarian Foreign Ministry, August 1962."
69. "Tang chojik saŏp kwa sasang saŏp ŭl kaesŏn kanghwa halde taehayŏ," 329.
70. Ibid.
71. Kurt Pätzold, Manfred Weißbecker, *Geschichte der NSDAP*, 358-359.
72. Song Jŏng-u, "Kyogwasŏ ŭi chil ŭl nop'igi wihayŏ," *Kŭlloja*, June 1962, 38.
73. Durcak, "Notes from a Conversation between Comrade Durcak of the Czech Embassy in the DPRK with the Soviet Ambassador, Comrade Moskovskii," 28 August 1962, translated by Adolf Kotlik, DA/WWC.
74. *Chosŏnmal sajŏn* (Pyongyang, 1962), 2948. Quotes from Kim's works were used throughout the dictionary to illustrate words of a political nature.

4

THE PARTY'S SUBJECT THOUGHT: 1962-1967

THE MOST FLATTERING explanation for North Korea's stability and longevity, and therefore the explanation that has prevailed in Western academia since the 1980s, is that the regime has been uniquely successful in adapting communism to Korean traditions. Along with the reduction of those traditions to a misrepresented Confucianism, this so-called indigenization model entails much exaggeration of the forthrightness with which North Korea deviated from East Bloc conventions. Hence, as we have seen, the glamorization of Kim Il Sung's so-called Juche speech of December 1955 as a "declaration of independence from Soviet control." It also inspires the claim, which can be encountered in various formulations, that in the 1960s the DPRK "frankly broke with Marxism-Leninism" in order to "establish the nationalist philosophy 'Juche' as the reigning state doctrine."[1] In this and the next chapter I will show that there was nothing nationalist or philosophical about *chuch'e sasang* as then defined, nor did the decade see any formal shift in ideology.

On December 5, 1962, the journal *Kŭlloja* carried an article on problems in ideological instruction. It is unremarkable except for the point where the writer, one Pak Ki-sŏn, calls for cadres to be armed with "the subject's thought" (*chuch'e ŭi sasang*) in opposition to "all anti-Marxist currents."[2] The context shows that this was to be seen, like Mao's *sixiang* (the Chinese equivalent of the Korean *sasang*), as but practical thought for the application of Marxism-Leninism to local conditions. Two weeks later, on December 19, the *Rodong Sinmun* published an editorial commemorating a Central Committee plenum held in December 1952, which had purportedly stressed the need to "establish the subject."[3] The most noteworthy part of the article:

> To implement the party's subject thought [*chuch'e sasang*] more thoroughly in real life, we must arm ourselves strongly with party policies that creatively apply the principles of Marxism-Leninism to our country's reality.[4]

An even clearer indication of the new term's importance was a long article commemorating the 1952 plenum which appeared in *Kŭlloja* on December 20.[5]

> Only by being equipped with the subject's thought could [the WP] overcome wartime trials and difficulties. . . . At the fifth joint plenum Comrade Kim Il Sung's teachings thoroughly armed all party members and officials with the subject's thought. He taught that dogmatism, formalism and national nihilism were to be overcome in all endeavors, and emphasized in particular that Marxism-Leninism must be regarded as a guide to action, and that in order to apply it creatively, research into our country's realities must be strengthened. . . .[6]

Although the article's alternation between the terms "subject(ive) thought" and "subject's thought" shows we are not yet dealing with a new official doctrine, the term *chuch'e* and its derivatives were used here in sloganeering fashion for the first time.

THE PARTY'S SUBJECT THOUGHT: 1962-1967

These articles may well have been innocently occasioned by the tenth anniversary of a plenum at which Kim Il Sung, as we saw in an earlier chapter, had called for creative application of Marxism-Leninism. The press often marked anniversaries of party events. But this one could have been fittingly celebrated with lip service to "Comrade Kim Il Sung's revolutionary thought," the usual umbrella term for everything the leader brought to the equation. Talk of "the subject's thought" or "subject thought" seemed intended to dissociate this construct from that older one, since the word *chuch'e* was far more common outside the leader's discourse than in it.

It is likely that the new catchphrase had to do with the fact that vice-premier Kim Ch'ang-man, who had initiated discussion of *chuch'e* and spoken the most on this topic at two congresses, was then at the height of his power. Only a few months earlier, he had managed to have the leader's top hagiographer purged.[7] It therefore seems safe to assume that by this time he had joined forces with the Kapsan faction in trying to widen the spotlight then focused on Kim Il Sung. Both the vice-premier and the Kapsan faction's leader Pak Kŭm-ch'ŏl, who was fourth in the formal hierarchy, had reason to fancy their chances of taking over someday. Since their offices gave them much control over propaganda, they were in a good position to make a difference.[8] It helped that neither the dictator nor his inner circle was interested in theoretical discussion.

In short, I agree with the South Korean researcher Sŏ Chae-jin that early praise of "subject(ive) thought" or "subject's thought" reflected an effort to restore some of the stature the party had lost to the personality cult.[9] Although Kim Il Sung's leadership of the WP was formally acknowledged — just as the USSR's leadership of the communist camp was — the relevant propaganda left no doubt that its body of thought was to be regarded as a collective product.

South of the DMZ, the word *chuch'e* and its cognates were being put to bolder use. Since taking power in mid-1961, Park Chung Hee had spoken more often of the need for national subjectivity than Kim Il Sung had done since 1945. This is from the presidential inauguration speech he held on December 17, 1963:

> To promote this great reform movement... we must first unfold an individual spiritual revolution in ourselves. Our citizens, starting with each individual, must foster an autonomous subject consciousness [*chajujŏk chuch'e ŭisik*], firmly establishing a spirit of independence and self-help, according to which one realizes one's own fate; and to build democracy and a flourishing welfare society in this land, national subjectivity, a public spirit of spontaneous active participation and a mental attitude of strong effort must be properly established.[10]

This was in no small part a response to Washington's determination to reduce its aid to Seoul.[11] All the same, for the first time since 1945, the ROK could make a strong case for being the more sovereign part of the peninsula. To make matters worse for Kim, Park's export-oriented policies began paying off just as the DPRK's economy ran out of steam. The rapid narrowing of the gap in living standards threatened Kim's plan to push for pan-Korean elections after his system had conclusively bested the other. The official media responded by going on the defensive — and making Park-like use of the word *chuch'e* in the process.

> Our enemies rattle on as if our republic were "subordinate" to another socialist country.... We do not act in accordance with anyone else's instruction or command. Instead, proceeding according to what is in the national interest of our masses and the shared

interest of the world's masses, we solve all problems in a subjective manner, on the basis of our own decisions. . . .[12]

It was at this early time, when the word *chuch'e* was more Park Chung Hee's word than Kim's, that American scholars began treating it as a uniquely North Korean term of great importance. Two of the academic articles anthologized in *North Korea Today* (1963) refer to it.[13] One does so only in passing.

> The key to Workers' Party behavior . . . is emergent Korean nationalism exemplified in an article published on the occasion of the fiftieth birthday of Kim Il Sung in April 1962, which stressed the establishment of *chuch'e* by the WP and mentioned neither Russia nor China.[14]

Note the misleading implication that Pyongyang was going it alone. Note also how the co-writers conveyed the impression that *chuch'e* defied translation, although they provided the words "autonomy" and "independence" in parentheses as if to offer at least a rough guide. (Confusion, then, from the very start.)[15] The co-writers of the other article referred with grudging respect to Kim's "now famous speech positing his thesis of 'Chuch'e,'" which they rendered into English as "national individuality" and "independence."[16] Let us keep in mind here that the speech in question was then far from famous in the DPRK itself, and that although the press had duly praised Kim Il Sung's guidance, it was years away from treating "subject(ive) thought" as his personal anything. American academics can therefore lay claim to having merged the Kim and Juche myths before the personality cult did. Their belief in *chuch'e sasang*'s originality and uniqueness may well have encouraged the regime to make more of it.

The irony is that the DPRK was then looking uncannily like an Asian Albania. From 1963 to late 1964 the *Rodong Sinmun* echoed

Beijing's every foreign-policy point while celebrating Korean-Chinese friendship more than it had done during the war. Although the WP remained averse to criticizing Moscow in its own voice, it published entire Chinese editorials and articles of an anti-Soviet nature.[17] (And to think Kim had once grumbled about the copying of *Pravda* headlines!) But like the Sovietophilia of the 1950s, the new Sinophilia featured mainly in showcase propaganda; in the inner track the regime continued tooting only its own horn.

As the East German ambassador complained to his home office, the North Koreans used "differentiated speech codes" when talking to representatives of communist countries on the one hand, and to sympathetic visitors from non-allied countries on the other.[18] The latter, it seems, were more likely to hear outbursts of inner-track sentiment. When the British economist Joan Robinson spent a week in Pyongyang in autumn 1964, she heard no term belabored so stridently by her hosts as that of (establishing) *chuch'e*.[19] Although her travelogue passed on the regime's formal assurances that it was merely applying Marxism-Leninism to local conditions, she realized "*chuch'e*" was functioning in the vernacular as a nationalist or even xenophobic catchword.

Published in January 1965, the Englishwoman's article gave rise to two fateful if understandable misconceptions. The first was that the outer-track term *chuch'e sasang* stood for the mindset expressed by inner-track use of the word *chuch'e*. The result was the West's assumption that Juche ideology consisted of a stridently nationalist Marxism-Leninism, something in fact propagated in neither track. The second misconception was that it manifested itself primarily in an obsession with attaining to self-reliance above the DMZ. B.C. Koh wrote along such lines the following winter in the Canadian journal *Pacific Affairs*.[20] Like Robinson, he took a rosier view of the DPRK's economy than did Eastern European observers,[21] and implied that self-reliance had become a goal as important as, and perhaps more important than, the goal of unification. In fact Kim continued to leave his allies in no doubt that the North needed to succeed, especially on the economic front, in order to win over the South Korean public.[22]

The DPRK had parted ways with China by the time Robinson's piece appeared. Far from living up to its new reputation as a bastion of autonomy, however, it swung back to alignment with the USSR, even if the official media did not wax as fulsome about the relationship as before. Diplomats in Pyongyang attributed Kim's change of heart to the inferior quality and quantity of Chinese aid, the military kind in particular.[23]

It was in April 1965 that he finally recurred to discussion of *chuch'e* (as opposed to merely mentioning it in passing).[24] Had he grasped the dangers of leaving meta-ideological discussion to his or his son's rivals in the WP? Or did he want more of the limelight the catchword was getting overseas? But perhaps the time and venue of the speech in question are sufficient explanation. Kim was then in Indonesia to commemorate the tenth anniversary of the Bandung Conference, which had laid the groundwork for the Non-Aligned Movement. The theme of autonomy virtually thrust itself upon him. But the Aliarcham Academy of Social Sciences at which Kim chose to speak was run by Indonesia's enormous communist party, which leaned toward Beijing. It was a school of Marxism-Leninism, and thus the last place at which Kim would have chosen to break publicly with that ideology, even had he wanted to. It seems likely, therefore, that Kim's real purpose in speaking at the academy was to let the world and especially the Chinese know that his country had not realigned itself as squarely with Moscow as appearances might suggest.[25]

Outside scholars have long regarded the Aliarcham speech, which appeared in the *Rodong Sinmun* a few days later, as the second great milestone in the history of Kim's unique Juche ideology. (The venue at which he chose to plant it does not strike them as odd.)²⁶ The North Koreans themselves had in fact heard the content before. Yet again, es-

tablishing the subject was defined as a matter of applying Marxism-Leninism creatively to local conditions. Kim was at obvious pains to make clear that "subject thought" or "the subject's thought" — he too vacillated between the terms — "is in accordance with this [international] communist movement's principles, indeed flows directly forth from it."²⁷ The speech's most famous part stands out more for its succinctness than anything else:

> While opposing revisionism and fighting in tenacious defense of the purity of Marxism-Leninism, our party has undertaken all possible effort to oppose dogmatism and serve-the-great-ism and to establish the subject. In practical thought, the subject; in politics, autonomy; in economics, independence; in national security, self-defense: this is the standpoint to which our party consistently adheres.²⁸

I depart here from the Western convention of mistranslating that second sentence as: "In ideology, Juche ... in economics, self-sufficiency," etc.²⁹ *Sasang* is practical thought for the application of the ideology of Marxism-Leninism. *Chuch'e* is "the subject." And yes, *charip* is "independence," the state of not being dependent on any foreign power. Park Chung Hee's references to *charip* have always been rendered into English that way; why should Kim's be translated differently?³⁰ To be sure, the latter spoke in Jakarta of the need to make full use of one's own nation's resources before looking elsewhere for assistance.³¹ But he promptly added, "Of course, we sufficiently acknowledge the importance of international support and aid, and acknowledge that we need other countries' aid. . . . By no means do we oppose economic cooperation between countries, nor are we proposing to build socialism after closing our doors."[32]

In the same speech Kim sought to put the DPRK's acceptance of aid in a better light by claiming that it was being used to develop subjective capabilities. Grossly understating the amount already received, he contrasted this stance with Seoul's alleged reliance on Washington's enslaving hand-outs.[33] His rhetoric must have been motivated to some extent by the need to counter South Korean propaganda, but Pyongyang's embassy row was no doubt right in assuming that he also wanted a) to preclude domestic criticism of his failure to improve living conditions, and b) to improve his chances of getting still more aid.[34]

That the speech was rather bold by Kim's standards goes without saying. His audience, however, can hardly have been very excited. Whether rightly or wrongly, the Indonesian communists had prided themselves for years on their independence from Beijing and Moscow, and since 1963 their leader had talked of the enervating effect of foreign aid and the need for "standing on one's own feet."[35] Kim had not said anything particularly daring even by East Bloc standards; Romania was then using much stronger language with impunity.[36] Let us stop treating the speech as a programmatic declaration of equidistance from Moscow and Beijing and see it for what it was: a profession of neutralism in the Sino-Soviet conflict aimed at maintaining *equiproximity* to two vital sources of aid and protection.[37]

Contrary to yet another fallacy, the Jakarta speech did not kick off a *bona fide* Juche era in Kim's discourse.[38] On October 10, 1965, the dictator ran through the WP's history in a long speech, pausing 66 times for "resounding applause."[39] At one point, he reiterated the line he had told the Indonesians: "In practical thought, the subject; in politics, autonomy; in the economy, independence." (*"Resounding applause."*)[40] There were only four other references to "the subject" — each in the familiar formula "establish the subject," used in the narrow 1955 sense of opposing dogmatism.[41] Especially conspicuous is the word's absence from the finale, in which he wished long life to the glorious WP (*"resounding applause"*), the heroic Korean people ("*resounding applause*"), and the "invincible banner of Marxism-Leninism" ("*standing ovation, extended applause like thunder*").⁴²

Even at this late date, in other words, "subject(ive) thought" loomed larger in the party's discourse than in Kim's. To be sure, due respect was paid to him as one who had always striven to "establish the subject," and his mentions of that phrase in Indonesia and in 1955 did not go unquoted.⁴³ But no claims were yet being made for the originality of the thing in question. It was country-specific, to be sure, but so, it was taken for granted, were the *sasang* of other states. In 1966 the country's official yearbook vaunted the WP's adherence to the "purity of Marxism-Leninism"; it would be another few years before the yearbook so much as mentioned *chuch'e sasang* in this context.⁴⁴ On the WP's list of assigned reading matter, Kim Il Sung's writings continued to occupy a lower place than Lenin's and Stalin's.⁴⁵ If cadres'  knowledge of the Soviet orthodoxy was as bad as East European diplomats kept claiming, their knowledge of Kim's work must have been worse.

Clearly, then, his talk of *chuch'e sasang* at this time was not intended to serve the personality cult or to agitate the masses to any other end. It seems to have been meant a) to insulate the WP against the ideological crosswinds blowing down from the USSR and China, and b) to project more sovereignty southward, while c) making the DPRK's refusal to choose between its main patron-states look less obviously like an effort to milk both. Far from posing as a generator of new ideology, Kim wanted to be seen in these years as a camp-uniting guardian of the golden mean between dogmatism and revisionism.⁴⁶ Points were to be scored with Beijing by rejecting Soviet-style reforms, and with Moscow by containing a personality cult that now seemed moderate in comparison to Mao's. Hence the conspicuous emphasis — not least in Kim's own speeches — on *chuch'e sasang* as a collective product. "Our party's subject(ive) thought":

THE PARTY'S SUBJECT THOUGHT: 1962-1967

this was the standard phrase.[47] Some articles on it made no mention of the leader at all.[48]

Having ridden high throughout the first half of the decade, Kim Ch'ang-man, the initiator of *chuch'e* rhetoric, disappeared from the political scene in early 1966. He was only fifty-nine. It is tempting to think that the leader got him out of the way in order to abduct his theoretical baby, but no evidence or testimony supports such an explanation. In any case, the DPRK was then still maintaining some semblance of party-democratic procedure. Kim Il Sung could not have eliminated such a powerful official so quickly and silently on his own whim. The Kapsan faction must have assented to the unfortunate man's purge, if only to strengthen its own chances of providing a successor to Kim Il Sung. His removal may also have been intended to palliate the Soviet embassy, which had long regarded him as a hostile element.[49] Yet the Kapsan faction was itself perceived by foreign diplomats as pro-Chinese, or at least unwilling to align the DPRK as squarely with Moscow as Kim Il Sung wanted. The latter's lack of subjectivity evidently came under criticism on the eve of a WP conference in October 1966.[50] This may have influenced his decision to refrain from explicit criticism of Beijing during his report, which did, however, make dogmatism out to be a greater threat than revisionism.

There followed a period in which chroniclers of the colonial past paid more attention to the exploits of members of the Kapsan faction.[51] An historical play glorifying Pak Kŭm-ch'ŏl's anti-Japanese activities was also staged.[52] Over the winter of 1966-1967 the personality cult cooled off enough for foreign diplomats to take notice, and for China's Red Guards to assert that a change in leadership was underway.[53] In January 1967 the Korean Central News Agency angrily denied these rumors, but the cult maintained a low profile in the outer track.[54] This was a time when a headline could still start with the words, "Comrade Kim Il Sung and other party and government leaders . . ."[55]

The man himself was yet to claim any great ideological attainments. At a gathering of party secretaries in March 1967, he made a remarkable admission.

> Up to 1956, although I was in the cabinet, I mainly occupied myself with administrative affairs, so I lacked the time to pay much attention to party-internal matters. Taking advantage of this . . . [factionalists] revised and implemented at will things that had been decided on in the party. Even worse, [Soviet Korean] people like Hŏ Ka-i and Pak Yŏng-bin went in and out of foreign embassies to get their orders instead of implementing the party's. Due to these factionalists' scheming no small number of people were unaware even of what the party's unitary ideological system was. . . . This is why I took control of party affairs and led them from 1956 on. In the ten years from that time to today, I have striven to establish a unitary ideological system inside the party.[56]

The implication is that Kim would not have assumed ideological leadership at all had the WP not run into difficulties without him.

Although the new catchphrase of "unitary ideology" may have been inspired by a similar Chinese term,[57] Kim invoked it only to urge support for WP policy-making; he was not yet laying claim to anything of his own conception. The situation was thus very different from that in China, which in 1966 was already wrapped up in what Martin calls the "pious veneration, the moralizing exegesis, and the absolutizing of all Mao's utterances."[58]

Kim evidently took action against Pak Kŭm-ch'ŏl and other members of the Kapsan faction in early spring 1967, when they stopped making public appearances.[59] He did not, however, immediately pass off *chuch'e sasang* as his personal product. How low a position it still occupied in the official culture can be seen from an article about the anti-Japanese struggle published in the May 1967 issue of *Kŭlloja*:

> And in this time was created the tradition of unlimited loyalty to the revolution and the Leader, of firm belief in Marxism-Leninism and unbending revolutionary spirit, of burning hatred for the enemies and warm love for the homeland and the masses, of subject

thought, of socialist patriotism and proletarian internationalism, and other elements of the Marxist-Leninist ideological system.[60]

A Central Committee plenum held in late May was used — at Kim Jong Il's urging, according to later hagiography — to publicize the imposition of a "unitary ideological system."[61] This announcement, which would henceforth be referred to as Kim Il Sung's "May 25 Teaching," is recalled by defectors as having transformed the DPRK from a dysfunctional party state into a one-man dictatorship. There certainly ensued a wide purge of the Kapsan faction's real and presumed followers.[62] Yet the effect of the May 25 Teaching was not immediately obvious to foreigners; the outer track reflected no great change in the leader's stature until the second half of 1967.

1. Cumings, *North Korea: Another Country*, 107.
2. Pak Ki-sŏn, "Tang sasang kyoyang saŏp esŏ chegi toenŭn myŏt' kaji munje," *Kŭlloja*, 5 December 1962, 6. This reference is overlooked by many scholars, who prefer to think of the first mention of the body of thought as having come later that month, in the *Rodong Sinmun* article which mentioned *chuch'e sasang*. (See the endnote below this one.) But there is no reason for taking only the latter term seriously, considering that *chuch'e ŭi sasang* and *chuch'e sasang* were used interchangeably until 1966. I suspect advocates of the conventional wisdom are discomfited by the fact that the term made its first appearance not in a newspaper editorial (which could conceivably have been ordered or even penned by Kim Il Sung himself), but in a journal article by a scribe who drew no great attention to it.
3. "1952-nyŏn tang chung'ang wiwŏnhoe che 5-ch'a chŏnwŏnhoe ŭi ryŏksajŏk ŭiŭi," *Rodong Sinmun*, 19 December 1962. The writer also mentioned Kim's "historic speech" of December 1955 — "historic" being an attribute now ascribed to virtually all the Leader's public words and deeds — which had constituted "a powerful guide" in the fight against dogmatism. But the editorial neither quoted from the speech nor made clear what it had added to an already-established line.
4. Ibid.
5. "Uri tang ŭi chojik sasangjŏk kanghwa paltchŏn esŏ ryŏksajŏk ŭiŭi rŭl kajinŭn chŏnwŏn hoeŭi," *Kŭlloja*, 20 December 1962, 2-25.
6. Ibid., 24.
7. The man in question was of course Han Sŏrya. Yi Hang-gu, "Pukhan ŭi chakka taeyŏl sok esŏ," *Pukhan* 118 (January 1974), 244-249.
8. Paek, *Pukhan kwŏllyŏk ŭi yŏksa*, 601. There were, for example, Kim To-man, head of the CC's department of propaganda, and Ko Hyŏk, chairman of its arts and culture section.
9. Sŏ Chae-jin, "Chuch'e sasang ŭi hyŏngsŏng gwa pyŏnhwa e taehan saeroun punsŏk" (Seoul, 2001), 37-38.

10. "Sŏngsŏ rŭl ingnŭndanŭn myŏngmok arae ch'otbul ŭl humch'inŭn haengwi ka chŏngdang hal su ŏpta," *Pak Chŏng-hŭi taet'ongnyŏng sŏnjip* 4 (Seoul, 1969), 16.
11. Nicholas Eberstadt, "Western Aid," in *North Korea in Transition* (Plymouth, UK, 2013), 142.
12. "Ch'ullo nŭn minjok ŭi chaju t'ong'il e itta," *Kŭlloja*, 20 April 1963, 12.
13. Key P. Yang and Chang-Boh Chee, "North Korean Educational System," in *North Korea Today*, ed. Robert Scalapino (New York, 1963), 129-130; and, in the same book, Glenn D. Paige and Dong Jun Lee, "The Post-War Politics of Communist Korea," 25.
14. Paige and Lee, 25.
15. Ibid.
16. Yang and Chee, "North Korean Educational System," 129-130.
17. "Excerpts from the report of the Soviet Embassy in Pyongyang 'Some new aspects of Korean-Chinese relations in the first half of 1965'," 4 June 1965. Note that as late as February 1963 the WP press, while defending China, was still referring to "the great USSR." "Sahoejuŭi chinyŏng ŭi t'ongil ŭl suho hamyŏ kukche kongsanjuŭi undong ŭi tan'gyŏl ŭl kanghwa haja," *Kŭlloja*, February 1963, 3. Some Western historians try to make even this shift to China seem nationalist by implying that it took courage to turn away from the USSR. In fact Moscow was disengaging itself from East Asia at the time in question (though this policy was later reversed). Richard Wich, *Sino-Soviet Crisis Politics*, 126.
18. Horst Brie, "Letter from GDR Embassy in the DPRK to State Secretary Hegen, December 12, 1966," translated by Karen Riechert, DA/WWC.
19. Joan Robinson, "Korean Miracle," *Monthly Review*, 16, No. 8 (January 1965), 541–549.
20. B.C. Koh, "North Korea and its Quest for Autonomy," *Pacific Affairs* 38, No. 3/4 (Autumn, 1965 – Winter, 1965/1966), 294-306. He has recently revised his first appraisal of *juche*. See "An Elusive Quest with Mixed Results," *Pacific Affairs* 87, No. 4 (December 2014), 809-814. I wish the scope of this

book did not confine me to making critical remarks about Prof. Koh's work, from which I have learned a great deal.
21. The Czech ambassador reported in 1965 that the DPRK media's sudden focus on foreign policy was meant to detract public attention from worsening economic difficulties. "On the Development of the Situation in the DPRK in May 1965," translated by Adolf Kotlik, DA/WWC.
22. "Report, Embassy of Hungary in North Korea to the Hungarian Foreign Ministry, 2 July 1960," translated by Balazs Szalontai, DA/WWC. Relevant in this context is also the statement of the DPRK ambassador to Prague in 1961 that the North needed to improve the quality of its consumer goods in order to make a good impression on visiting South Koreans. Szalontai, "You Have No Political Line of Your Own," 96.
23. Wegricht, "Changes in the leadership of the Korean Workers Party and the government of North Korea," 12 July 1965, translated by Bernd Schaefer, DA/WWC.
24. Kim Il Sung, "Chosŏn minjujuŭi inmin konghwaguk esŏ ŭi kŏnsŏl kwa nam chosŏn hyŏngmyŏng e taehayŏ," *Kŭlloja*, 20 April 1965, 17.
25. "Excerpts from the report of the Soviet Embassy in Pyongyang 'Some new aspects of Korean-Chinese relations in the first half of 1965," translated by Sergey Radchenko, 4 June 1965, DA/WWC.
26. See for example Sung Chull Kim's *North Korea Under Kim Jong Il* (Albany, NY, 2006), 108; Heonik Kwon and Byung-Ho Chung's *North Korea: Beyond Charismatic Politics* (Plymouth, 2012), 145. When historians talk vaguely of how North Korea broke with Marxism-Leninism in the 1960s, I have to assume that they consider this the event at which the break took place. Little to no attention is devoted to the nature of the venue, or to what the Indonesian communists already believed. Readers are usually given to understand that Kim proclaimed his original Juche principles or philosophy to a non-communist audience, to great international effect. (See for example Kwon and Chung, op. cit, 139-140; Armstrong, *Tyranny of the Weak*, 148.)
27. Kim Il Sung, "Chosŏn minjujuŭi inmin konghwaguk esŏ ŭi kŏnsŏl," 17-18.

28. Ibid., 18. Jae-Jung Suh has asserted that this sprinkling of words "formalized Juche in terms of a set of concrete programs." See "Making Sense of North Korea," 11.
29. See for example Mitchell Lerner, "'Mostly Propaganda in Nature,'" NKIDP Working Paper # 3 (December 2010), 88; David Maxwell, "What to Make of North Korea," *The Diplomat*, 11 April 2013; Armstrong, *Tyranny of the Weak*, 216.
30. See for example Hyung-A Kim, "Heavy and Chemical Industrialization, 1973-1979," in *Reassessing the Park Chung Hee Era, 1961-1979* (Seattle, 2011), 19. The DPRK's own translators talk only of an "independent economy" in the constitution and in Baik Bong's Kim Il Sung biography, *From Independent National Economy to 10-point Political Programme* (Tokyo, 1970). There is no justification for the Western tradition of translating only Kim's references to *charip* as "self-reliance," "self-sufficiency" or "self-sustenance," to say nothing of the reader-bullying practice of leaving the word untranslated, and sometimes capitalized to boot, as if it were yet another mysterious concept unique to the DPRK. Westerners' susceptibility to this sort of thing has induced North Korea's own translators to give similar treatment to words they once saw no reason not to translate. See for example Jajusong (to be dimly understood as meaning autonomy *and so much more*).
31. Kim Il Sung, "Chosŏn minjujuŭi inmin konghwaguk esŏ ŭi kŏnsŏl," 20.
32. Ibid., 19-20.
33. Ibid., 25. Kim claimed that aid totaled 500 million rubles or $550 million. (Ibid., 20.) Yoon T. Kuark, referring to published academic sources, arrived at an estimate of about ten times that much — excluding military aid — between 1946 and 1961. See "North Korea's Industrial Development during the Post-War Period," *North Korea Today*, 61.
34. "Telegram from Pyongyang to Bucharest, No.76:208," June 15, 1967, translated by Eliza Gheorghe, DA/WWC. In 1965, the regime criticized the Chinese for giving less than before. Bernd Schaefer, "North Korean 'Adventurism' and China's Long Shadow, 1966-1972," Cold War International History Project, Working Paper #44 (Washington, DC, 2004), 5.

35. Rex Mortimer, *Indonesian Communism Under Sukarno* (Jakarta, 2006), 235-237.
36. Richard Wich, *Sino-Soviet Crisis Politics* (Cambridge, MA, 1980), 131.
37. Such neutralism was common in the communist camp at the time. Ibid., 137.
38. See for example Armstrong, *Tyranny of the Weak*, 53 and 129.
39. "Chosŏn rodongdang ch'anggŏn 20-chu'nyŏn e chehayŏ," *Kŭlloja*, 20 October 1965, 2-24.
40. Ibid., 11.
41. Ibid., 11-13.
42. Ibid., 24.
43. A relevant article printed in October 1965 contained several quotes from Kim's Indonesia speech. Sin Chin-gyun, "Chuch'e sasang ŭn kongsanjuŭijŏk chaju charip ŭi sasang ida," *Kŭlloja*, 5 October 1965, 7-21. It also recalled his speech of December 1955 as the first "comprehensive" elucidation of "the Party's subject thought," yet quoted only a few words from it, which, unlike the other excerpts from Kim, were not printed in bold. Ibid., 18-19.
44. See *Chosŏn chung'ang nyŏn'gam* from 1961 (page 145) to 1968 (page 64).
45. Hwang, *Ŏdum ŭi p'yŏn i toen haetbyŏt'*, 48.
46. Sŏ Chae-jin, "Chuch'e sasang ŭi hyŏngsŏng gwa pyŏnhwa e taehan saeroun punsŏk" (Seoul, 2001), 37-38.
47. Ch'oi Sŏng-uk, *Uri tang ŭi chuch'e sasang gwa sahoejuŭijŏk aegukchuŭi* (Pyongyang, 1966).
48. See for example the lead-off article "Munhak esŏ ŭi chuch'e hwangnip kwa sahoejuŭi aegukchuŭi kyoyang ŭi kanghwa rŭl wihayŏ," *Chosŏn Munhak*, July 1966, 2-3. See also the concluding chapter of the pointedly-titled *Uri tang ŭi chuch'e sasang kwa sahoejuŭijŏk aegukchuŭi*, edited by Hong Sŏn-bong *et al* (Pyongyang, 1966), 90-91.
49. Kim Ch'ang-man had long been considered pro-Chinese by the Soviet embassy. A. Puzanov, "Journal of Soviet Ambassador in the DPRK A. M. Puzanov for 25 June 1960," translated by Gary Goldberg, DA/WWC.
50. See Document No.1, "Telegram from Pyongyang to Bucharest, No. 76.203, Top Secret, June 13, 1967," translated by Eliza Gheorghe, DA/WWC.
51. Paek, *Pukhan kwŏllyŏk ŭi yŏksa*, 588-589.

52. Some South Korean researchers refer to *Ilpyŏn tansim* as having been a movie (which is not impossible, considering that the Kapsan faction then had a hold on the film studio), but North Korean sources say it was a play. *Kim Chŏng-il chidoja* (Tokyo, 1984), 141-142.
53. "Telegram from Pyongyang to Bucharest," 13 June 1967, DA/WWC.
54. "Chosŏn minjujuŭi inmin konghwaguk chungang t'ongsinsa sŏngmyŏng," *Rodong Sinmun*, 27 January 1967.
55. "Kim Il-sŏng tongji rŭl pirot han tang kwa chŏngbu chidojadŭl i chaeil tongp'odŭl i mandŭn ch'ŏnyŏnsaek changp'yŏn kirok yŏnghwa <choguk ŭi haepit' arae> rŭl posiyŏtta," *Rodong Sinmun*, 23 March 1967.
56. "Tangsaŏp ŭl kaesŏn hamyŏ tang taep'yojahoe kyŏljŏng ŭl kwanch'al halde taehayŏ," *Kim Il-sŏng chŏjakchip* (Pyongyang, 1983), 21:136-137.
57. Lin Biao had begun making much of the need for a "unified ideology" (*tongyi sixiang*) in 1966. Martin, *Cult and Canon*, 26. Directly translating that phrase into Korean as *t'ongil sasang* would not have been feasible, because it would have been assumed to refer to the unification of the peninsula.
58. Ibid., 27.
59. "Telegram from Pyongyang to Bucharest, No. 76.203, June 13, 1967," DA/WWC.
60. "Poch'ŏnbo ch'ŏnt'u sŭngni 30 chu'nyŏn," *Kŭlloja*, May 1967, 5.
61. *Kim Chŏng-il, chidoja*, 141-142.
62. Kim Min-su, "5.25 kyosi ga Pukhan sahoe e mich'in yŏnghyang," Radio Free Chosun, 26 May 2014.

5

KIM IL SUNG'S SUBJECT THOUGHT: 1967-1971

THE DICTATOR'S TRIUMPH over his Kapsan rivals was followed by increasing talk of a policy of "parallel advance," according to which the tasks of military armament and economic development would receive equal attention.¹ In practice the regime was putting guns before rice, as the East German embassy reported home.² Party and public were urged to prepare for liberation of the South; even women and children had to undergo weapons training. The 1960s thus saw the *de facto* start of the "Military-First" policy which the regime did not exoterically own up to for another few decades. Diplomats in Pyongyang were no doubt correct in concluding that the "warmongering psychosis" (as a North Vietnamese diplomat called it) was meant to distract public attention from economic problems while encouraging Moscow to send more aid.³ But such motivations do not preclude the possibility that the regime was planning another invasion in earnest.

Boasts of non-alignment and neutralism were accompanied by no real-world movement away from the USSR. In August 1967 a Soviet embassy official bragged to his Romanian counterpart of the renewed closeness of Moscow-Pyongyang relations.⁴ Soviet-Korean trade was predicted to increase by almost 50% in 1968.⁵ But Kim was naturally reluctant to burn his bridges with his other main patron. Criticism of Mao and the Cultural Revolution was therefore limited to party lectures and other inner-track propaganda.⁶ Kim's vague public criticisms of dogmatism or "left opportunism" were decoded for cadres in explicitly anti-Beijing instruction.⁷

The Chinese were not deceived. A Romanian diplomat in Pyongyang reported in April 1967 on a conversation with a counselor from the PRC embassy, who said that

> whoever knew the North Koreans was aware that one should not listen to what they said in public but pay attention to what they did in practice.... [He said:] The North Korean leadership are asking for and receiving from China wheat (200,000 tons), soy beans for oil (60,000 tons), coke, coal, crude oil. In spite of all this, they are misinforming the population about how China is not delivering the aforementioned goods, how it does not respect its treaty obligations, all this in order to starve off the population and economically strangle the DPRK.⁸

Bill Clinton was therefore not the first to be accused of wanting to "strangle" the country even as he pumped aid into it. We see here that the national attitude Western observers flatteringly refer to as self-reliance — i.e., the proud forgoing of help as a virtue in itself — was in fact called for in response to the outside world's alleged refusal to help the DPRK, or even to conduct fair trade. The Chinese diplomat astutely interpreted this misinformation as an effort to squeeze more aid out of Moscow.

Sure enough, Kim asked the Russians in 1967 to increase their supply of the very goods in question, claiming that Beijing had refused to deliver them.⁹

The leader had hitherto been praised far more effusively in the inner than the outer track. The gap narrowed drastically in late summer 1967.[10] Kim was touted ever more stridently, the East German embassy noted, as a brilliant theoretician admired by revolutionaries everywhere.[11] The press ran crudely-doctored photographs of his portrait adorning the front pages of foreign newspapers.[12] His speech to propagandists in 1955 was commemorated on December 28, 1967 in a *Rodong Sinmun* piece that praised "great Subject Thought" in effusive if vague terms. It was still defined only as practical thought for the application of Marxism-Leninism.[13]

Although the regime demanded loyalty to Kim's leadership in all things, it wanted to keep up the appearance of a party state, for which reason the old practice of referring to his "revolutionary thought" on the one hand and the WP's "subject(ive) thought" on the other did not disappear overnight. In October 1967 Kim announced that "Our party's subject(ive) thought is the most correct Marxist-Leninist guiding practical thought."[14] The official media, however, were careful to describe it as the virtual product or embodiment of his "revolutionary thought," which thus enjoyed pride of place. Even in panegyric poetry it was mentioned more often than *chuch'e sasang*.[15]

Let us take a step back from this dry ideological talk to remember that it played only a small part in the official culture, which generally dealt in matters more likely to interest average people. The detainment of the USS Pueblo's crew, the top story of 1968, boosted national pride while spurring the militarization of society on to a new height. The Vietcong's early successes in the Tet offensive raised hopes that the Yankees could soon be forced off the peninsula. Domestic news focused — probably to less crowd-pleasing effect — on the purported successes of the Ch'ŏllima industrialization movement. Even the personality cult had better things to talk about than *chuch'e sasang*; there were plenty of lacunae in Kim's legend still to be filled in with tales of deep-forest warfare and motherly solicitude. Entire weeks went by in 1968 and 1969 in which the word *chuch'e* did not appear in a newspaper headline.[16]

Even on those occasions when the phrase "Comrade Kim's Subject Thought" was used, it seemed to stand for something narrower than the all-encompassing body of thought which the WP had attributed to itself. It tended to be reduced to his insight into the need for doing things "mainly" by one's own efforts. The stock quote was the one from his Jakarta speech: "in practical thought, the subject," etc. Official translators were therefore not wholly wrong in rendering *chuch'e sasang* into English as "the Juche idea." The choice of words had the added advantage of not seeming to put the thing in question on the same  level as Mao Zedong Thought.¹⁷ Marxism-Leninism remained the central object of praise. The *Rodong Sinmun* asserted Kim's loyalty to it in all its "purity."¹⁸ He had applied it creatively to local conditions, to spectacular effect: there was still little more to *chuch'e sasang* than that.

We mustn't think the regime was too stupid to come up with anything deeper or more original. Kim's appeal had always derived from his perceived embodiment of rustic spontaneity and other ethnic virtues. He could not hope to continue appearing as the quintessence of Koreanness while putting his name on something abstruse or erudite. Besides, nothing good could come of focusing public attention on theory, as China's Cultural Revolution had already made clear. It was enough for the masses to know that *chuch'e sasang*, whatever that was exactly, constituted the world-famous perfection of Marxism-Leninism, whatever *that* was exactly, for which reason they had to obey Kim's every current command. To look for guidance to treatises appearing under his name was to miss the whole point of a monolithic ideological system, namely, for everyone to buckle down and work.

In the dictionary of the Korean language published in 1968, the political meaning of the word *chuch'e* at last rose to the first entry given, and it was defined in more Jakarta-esque terms than it had been in 1962, namely, as "the autonomous and creative ideological standpoint and work attitude of solving all problems of revolution and construction independently, in accordance with the actual conditions of one's country, and mainly through one's own power."[19]

Despite its currency in the North the word *chuch'e* remained in common use across the DMZ. It is striking how similar the rival dictators' main points were, and how much more forcefully Park Chung Hee got them across. In February 1968, a month after KPA commandos had attempted to attack his official residence, he spoke the following words at a university graduation ceremony.

> It's natural that we should accept help from others when our own strength is insufficient. But we must remember that help is always just that, help, and not hope that others will protect us. I call this the subjectivity of national defense. When it comes to others helping us, we must keep in mind that we will only be able to get help if there is subjectivity in national defense. Is it not impossible that others will come and help a people who don't have the resolve to protect themselves?
>
> The life of a nation lies in its subjectivity. To put it in a nutshell, one can say that the nation's subjectivity consists in its acting and exerting influence in accordance with its determination to serve the nation's life and interests. We as an entire citizenry must unite and, stimulating the new spirit of "fighting while working, working while fighting," cultivate our subjective capabilities for self-developing the nation's fate.[20]

To read both dictators' works, and compare the Koreas they left behind (the one after 18 years, the other after 46), is to see the wrongness of the common notion that Kim was "always the major interpreter of Korean self-reliance."[21]

In the North, the media increased their coverage of *chuch'e sasang* while keeping the focus on its fame overseas. The first research institute devoted to it was supposedly established in Mali in April 1969, a good ten years before the DPRK got one of its own.[22] International institutions like the Organization of Solidarity of the People of Asia, Africa and Latin-America or the International Confederation of Arab Trade Unions; periodicals from Ecuador's *Mañana* to India's *Janwarta*; everyone from revolutionary functionaries in the Congo to Latin-American exchange students in Iraq: all were said to be celebrating Kim as "the Marxist-Leninist theoretician of our time" and "the pre-eminent leader of the world revolution."[23]

The same regime that had once used the Japanese loanword *chuch'e* to translate Marx was now determined to present it as an ineffably Korean concept. The following is from "Juche, This is the Banner of Revolution" (1971), purportedly by a Mauritanian devotee.

> Juche, this may be Korean language
> But it is a word shared by revolutionary masses the world over!
> Like a torch of revolution,
> Juche, Juche, Juche!
> ....
> You have more firmly consolidated Marxism-Leninism
> Made a precious contribution to its store of treasures
> Strengthened it and made it perfect.[24]

Considering South Koreans' insatiable need to hear of their athletes' and entertainers' popularity overseas, it is safe to assume that this propaganda went down well in the North. But although talk of Kim's fame appealed to national pride, we must not conflate *chuch'e sasang* itself with nationalism. What communist would oppose the notion that every country must adjust Marxism-Leninism to its own conditions? All that was nationalist was the claim that Kim had hit upon this idea himself, but it was stated less stridently in English. Foreign communists were therefore ready to praise "the Juche idea" in carefully chosen terms, though in Korean translation they ended up praising "Subject Thought" instead. Reidar Larsen, chairman of the Communist Party of Norway, was quoted as saying, "We believe that the Subject Thought put forward by Comrade Kim Il Sung is Marxism-Leninism as applied to Korean conditions, and constitutes experience and encouragement for other communist parties too."[25]

The more likely propaganda was to be read by the country's allies, the more mildly it was formulated. The WP's fifth congress took place in November 1970. It ended with the issuance of new bylaws, according to the preamble of which, "The Workers' Party of Korea is guided in its activities by Marxism, Leninism and the Subject Thought of Comrade Kim Il Sung, which is the creative application of Marxism and Leninism to the reality of our country."[26] The wording was more modest than the CCP's statement the year before, according to which it regarded "Marxism-Leninism-Mao Zedong Thought as the theoretical basis guiding its thinking."[27]

Meanwhile the regime undertook efforts to bring Kim's international stature more in line with the domestic hyperbole about it. Some headway was made. In answers to the written questions of foreign delegations, Kim came across as a genial, moderate communist, a man as friendly to non-aligned countries as to signatories of the Warsaw Pact. Hungry as always for loans and aid, he sought to counter the notion, already a widespread one, that he advocated radical self-reliance. "By establishing the subject and relying on our own efforts we do not mean, on any account, building 'Socialism in isolation.' We fully recognize that it is necessary for states to supply each other's needs and cooperate with each other."[28]

In 1971, at what must have been great expense, Pyongyang established the so-called American-Korean Friendship and Information Center in downtown Manhattan. Nominally run by local communists, it published a journal, arranged trips to Pyongyang, and inserted advertisements in newspapers calling for the withdrawal of US troops from the peninsula.[29] That same year, a one-volume distillation of Kim's speeches was published in the USA, this too, no doubt, with financial support from Pyongyang.[30] North Korea's media celebrated the appearance of such books as proof of foreign demand for Kim Il Sung's guidance.

Considering the length and dullness of his speeches, it made good sense for the regime to publish them in excerpted form, but as an academic reviewer noted at the time, the important parts were left out.[31] *Juche! The Speeches and Writings of Kim Il Sung* (1972), which came with an effusive if empty foreword by the Black Panther Party's Eldridge Cleaver, did not even include the 1955 speech.[32] Nevertheless, these books' presence in shops and libraries sufficed to establish Kim in foreigners' minds as an original thinker of *some* sort, and thus as a more intellectual and autonomous man than his rival to the south.

A North Korean who sought to understand US foreign policy by studying State of the Union addresses would rightly be thought ridiculous. Why, then, have Westerners always been ready to impute both ideological sincerity and canonicity to Kim Il Sung's writing?[33] The answer lies in their misperception of the DPRK as a communist state. They are at least correct in thinking theory central to such states. The USSR's only source of legitimacy was the alleged infallibility of the philosophy its leadership espoused.[34] For this very reason the theoretical discourse was too important to be dictated by the needs of public diplomacy.

I dare say this is why so many Western observers who got to know Lenin before Hitler regarded the latter's "peace speeches" as coursechanging texts while shrugging off his party's anti-Semitic propaganda as hollow populism.[35] They failed to understand that a far-right state does not study its leader's words the way a communist one does, nor does he demand that kind of loyalty.[36] Although praised for his intelligence, he is the opponent of intellectualism and thus of theory; his role is to articulate and implement the race's healthy common sense.[37] Hitler needed only to assume a high-flown tone (as when disavowing designs on France) for the German masses to realize who he was talking to, and to switch off accordingly.

The West learned the truth about the Third Reich soon enough, but in the 1970s the DPRK was still putting on a good show of redness. With no opportunity to visit the country, and not enough language skills to study it from a distance, Pyongyang watchers tended to extrapolate from Chinese communism, a better-researched phenomenon. The official cultures looked similar enough in photographs: here and there the same uniform tunics and haircuts, the red flags, the same pledges of loyalty to a man whose portrait hung on every wall. The introduction of Kim Il Sung badges in 1970, a year after the CCP had stopped producing Mao badges, made North Koreans look more fanatical, hence even more likely to be memorizing their leader's every utterance. In fact Mao's Little Red Book had been disseminated in China in order to enfranchise the non-party masses, something Kim never had any intention of doing.[38] No matter; the extrapolation continues today. Although the export of Kim's writings may not have made many converts, then, it strengthened the West's impression of a country under left-theoretical governance.

1. The term *pyŏngjin*, which first surfaced in the early 1960s, has experienced a comeback under Kim Jong Un.
2. "Report from the East German embassy to North Korea, Plenum of the North Korean Workers' Party on 18 July 1967, 14 August 1967," translated by Bernd Schaefer, DA/WWC.
3. N. Popa, "Telegram from Pyongyang to Bucharest, No.76.108, Top Secret, March 28, 1967," and "Telegram from Pyongyang to Bucharest, No. 76137, Top Secret, April 18, 1967," both sources translated by Eliza Gheorghe, DA/WWC.
4. "Telegram from Pyongyang to Bucharest, No. 76.279," 3 August 1967, translated by Eliza Gheorge, DA/WWC.
5. Jószef Oláh, "Report, Embassy of Hungary in the Soviet Union to the Hungarian Foreign Ministry, November 25, 1967," translated by Balazs Szalontai, DA/WWC.
6. "Excerpts from a 30 December 1966 memo of the Soviet embassy to the DPRK (A. Borunkov) about embassy measures against Chinese anti-Soviet propaganda in the DPRK"; "The DPRK attitude toward the so-called 'Cultural Revolution' in China," 7 March 1967, both sources translated by Gary Goldberg, DA/WWC.
7. Ibid.
8. N. Popa, "Telegram from Pyongyang to Bucharest, No.14.213, Top Secret, April 7, 1967," translated by Eliza Gheorghe, DA/WWC. Everard writes in his memoir: "In a conversation about an Iranian delegation many years ago, a senior Chinese official told me that 'they were awful, they were devious, they were sly, they were . . . ' (he groped for a comparison) 'they were as bad as North Koreans!'" *Only Beautiful Please*, 227.
9. Popa, op. cit.
10. It was at this time that the use of honorative verb forms (*hasiŏtta*, say, for *hayŏtta*) became mandatory in connection with the "Great Leader" (*widaehan suryŏng*).
11. "Information About Some New Aspects on Korean Workers' Party Positions concerning Issues of Domestic and Foreign Policy, 18 August 1967,"

translated by Bernd Schaefer, DA/WWC. The Germans also reported on "the replacement of Marxism-Leninism through 'the ideology of Kim Il Sung.'" This misperception must have derived either from conflation of the inner and outer tracks or from a failure to grasp the deference to Marxism-Leninism implicit in the word *sasang*. One is reminded of how Western journalists annoyed Beijing by referring to Mao's *sixiang* as "Maoism," as if it were a pure ideology in its own right. Nothing more was being laid claim to in these years, in Pyongyang or Beijing, than practical thought for the application of Marxism-Leninism to national conditions.

12. "Kim Il-sŏng ŭi ronmun <Panje panmi t'ujaeng ŭl kanghwa haja> nŭn segye ŭi ssaunŭn hyŏngmyŏngga'dŭl ege nŭn muhan han yonggi wa sinsim ŭl an'gyŏjunŭn kyogwasŏ ro toemyŏ wŏnssu'dŭrin chegukchuŭija'dŭl egenŭn pokt'an ŭro toenda," *Rodong Sinmun*, 10 December 1967.

13. "Chuch'e sasang ŭl ch'ŏljŏ hi kuhyŏn hanŭn kŏs ŭn uri hyŏngmyŏng sŭngni ŭi hwakko han tambo," *Rodong Sinmun*, 28 December 1967.

14. Ibid.

15. See for example Kang Hyŏn-se's "Suryŏngnim ŭi hyongmyŏng sasang ŭl simjang e saegimyŏ," *Chosŏn Munhak*, January 1970, 26. A page-long paean to Kim's thought, it makes no mention of *chuch'e sasang*.

16. Meanwhile the once-famous plenum of 1952 ceased to be commemorated as a watershed, despite the regime's tendency to backdate its every tradition as much as possible. I suspect the event had seen others discuss subjectivity more than the leader had.

17. Implicitly conceding that vast reaches of policymaking were outside its scope, journalists used formulations that were soon to become unthinkable, such as "Long live *chuch'e* and *ch'ŏllima sasang*!" "Chuch'e wa ch'ŏllima sasang manse," *Rodong Sinmun*, 13 September 1968.

18. See for example, "Uri tang ŭi widaehan chuch'e sasang kwa chaju, charip, chawi ŭi hyŏngmyŏngjŏk rosŏn," *Rodong Sinmun*, 18 April 1968.

19. *Hyŏndae chosŏnmal sajŏn* (Pyongyang, 1968), 809.

20. Quoted in Cho Kap-che, *Pak Chŏng-hŭi ŭi kyŏljŏngjŏk sungandŭl* (Seoul, 2009), 459.

21. Cumings, *Origins of the Korean War* 2, 313.

22. Kim Hyŏn-hwan, *Na wa chuch'e sasang kwa ŭi taehwa* (1998), 24.
23. Kim Chŏng-ja, "Kim Il-sŏng tongji ŭi chuch'e sasang ŭn maksŭ–reninjuŭi paltchŏn e kiyŏ han sasangimyŏ chegukchuŭi wa sin'gu singminjuŭi rŭl pandaehanŭn t'ujaeng ŭi sŭngni rŭl tambo hanŭn widaehan sasang," *Kŭlloja*, April 1970, 4-6. The foreigners' praise was printed in bold, an honor soon to be reserved for the leader's own statements.
24. Erŭman Elleiruarŭ, "Chuch'e, i nŭn hyŏngmyŏng ŭi kich'i," *Chosŏn Munhak*, April 1971, 58.
25. Kim Chŏng-ja, "Kim Il-sŏng tongji ŭi chuch'e sasang," 6.
26. Dae-Sook Suh, *Korean Communism, 1945-1980*, 526.
27. Tang Tsou, *The Cultural Revolution and Post-Mao Reforms* (Chicago, 1986), 290.
28. Kim Il Sung, *Answers to the Questions Raised by the Iraqi Journalists Delegation, Pyongyang 1971*, MIA.
29. Brandon Gauthier, "'Bring All the Troops Home Now!' The American-Korean Friendship and Information Center and North Korean Public Diplomacy, 1971-1976" (Unpublished manuscript, 2014).
30. *Revolution and Socialist Construction in Korea* (New York, 1971).
31. Dae-Sook Suh, "*Revolution and Socialist Construction in Korea* (review)," *Pacific Affairs* 45, No. 2 (Summer 1972), 292-293.
32. *Juche! The Speeches and Writings of Kim Il Sung*, ed. Li Yuk-sa (New York, 1972).
33. Robert Winstanley-Chesters is representative of the consensus according to which the Kims' writings comprise the country's primary canon. *Environment, Politics and Ideology in North Korea* (Lanham, MD, 2014), 8.
34. Boris Groys, *Das kommunistische Postskriptum*, 35.
35. Carl Zuckmayer: "Even many Jews considered the savage anti-Semitic rantings of the Nazis merely a propaganda device." Quoted by Erik Larson, *In the Garden of Beasts* (New York, 2011), 58.
36. Buchheim writes of the great range of opinion which Hitler tolerated even inside the Nazi party, so long as everyone was fully loyal to his person. *Totalitäre Herrschaft*, 37.

37. Outside scholars have long pointed to the WP flag's inclusion of a writing brush along with the standard hammer and sickle as a sign of the party's unique soft spot for intellectuals. In fact the writing brush simply stood for white-collar workers (*samuwŏn*), as part of an effort to appeal to the middle class on both sides of the peninsula. (One is reminded of the Nazis' early appeals to "*Arbeiter der Stirn und Faust*.") For more on *samuwŏn* see Cumings, "Corporatism," 292.
38. Lowell Dittmer, *Liu Shao-ch'i and the Chinese Cultural Revolution* (Berkeley, 1974), 224.

6

THE GREAT CHARM OFFENSIVE: 1972

THE CONVENTIONAL WISDOM is that Kim Il Sung introduced his "human-oriented" version of Juche in September 1972, in answer to questions from Japanese journalists.[1] So familiar has this assertion become over the past forty years that people no longer see anything strange in it. One might almost think it were normal for a dictatorship to let foreigners scoop a declaration of epochal domestic importance. Too often overlooked is the North Korean charm offensive underway at the time in question.

The year before, the White House had announced that President Nixon planned to call on Mao in Beijing. The two Koreas had received this news with equal fear that their fate might be decided without them. In response they explored possibilities of bringing about an inter-Korean rapprochement on their own. In late summer 1971 the rival states' Red Cross societies began communicating in preparation for formal talks.

South of the DMZ, reports of these developments excited popular hopes for unification which Park Chung Hee had difficulty containing.[2] The relaxation of hostility to the North emboldened dissident elements;

students demonstrated against a military training program, and the citizens of Kwangju battled police in large-scale riots. The expulsion or withdrawal of Taiwan from the UN in October 1971 made conservative South Koreans worry that economic prosperity would not legitimize their state in the world's eyes. It was no good, editorials warned, to trust in an America in decline; if the ROK took a passive role in the unification issue, it might end up the absorbed and not the absorbing party. Centrists and conservatives alike called for better relations with Pyongyang, even if it meant loosening restrictions on pro-North expression.

Responding to these fortuitous developments, Kim Il Sung mounted a public-diplomacy campaign in order to — as a Romanian diplomat later summarized the official explanation — "obtain support for [reunification] and push for the isolation of South Korea to such an extent that it will have to accept the proposals and the line imposed by the North."[3]

Although delegations were sent around the world, the regime concentrated its lobbying efforts on Japan. While North Korean officials visited Tokyo, Japanese politicians and journalists were invited to Pyongyang, where some enjoyed audiences with the dictator himself. Upon returning home, conservative politicians vied with their left-wing counterparts in praising the DPRK. Intent on keeping open this new window to a hitherto closed society, Japanese media relayed Kim's statements in an uncritical tone.[4]

Pyongyang's focus on Japan is easily explained. The North's most important capitalist trading partner since the mid-1960s, it was also a main creditor and trade partner of South Korea. By improving relations with Tokyo, Kim hoped to effect a drastic reduction of Japanese economic support for Park Chung Hee — as in fact soon happened.[5] Positive coverage of the DPRK and its reunification efforts could also be expected to reach the many Koreans still residing in Japan, as well as intellectuals in Seoul, among whom proficiency in Japanese was then still common.[6] Finally, Kim wanted to show his own people that even the richest nations looked up to him. It was one thing to print panegyrics

THE GREAT CHARM OFFENSIVE: 1972

from Mauritanians, and another to point to respectful treatment by the erstwhile colonial power.

Central to the public relations drive were answers that Kim provided in purported response to questions from Japanese periodicals. This approach kept his statements from being judged by the demanding standards of a monograph; everything could be phrased as shallowly and equivocally as was necessary to satisfy various constituencies. The Japanese needed to hear tones of moderation and reconciliation, while expressions of autonomy would go down better on both sides of the DMZ. Moscow and Beijing, on the other hand, needed to know that Kim was not straying from the Marxist-Leninist fold.

The first interview was excerpted in January in the conservative *Yomiuri Shimbun* before being published in the DPRK.[7] In it Kim boasted of successes on every front, denied an interest in exporting revolution, and called for the improvement of Tokyo-Pyongyang relations. Of special interest for our purposes are the paragraphs on "Subject Thought." (Note that since my interest lies more in domestic than in export propaganda, I translate the term *chuch'e sasang*, so as to convey the less impenetrably exotic message the North Korean readers got.) Kim promised to give his interviewers a brief explanation of the thing in question, but added, "I think you will get a clearer idea of it if you read some of my books on it."[8]

Some of my books! He had never so much as devoted a full speech to Juche. Had he been called upon to explain himself, he might have argued that his published works reflected a Juche mindset, but that (apart from being untrue in itself) is clearly not the meaning he sought to convey. The *Yomiuri* journalists and their readers were to assume he had already explained his doctrine to his own people. This sort of bluster has remained integral to the Juche discourse ever since. No matter what text one consults, one is made to feel, through a kind of infinite regress, that the argumentative groundwork must have been laid elsewhere.

Kim went on to dilute the old bloc-conform definition of *chuch'e sasang* with truisms that were not specifically communist in nature.

> Establishing the subject means that the people approach the revolution and construction in their own country as masters. In other words, it means the embodiment of independent and creative spirits; the people must adopt an independent and creative stand to solve mainly by themselves all the problems arising from the revolutionary struggle and constructive work, in the context of their own country's actual conditions.⁹

The traditional emphasis on the independent, creative application of Marxism-Leninism has here become a call for independence and creativity *per se*. This brings the sentiment close to the can-do rhetoric of Park Chung Hee, as was probably intended. Kim then recalled the WP's resolute opposition to serve-the-great-ism or *sadaejuŭi*, which he explained — did he not know the term had originated in Japan? — as a matter of blindly following foreign countries. "We do not act on orders or instructions from any foreigners."¹⁰ At the same time Kim had to cover himself:

> Subject Thought is based on Marx's principle "Workers of all countries, unite!". . . It does not befit a communist to turn his back on proletarian internationalism under the pretext of maintaining independence. This means simply sliding into nationalism.¹¹

Contrary, then, to the Western assumption that Juche equals Korean nationalism, it was conceived and formulated in large part to hide the *de facto* ideology from outsiders, or at least to dress it up as a belief in every country's need to do its own thing.

THE GREAT CHARM OFFENSIVE: 1972

In the following month, Nixon visited Beijing. The Sino-US Joint Communiqué issued on February 27, 1972 recommended the peaceful solution of the Korean problem by the two parties most affected.[12] Whether or not this constituted tacit American recognition of the DPRK, it undermined Seoul's plan to have the UN solve everything. Park Chung Hee's foreign minister called the international situation "the most difficult one for the ROK since the Korean War."[13] As the mood of crisis deepened, media and opposition leaders in Seoul called for better relations with the Kim regime. Bowing to the pressure, Park sent emissaries to Pyongyang in the spring of 1972 while receiving the rival leader's in return.

The personality cult reached a new height during celebrations for Kim's sixtieth birthday on April 15. An enormous bronze statue of the leader, one arm outstretched, was unveiled on Pyongyang's Mansudae Hill. To this day it remains the country's best-known landmark.[14] I mention it to enforce the point that the DPRK of April 1972 was recognizably the DPRK of 1982 and 1992. Both the cult and the national economy had reached their respective peaks before Kim explained "his" human-oriented doctrine at any length.

A conference on "the role of US imperialism in Asia" was hosted in April in the birthday boy's honor. When participants arrived from around the developing world, they were asked to present on Kim's contributions to Marxism-Leninism instead. No effort to enlighten them as to the nature of those contributions ensued. According to Tariq Ali, one of the invitees, an "apparatchik" went from room to room in the hotel, offering bribes of about $5000.¹⁵ When Ali balked, the bribe was doubled — and again refused. All this bespeaks the lack of a serious intent to proselytize, for the regime cannot have thought visitors would respect Juche more after these sordid proposals. (Ali noted that the dictator's "bloated neck seemed to be inviting a bullet.")¹⁶ On the other hand the regime did not need to go to such expense just to make the locals think the world looked up to Kim. The greater goal was evidently to induce prominent foreigners to commit themselves to a pro-Pyongyang position, thereby burning their bridges with Seoul.

The first volume of a new version of Kim Il Sung's biography came out in August 1972. In contrast to the one published in 1968, which had gone into the pipeline too early to reflect the burgeoning Juche myth, it told how the eighteen-year-old hero had conceived *chuch'e sasang* by the time of his release from a Manchurian prison in June 1930.¹⁷

> The most precious and powerful being in the world is man, and the master who rules everything and decides everything is none other than man.
>
> That man is the master of all things and the decider of all things was General Kim Il Sung's unwavering belief. . . . The General taught that if man is to support his rights as a master of revolution . . . he must regard it as his guiding principle in all activities to forbear depending on others, and instead to think with his own head, to believe in his own power, to cultivate the revolutionary spirit of revitalization by one's own efforts [*charyŏk kaengsaeng*], always to take responsibility for his own problems, to solve them autonomously, and to solve them creatively in accordance with his concrete conditions. This meant the origination of Subject Thought, according to which man is the master of all things and decides all things.¹⁸

I would like to linger on the assertion that "man is master of all things." Some Western observers seem to think it countered a dominant

Asian belief in the need to live in harmony with nature.[19] In fact the idea has as long a recorded history in the East as in the West. The millennia-old Chinese *Book of Documents* (*Shujing*) contains the words "Man is the spirit [*ling*] of all creatures."[20] This engendered the Japanese saying "Man is the supreme spirit of all creatures" ("*Ningen wa banbutsu no reichō desu*"), which, as Tessa Morris-Suzuki has written, "conveys a strong sense of humanity as the most active, potent, creative force in a numinous natural order."[21] It was not perceived as a distinctly Confucian sentiment; Japanese Buddhists invoked it to discourage infanticide.[22] The exact Korean equivalent, "*Ingan i manmul ŭi yŏngjangida*," is still current in the ROK, though few people seem to know where it came from.

Let us trace the Western history of the same idea at least as far back as Lorenzo Ghiberti (1378-1455), the Florentine artist who said, "People can do everything if they only want to." The German philosopher Peter Sloterdijk has called these words "the proud motto of the modern era," rightly adding that they can be squared with Marx by adding the words: "so long as social conditions are right."[23] True, the lack of such a qualifier in the philosophy attributed to Kim above would have given a Soviet censor pause, but the CPSU had long used voluntarist hyperbole in its own mass-oriented propaganda, if not in the theoretical discourse *per se*.[24] Bernd Stevens Richter has written of how "nature reached the status of a 'class enemy'" during the Stalin era: "Man was God and master of everything and could change everything at will."[25]

Mao Zedong, for his part, had made similar statements even while arguing the rightness of dialectical materialism.

> Things under heaven depend solely on one's strength, so it is no use blaming heaven or other people; man is the master of his own fate, difficulties can be overcome, and external conditions can be changed; this is our philosophy.[26]

We must keep in mind that the USSR was then well into an era of so-called Marxist humanism. It was claimed that the erroneous view of man as a mere product or function of his environment had led directly to Stalin's excesses. Intellectuals in and outside the East Bloc pored over Marx's earlier writings ("communism . . . equals humanism"),[27] while propaganda aimed for a people-friendlier tone; "All for man!" as the Soviet slogan went.[28] The regime in Cuba had been vaunting its humanist approach to revolution.[29] The efficacy of such talk in broadening support for the cause was well-known. Humanism had also been playing a key role in Kenneth Kaunda's ideology and other so-called African socialisms.[30]

The mytho-biography of Kim claimed that *chuch'e sasang* derived from the teenage hero's prodigious grasp not only of local conditions, but of the international situation as well, for which reason it had ushered in a "glorious era of the subject" for people around the world.[31] It also told of a Kalun Conference in June 1930 — Kalun, now part of Changchun, was then a town in Manchuria — at which Kim had allegedly put forth his revolutionary ideas. An illustration showed the black-clad, blank-faced youth holding forth to a rapt audience of young exiles.[32] Han Sŏrya's hagiographies had mentioned no such event. The fact that the doctrine's shift to ostentatious humanism first took place in a fraudulent account of Kim's boyhood makes its domestic function as a prop in the personality cult all the more obvious.

It is important to keep in mind how well things were then going for North Korea on the international front, and how bad a time the rival state was having despite its spectacular economic growth. That the first round of Red Cross talks took place in August 1972 in Pyongyang and not Seoul was a great symbolic victory for Kim. International media took due note of the hospitality lavished on his wary visitors. Thus did the leader who in 1968 had tried to have the other assassinated now appear as the more reasonable of the two. The ROK government did itself no favors by expelling a *Yomiuri* correspondent in retaliation for the newspaper's puff piece on "(North) Korea, the Country of the Subject" (*Shutai no kuni Chōsen*).

One would never know any of this from the defector Hwang Jang Yop, who pretends in his memoirs that a *bona fide* philosophy ripened in him  independently of current events.³³ He talks of returning with Kim Il Sung from a shared summer vacation to learn that the *Mainichi Shimbun*, another Japanese newspaper, had requested an interview with the leader. The theme, according to Hwang, who was then a member of the party's Central Committee, was to be "Subject-Thought-based domestic and foreign policies of the Korean Workers' Party." Kim agreed to provide a written response.³⁴ Hwang would have us believe that he seized on the ghost-writing job so as to smuggle his own world-improving ideas into print. He says he composed the text with the assistance of two party departments in order to forestall factional opposition to its content.³⁵ It was handed over to the Japanese on September 17, 1972, a Sunday.³⁶ To uphold the pretense of an actual interview, Kim Il Sung spent four hours chatting with them.³⁷ Evidently the hosts and their guests agreed to release the text simultaneously on Tuesday, September 19. It took up the first and second pages of the North Korean newspaper and the fourth and fifth pages of the *Mainichi*.³⁸

Now, one may well wonder how Hwang could have defined something for the first time — and in expectation of elite opposition, at that — while at the same time calling it the basis for current and even past policies, but this is not necessarily as mendacious as it might appear. He, or whoever else penned the text, could well have looked back over the WP's policy-making, then distilled the apparent essence of it. Still, to claim that *chuch'e sasang* functioned as the guiding ideology well before it was even articulated (as so many Western academics now do) is to stretch the definition of ideology into meaninglessness, and to impose a spurious unity on policies conceived in a less monolithic era.

Granted, even a retrospective text can spread an urgent message, but had it been Kim's intent to make an ideological statement to his own people, he would hardly have let the Japanese see it first, nor would he have restricted it to the first of the speech's three parts. Hwang's self-dramatizing version of events aside, then, the piece was obviously conceived as a textual salvo in the "peaceful offensive" against the ROK.

The lion's share of it summarized the regime's stance on various issues of the day, with plenty of criticism of the rival state. Park's decision to allow the Red Cross talks, the second round of which had just ended in Seoul, was explained away — with some truth — as the result of domestic pressure on his government.[39] The absence of foreign troops from the DPRK was contrasted with the ROK's insistence on the presence of American forces. According to Kim, his republic had no intention of invading the South or imposing socialism on it any other way. Instead it wanted to bring about negotiations between the peninsula's two law-making assemblies with a view to creating a confederation. Pyongyang also sought better ties with Japan, provided the latter rein in its militarism.[40]

But all the above came later in the speech, the first third or so of which was taken up with a rambling discussion of *chuch'e sasang*. What Kim had often explained as a matter of applying Marxism-Leninism creatively to national circumstances was now defined as "the idea that the masters of revolution and construction are the masses."[41] This was old hat. Communist theory had long regarded the masses as the driving force of revolution and the makers of history.[42] The Chinese party had since the mid-1960s been stressing the need for the workers and peasants to become "masters of society."[43] This was not to be taken so literally as to imply that they did not need guidance. I draw attention to the unoriginality of the *Mainichi* text not to discredit it, but only to counter the notion that it represented a conscious challenge to Marxist-Leninist orthodoxy.

Kim continued:

> In other words, it is the idea that one is the master of one's own fate and that the power to develop that fate lies with oneself. We

are by no means the first to develop this idea. Every Marxist-Leninist thinks along these lines. It is only that I place a special emphasis on this idea.[44]

This can be compared to an American's saying, "You can do whatever you set your mind to. Every rational person thinks along these lines." While the first sentence would be indulged even at an MIT commencement ceremony, the second one calls on us to take the first literally, which no rational person would do. For comparable reasons, a Soviet theorist might have nodded upon hearing of man's mastery of his fate (a line Mao had used) only to frown at the follow-up implication of a truth backed up by theory. Was not the whole point of revolution to liberate man from the limitations preventing his "self-activity" (Marx), his fate-mastery, as it were? Did Kim really mean to deny that? No. A little later in the *Mainichi* piece came these words:

> Our struggle for the building of socialism and communism, too, is, in the long run, to enable the people to extricate themselves from many forms of subjugation and lead independent and creative lives as masters of nature and society.[45]

So we see that the "man is master of all things" line was by no means that audacious turning of Marx on his head (or of Hegel back on his feet) which so many observers regard it as.[46] The article continued with Kim's assertion that he had begun thinking along these lines during the anti-Japanese struggle, when his guerrilla army had had to fend for itself. In keeping with the chronic vagueness of his reminiscences — which sharpened miraculously in the 1990s — he provided no concrete illustrations. He also skipped past the country's liberation entirely. No doubt he knew that Japanese were the last people who would swallow the core of his legend.

Moving on to the years that followed (sans mention of the Soviet occupation) he explained that his party had been unable to implement socialism at once. Needing to unite the masses into a broad front, it had tailored policies to the country's special needs. The WP had conducted research in rural areas before carrying out land reform. This first success had proven the efficacy of taking national conditions into account instead of imitating other countries' experiences.[47] In fact the land reform of 1946 had been planned by the Soviet military administration.[48]

He then elaborated a little on *chuch'e sasang* itself, starting with a shorter version of the Jakarta slogan.

> You all have asked if it is right to understand Subject Thought as something embodied by autonomy in politics, independence in economic affairs, and self-defense in military affairs; it is indeed correct . . . . Establishing the subject means approaching revolution and construction with the attitude of a master. Because the people are the master of revolution and construction, they must assume a master's attitude in regard to revolution and construction. A master's attitude is expressed in an independent position and creative activity. Revolution and construction are endeavours for the sake of the people, and endeavours that the people themselves must carry out. Therefore, in reshaping nature and society an independent position and creative activity are called for.[49]

The repetitive sententiousness is at odds with the rest of the article. Kim cannot have believed this prose style would appeal to his own people, whose need for folksy, concise propaganda his speechwriters had been emphasizing since the 1940s.[50] In all likelihood the deliberate dullness was meant to serve the same twofold function it serves among our own politicians and academics, namely, to imbue trite content with an air of profundity while discouraging readers from paying close attention. Had Kim wanted to rouse Koreans

to pro-activeness, he could have done so straightforwardly and without Japanese go-betweens, as Park Chung Hee had been doing for ten years. But such a message would have clashed with the myth of a Parent Leader from whom all blessings flow. To keep the showcase ideology ("Man is the master of all things") from competing with the real one ("We cannot live away from his breast"), the former had to be presented as bone-dry theory with a capital T.

The *Mainichi* journalists had hoped for firmer answers. Kim refused to be drawn out.

> You asked me to give a more concrete explanation of Subject Thought. But if I were to do so there would be no end to it. All the policies and lines of our party emanate from Subject Thought and they embody it. It is not a theory for theory's sake. . . . To have a deep understanding of Subject Thought it is necessary to make a detailed study of our party's policy and our country's reality.[51]

In other words, one was not to study the doctrine in order to understand the party's policies; one was to study the policies in order to understand the doctrine.

In his memoirs Hwang writes that in the *Mainichi* monologue he "gave the earliest definition of Subject Thought, and revealed the policies of the Korean Workers' Party as based on human-oriented socio-historical principles."[52] That sounds like deep stuff indeed, but the main points of the relevant section can be summarized as follows:

1) Man is the master of his fate.
2) The masses are the masters of revolution, and should behave accordingly.
3) It is necessary to solve problems in accordance with conditions in one's own country, rather than imitate the experiences of others.
4) One should solve one's own problems rather than rely too much on others.

5) Autonomy in politics, independence in the economy and self-defense in national defense.
6) The main goal of socialism and communism is to enable people to live independent, creative lives as masters of nature and society.

Let us review these points in reverse order. The sixth accorded with Marx's own hazy vision for the future. The fifth echoed the Jakarta speech, but sounded even milder in the context of 1972. The fourth was a much more moderate notion of self-reliance or self-determination than we find in our own Emerson and Kant. The third was international communist orthodoxy. The second was as familiar to North Koreans as to Chinese.[53] This leaves us with the bit about man's mastery of his fate, which, as we have seen, was one of Mao's sayings too. Far from developing it, the *Mainichi* piece waters it back down to Soviet orthodoxy by explaining that the whole point of communism is to *enable* people to live as masters.[54]

The regime occasionally touts all this as an actual philosophy, but the assertions are too inconsecutive to amount to a system of any kind.[55] As F.R. Leavis said of Wordsworth's so-called philosophy: "If you find anything to discuss, to a great extent you put it there yourself."[56] But whether we can at least call it an ideology depends on which definition of this word we choose to accept. If it "presupposes an apparently systematic formalization of facts, interpretations," etc, as Raymond Aron wrote,[57] the *Mainichi* monologue fails the test. Yet few people would deny the status of an ideology to Nazism, the leading spokesmen of which — the absurd Rosenberg aside — never pretended to an intellectual system. For my part, I have always applied the word to Korean race-nationalism, which any child can grasp, so I can hardly hold *chuch'e sasang* to a higher standard. Aron concedes that ideologies often reveal "a simple structure with one or two guiding ideas."[58] Surely we can all give this little doctrine that much.

Therefore my goal in this book, as I have said already, is not to deny that *chuch'e sasang* qualifies as an ideology *in vacuo*, but to deny that it has ever functioned as ideology — to deny that it has ever energized and guided North Koreans in political activity. There can be no contending that

THE GREAT CHARM OFFENSIVE: 1972

the pap Kim dished out to his Japanese guests reflected the worldview that had made the DPRK a society like no other. The mild bits about solving one's own problems offer no hint of either the country's extreme isolation or its abject reliance on foreign aid. Nor could any reader without background knowledge dream that Kim, this champion of the human spirit, led a propaganda apparatus that likened his people to babies. Sympathetic and critical observers alike try to reconcile the man-as-master rhetoric with the personality cult by pointing to official talk of every nation's need for a leader. Even if that did settle the contradiction — and it doesn't — no "leader theory" is espoused in the *Mainichi* text itself. This must be taken into account when judging whether it was conceived as an earnest political manifesto or as public-diplomatic cant. There can be no claiming it was both. The same vague innocuousness that made it acceptable to a wide range of external constituencies unfitted it for use in domestic policy-making and agitation.[59]

I hasten to add that Juche was not meant to become a political force overseas either. That would have undermined the whole mission, which was to win the support of non-aligned governments without estranging Moscow and Beijing. So-called Juche conferences and other pseudo-missionary activities were mere pretexts to bring foreigners together for the sake of favorable media attention, lobbying or outright bribery. (Of course smuggling and spying went on as well.) To make it easier for them to pay lip service to *chuch'e sasang* without contradicting their own party platforms, the regime stuck to the earlier English translation "the Juche idea," although the thing had since become a sprawl of different points.

South of the DMZ, in November 1972, a referendum approved Park Chung Hee's so-called Revitalization (*Yusin*) Constitution. It was the first constitution on the peninsula to include the word *chuch'e*: the new electoral college was called *T'ongil chuch'e kungmin hoeŭi*, literally, the Unification Subject Citizens' Assembly. The DPRK followed suit in December with a new "Socialist Constitution," so called to underscore the difference from the 1948 constitution, which had protected private ownership.

I have to break with the common practice of taking the North Korean constitution as seriously as if the regime had not become a one-man

— 133 —

dictatorship in 1967. Since then the leader has throned far above state and party alike. He therefore stands in an adversarial relationship to the very laws and regulations those institutions routinely issue, because their enforcement would impose unacceptable limits on his initiative. It is therefore more proper to describe the DPRK as a "total despotism" than a "total state." To borrow a phrase which a German scholar has used in regard to the Third Reich, the North Korean leader was, and remains today, "beyond all normativity."[60] (I would only add that, as with Hitler, this does not mean "beyond all ideology.")

The constitution of 1972 should therefore be recognized as outer-track propaganda. It declared that the "Democratic People's Republic of Korea is guided in its activity by the Korean Workers' Party's Subject Thought [*chuch'e sasang*], which has creatively applied Marxism-Leninism to our country's reality, as its guide to action."[61] These words are often seen as having weakened or even ended the DPRK's commitment to Marxism-Leninism while strengthening Juche's grip on politics and everyday life.[62] But when one keeps in mind that *sasang* is but a practical adjunct to Marxism-Leninism, it becomes clear that the regime was not implying that anything had been dropped or replaced.[63] Contrary to a common assertion, the 1972 constitution did not attribute *chuch'e sasang* to Kim Il Sung.[64] (In that respect, it was a step back from the preamble to the WP bylaws that had been issued in 1970.) Nor did it so much as hint at any re-casting of its main principle to "man is the master of all things." It was a constitution to which even Kim's old Kapsan rivals would not have objected.

1. For example, Jae-Cheon Lim describes the *Mainichi* interview as the "first publication on *chuch'e* philosophy." *Kim Jong Il's Leadership of North Korea* (New York, 2008), 62.
2. Kim Hakjoon, *The Domestic Politics of Korean Unification*, 170-179.
3. Aurelian Lazar, "Telegram from Pyongyang to Bucharest," 1 March 1973, translated by Eliza Gheorghe, DA/WWC.
4. Chong-Sik Lee, *Japan and Korea* (Stanford, 1985), 80. For obvious reasons, this is one of those aspects of North Korean history that many scholars prefer to overlook. Armstrong, for example, makes no mention of Kim's wooing of Japan in *Tyranny of the Weak* (2013), which presents itself as a history of the DPRK's foreign policy.
5. In 1973, the amount of money Tokyo annually loaned to South Korea was cut to a third of the previous year's level. Lee, *Japan and Korea*, 87.
6. This may well be why dealings with Japanese bourgeois parties later became the responsibility of the WP's department for anti-South activities. Hwang, *Hoegorok*, 268.
7. No doubt the DPRK version contained things that had not been communicated to the Japanese either orally or on paper. Harrison Salisbury, a *New York Times* reporter who met Kim in July 1972, later said that his interview was quite different from what was published in North Korea. *A Time of Change* (New York, 1988), 247.
8. Kim Il Sung, "On Present Political and Economic Policies of the Democratic People's Republic of Korea and Some International Problems," in *On Juche in Our Revolution* 2 (Pyongyang, 1975), 392.
9. Ibid.
10. Ibid., 395.
11. I have changed the word Juche in this English translation to Subject Thought. Ibid., 398.
12. Kim Hak-joon, *The Domestic Politics of Korean Unification*, 178.
13. Ibid.
14. A similarly posed and sized statue of a smiling Kim in suit and tie took the old one's place in 2012, while a new statue of Kim Jong Il went up alongside it.

The DPRK is now in the middle of a statue-erecting boom. (Whoever doubts that the regime would print Juche books as mere doctrinal place-markers and library props should consider the enormous annual costs of the personality cult as a whole.)

15. Tariq Ali, "Diary," *London Review of Books*, 26 January 2012.
16. Ibid.
17. The cult does not date his conception of *chuch'e sasang*, lest anyone think he was less perfect before it. A high-school textbook published in 2003, for example, only says that the seventeen-year old Kim already had its constituent ideas in mind when he went to prison in 1929. *Widaehan suryŏng Kim Il-sŏng taewŏnsunim hyŏngmyŏng ryŏksa: chung 4* (Pyongyang, 2003), 21. In keeping with the ahistoricity of the official culture as a whole, there is little sign of Kim's intellectual maturation in the mytho-biography. Hence the anime-like smoothness and blankness of the face we see in portraits of the older Kim Il Sung, as opposed to the lived-in, experienced face we see in portraits of Stalin.
18. Paek Pong, *Illyu haebang ŭi kusŏng Kim Il-sŏng wŏnsu* (Tokyo, 1972), 32.
19. See for example Richard Saccone, *Negotiating with North Korea*, 30-31.
20. James Legge translates this a shade too freely as "Of all creatures, man is the most highly endowed." *The Chinese Classics* (1865; reprinted Hong Kong, 1960), 3:281.
21. "Environmental Problems and Perceptions in Early Industrial Japan," in *Sediments of Time,* edited by Mark Elvin, Liu Ts'ui-jung (Cambridge, UK, 1998), 756-780, 773.
22. Fabian Drixler, *Mabiki* (Berkeley, 2013), 14.
23. Sloterdijk, *Du mußt dein Leben ändern* (Frankfurt am Main, 2009), 493-494.
24. For a superb explanation of the USSR's own gap between Marxist-Leninist theory and mass-oriented Marxist-Leninist myth (a very different gap from that between the DPRK's inner and outer tracks), see Carol Barner-Barry and Cynthia Hody's "Soviet Marxism-Leninism as Mythology," *Political Psychology* 15, No. 4 (December 1994), 609-630.
25. Bernd Stevens Richter, "Nature Mastered by Man," *Environment and History* 3, No. 1 (February 1997), 90.

26. *Mao Zedong on Dialectical Materialism*, ed. by Nick Knight (Armonk, NY, 1990), 158.
27. Marx, "Private Property and Communism," *Economic and Philosophic Manuscripts of 1844*, MIA. Loren R. Graham wrote in 1972 of the "current turn toward humanism" in Marxism in his book *Science and Philosophy in the Soviet Union*, 31
28. As quoted by Louis Althusser, one of those opposed to the trend, in "Marxism and Humanism" (1964), MIA.
29. Clive Kronenberg, "Manifestations of Humanism in Revolutionary Cuba," *Latin American Perspectives* 36, No. 2 (March 2009), 66-80.
30. Joseph C. McKenna, *Finding a Social Voice* (New York, 1997), 183-184.
31. Pong, *Illyu haebang ŭi kusŏng Kim Il-sŏng wŏnsu*, 33.
32. Ibid., 34.
33. Hwang's intellectual charlatanry is comically obvious in the relevant passages. "Opening Marx's most difficult texts I could clearly understand where the errors in his theory were, and my illusions about him disappeared. . . . I again opened Hegel's study of logic. Just by looking at the sub-headings, I could guess where he had gone wrong." *Hoegorok*, 197.
34. This would remain his preferred way of handling interview requests. Mark Barry, "Meeting Kim Il Sung in his Last Weeks," *NK News*, 15 April 2014.
35. Hwang, *Hoegorok*, 201.
36. Ibid.
37. "Kim Il Sung shushō 'tōitsu' de kataru," *Mainichi Shimbun*, 19 September 1972.
38. A version in much larger print appeared in the October 1972 issue of the (no longer biweekly) magazine *Kŭlloja*. Kim Il Sung, "Uri tang ŭi chuch'e sasang kwa konghwaguk chŏngbu ŭi taenaewoe chŏngchaek ŭi myŏt' kaji munje e taehayŏ," *Kŭlloja*, October 1972, 2-18.
39. Ibid., 12. This same line would be used decades later, with much less justification, to explain away the Sunshine Policy.
40. Ibid., 13-17. He was too diplomatic to mention the Liancourt Rocks.
41. Ibid., 2.

42. Aryeh L. Unger, *The Totalitarian Party*, 7; Tian Chih-sung, "The Masses are the Makers of History," *Peking Review* 29, 21 July 1972, 7-11.
43. "Study the 16 Points, Know Them Well and Apply Them," *Renmin ribao* editorial of 13 August, published in English, 19 August 1966. See also Joel Andreas, *The Rise of the Red Engineers* (Stanford, 2011), 120.
44. Kim Il Sung, "Uri tang ŭi chuch'e sasang," 2.
45. Ibid., 5.
46. See for example Armstrong, *The North Korean Revolution*, 6; Rüdiger Frank, "North Korea's Autonomy 1965-2015," *Pacific Affairs*, Vol. 87, No. 4, December 2014, 797. In *Nordkorea: Innenansichten eines totalen Staates* (Munich, 2014), 98, Frank goes so far as to talk of "a frontal attack on Marx." (The remark is not representative of what is on the whole a refreshingly thoughtful book.) I should add, by the way, that humanist talk was far from new to North Korea. We find comparable truisms in the 1950s, e.g., "The most precious thing in our national and social life is man." "Chŏnghwakhan kunjung kwanjŏm ŭi hwangnip ŭl wihayŏ," *Rodong Sinmun*, 11 December 1955.
47. Kim Il Sung, "Uri tang ŭi chuch'e sasang," 3.
48. Lankov writes that the law on land reform was formulated by "two consultants on agricultural economics specially invited [by Soviet authorities] from Leningrad." *From Stalin to Kim Il Sung*, 32-33.
49. Kim Il Sung, "Uri tang ŭi chuch'e sasang," 4.
50. Let no one claim (à la Cumings) that this sort of writing is more readable to the native speaker. As I know from teaching in South Korea, the almost immediate effect of Juche prose on people here is bafflement — not at the trite ideas themselves, of course, but at the numbing tautology and claim to profundity with which they are expressed. Even veterans of the South's Subject Thought movement attest, as we shall see in a later chapter, to having had this same reaction.
51. Kim Il Sung, "Uri tang ŭi chuch'e sasang," 8.
52. *Hoegorok*, 201.
53. The idea that the masses were the "true creators of history" had always been attributed to Marxism-Leninism itself. See for example Pak Chong-t'aek, "Tangsaenghwal e chuindapge ch'amga hara," *Rodong Sinmun*, 5 February

1954, "Sahoejuŭi hyŏngmyŏng kwa charyŏk kaengsaeng," *Kŭlloja*, November 1962, 3-4. See also "Ro-nong tongmaeng ŭi kanghwa nŭn sahoejuŭi sŭngni ŭi chungyohan cho'gŏn," *Rodong Sinmun*, 16 November 1955.

54. So much, then, for Hwang's claim to have "developed" Juche in order to correct what Marx and Lenin had got wrong. His refusal to explain these holes in his version of Juche's history reflects his confidence that South Korean readers would not seek out the *Mainichi* article, let alone the earlier *Yomiuri* article he chose to overlook entirely.

55. The terms Subject Thought and Subject Philosophy (*chuch'e ch'ŏrhak*) are not used interchangeably in North Korea. The latter construct, which has always been mentioned far less often, is praised in even airier language as the solution to fundamental problems of human existence. It is usually referred to as something foreigners are studying.

56. "The Literary Mind," *Scrutiny* 1, No. 1, May 1932, 26.

57. "The End of the Ideological Age?" *The End of Ideology Debate*, 28.

58. Ibid.

59. The regime's own mythmaking made clear that it was primarily Kim-deprived Third Worlders who needed to have the Juche gospel articulated; the locals had lived its wisdom by carrying out the great man's policies.

60. Hans Buchheim, *Totalitäre Herrschaft,* 109-126; Herbert Jäger, *Verbrechen unter totalitärer Herrschaft*, 199.

61. See Article 4 in "Chosŏn minjujuŭi inmin konghwaguk sahoejuŭi hŏnbŏp," *Kŭlloja*, January 1973, 29.

62. See for example Buzo, *Guerrilla Dynasty*, 37.

63. The CCP constitution of 1946 had stated, in similar fashion, "The thought that unifies the theory of Marxism and the praxis of the Chinese revolution ... Mao Zedong Thought, has become the guideline for all [the party's] own work." Martin, *Cult and Canon*, 10.

64. See for example Maretzki, *Kim-ismus*, 54; and Armstrong, "The Role and Influence of Ideology," 4. The Kim-glorifying preamble now associated with the 1972 constitution was not included in the first published versions. Also erroneous is Armstrong's assertion (ibid.) that there was "no mention of Marxism" in the 1972 constitution.

7

"THE ERA OF THE SUBJECT": 1973-1981

It cannot have been a secret to anyone of importance in Pyongyang that the things published under Kim Il Sung's name in 1972 had been ghostwritten, like most if not all texts attributed to him. The elite must have also drawn the obvious lesson from the fact that Japanese journalists, of all people, had got the latest version of the doctrine days before everybody else. Granted, a personality cult was in full swing, but this would only have enhanced resistance to something that had so obviously not originated with Kim himself, who for a quarter-century had done no theorizing to speak of, even at the low level of the *Mainichi* interview. If Hwang Jang Yop really did formulate *chuch'e sasang*, and his authorship were as open a secret as his memoirs indicate, its irrelevance to policy-making would have been even more obvious. And indeed, he recalls that top officials balked at taking the new "philosophical principles" seriously.[1]

No less plausibly does Hwang write of Kim's initial embarrassment about the attendant hyperbole, which included the claim that longer experience of holding power had granted him insight denied to Lenin.[2] It did not help that the Chinese used the same logic in praise of Mao.[3] Kim knew that he had to continue showing deference to Moscow and Beijing, and that his cult was already too extreme to benefit from puffing his doctrine up much further. It made little sense to draw mass attention to his published work, that patchwork product of disparate speechwriters, many of whom had since been purged or executed. There was great potential for Chinese-style "quotation wars" down the road, particularly after the hereditary succession he had already begun preparing. It was better to keep the spotlight on his biographical legend instead, where it remains to this day.

The regime therefore refrained from issuing an authoritative manifesto or treatise under the Great Leader's name. Officials responsible for so-called theoretical propaganda (*riron sŏnjŏn*) had to root around in his collected works for quotable scraps. A few texts attributed to the young Kim Il Sung were "discovered" and published, like the seminal declaration of basic *chuch'e sasang* principles which the eighteen-year-old was supposed to have made in Manchuria in 1930.[4] No explanation was given as to why they had not been brought out earlier. Only rarely were they quoted; their main function was to back up the biographical legend. Meanwhile propaganda made sure everyone understood that *chuch'e sasang* had not resulted from anything so un-Korean as solitary cerebration, but rather had crystallized within the teenage General during practical revolutionary work. Kim could thus preen himself on a world-changing insight while remaining the embodiment of Korean spontaneity and sociability.

In his *Mainichi* interview, the sixty-year-old had denied theoretical originality on his part. He had also explained that communism was needed to enable man to *become* master of all things. This did not prevent the cult from now touting Kim as the first thinker to recognize man's inherent mastery of all things, and even the first to grasp that the masses are the masters of revolution.

Granted, Stalin's so-called Marxism-Leninism was no less an ideology for misrepresenting Marx and Lenin. Nor is Christianity any less a religion for overriding Jesus' own insistence on the integrity of Jewish law. But at least the communists and Christians saw the inconsistencies, and took appropriate counter-measures. In contrast, North Korean propaganda misrepresented Kim's published works during his lifetime, without

"THE ERA OF THE SUBJECT": 1973-1981

his either objecting, or, conversely, ordering changes to those works. The same regime which had pulled almost every book published before 1967 included the Japanese newspaper interviews in unaltered form in every new edition of Kim's speeches. It even reprinted his "Juche speech" of 1955 without deleting its reference to "the day the Soviet army advanced into our homeland."[5] It also reprinted his equally problematic statement that he had not begun leading party-internal ideological discussion until 1956.[6] The only possible explanation is that neither Kim's writing nor the propaganda apparatus' version of the doctrine was being taught in earnest.

Even after the infusion of the *Mainichi* content, *chuch'e sasang* remained too thin to inform substantive articles, let alone books, not least because the regime, wary of distracting attention from the real ideology of ultra-nationalism, refrained from applying it to topical issues. How right Stalin was in saying, and Mao in repeating, that "theory becomes aimless if not connected with revolutionary practice."[7] The political dictionary of 1973 had to resort to plenty of tautology and praise just to drag the entry on *chuch'e sasang* out to six little pages.[8]

The DPRK's own historiography would eventually look back on the 1970s as a time when the young Kim Jong Il took on the task of systematizing his father's insights. Such an admission of the unsystematic nature of the latter would have been unthinkable had the old man's legitimacy

rested, as Stalin's had, on a claim to perfect brilliance. Unfortunately we cannot be sure what Kim Jong Il really said or wrote. Although pictures of him already hung on office walls, the only sign of his budding cult in newspapers and journals was a rise in references to advice issued by "the party center."[9] I see no reason, however, to doubt Hwang's testimony that although the young man had little interest in *chuch'e sasang* itself, he was the most vigorous promoter of the myth of it. By touting the doctrine he could bolster his own credentials while undermining rivals for the succession, who might otherwise have been able to make more of their education abroad. If *chuch'e sasang* were the answer to all challenges facing the DPRK, yet could only be mastered through long study of its practical application, it followed that the man best suited to take over was the one who had been around the Great Leader the most. If any logic could lend revolutionary respectability to a hereditary succession, it was that.

This does not mean that Kim Jong Il really did systematize the doctrine, which to this day evinces, as Yeats said of Swinburne's poetry, all the internal logic of a bag of shot. All he apparently did was to institute the practice of referring to a great system of which *chuch'e sasang* was but the essence.[10] This may well have been in response to the elite's reluctance to take the *Mainichi* platitudes seriously. It made more sense for the regime to enjoin allegiance to all the old man's thought and deeds, past and present — especially present.

We often read in South Korean sources that in 1974 Kim Jong Il praised his father's thought under the name Kimilsungism, the suffix of which allegedly implied a claim to its being a stand-alone ideology, independent of Marxism-Leninism.[11] We have no contemporaneous evidence that he was responsible, but the word *kimilsŏngjuŭi* did begin appearing in mass-oriented propaganda.[12] On a visit to the DPRK in 1981 the scholar B.C. Koh spotted the slogan "Long Live Kimilsungism" carved into a mountainside.[13] In the outer track, however, uses of it were seldom, and almost always attributed to foreigners or South Koreans, thus giving the regime a way out should Moscow or Beijing take offense.[14] The preferred name for the alleged system of which *chuch'e sasang* formed the core was the safer term "Comrade Kim Il Sung's revolutionary thought," which went back to the days when he had been presented as Stalin's loyal student. The new claim that it included its own original theory or *riron*[15] does not appear to have been meant or understood as a challenge to the Soviet orthodoxy, to which, as we shall see, the DPRK continued pledging loyalty.

Tellingly enough, what North Korean migrants recall as the main ideological event of the decade was not directly linked to *chuch'e sasang*. I

"THE ERA OF THE SUBJECT": 1973-1981

am referring to the revision, evidently made public in the inner track in April 1974, of the Ten Principles originally issued in 1967. The new principles, which repeated and overlapped with each other, demanded unconditional loyalty to a) the Leader, b) his "revolutionary thought" and c) his "instructions," while making no clear distinction between the three. This amounted to an only superficially left-theoretical version of a *Führerprinzip*. Although *chuch'e sasang* received dutiful mention in the official gloss, it did not feature in the principles themselves.

Small wonder, then, that the official media showed less interest in explicating the doctrine than in calling for perfect obedience to the man who had conceived it: "Showing endless loyalty to the Leader is the most basic character of the Subject-type communist."[16] There was less talk of a specific consciousness than of "hearts boiling with Subject-type blood," of turning "Subject Thought into flesh and bone."[17] The dictator's own assertion that his thought was best grasped by studying history, not doctrine, helped ensure that public attention remained safely focused on his biographical legend.

If *chuch'e sasang* could not be made to look prohibitively difficult without undermining the general opposition to intellectualism, it could still be made unreadable. Newspaper and journal articles set aside each month for token meta-ideological discussion repeated the same few banalities while offering no examples of application. This is from an article in the June 1974 issue of the magazine *Ch'ŏllima*.

> The beloved Leader Comrade Kim Il Sung has taught as follows:
> "In a word, Subject Thought is the idea that the masters of revolution and construction are the masses, and that also the force behind revolution and construction lies with the masses. To put it another way, one is the master of one's own fate, and the

force behind the realization of that fate also lies with oneself." ("Answers given to foreign journalists' questions," page 310.)

If I may interrupt here: Note how the *Mainichi* journalists have become "foreign" ones. (This strengthens the assumption that the interview was originally intended to serve only a public-diplomatic end.) The lack of a date reflects embarrassment about the advanced age at which the Leader had chosen to unburden himself of his teenage insights. The page number, cited without reference to a book, is meant to suggest a monograph of great length.

The article continues:

> Above all, Subject Thought revealed the truth that the masses are the masters of revolution and construction. The statement that the masses are the masters of revolution and construction means that the masses are in charge of revolution and construction and an autonomous entity responsible for revolution and construction. The thesis that the masters of revolution and construction are the masses is an idea illuminating the masses' place in revolution and construction.[18]

This sounds just as ludicrously repetitive in the original. Nabokov may have called the Soviet press "a hell of boredom," but it did not try to be dull, and to less hostile readers much of it was interesting. The same holds for most of North Korea's official culture. What tends to fatigue Western readers is the constant straining for maximum emotional effect, the last thing one could impute to the *chuch'e sasang* discourse. To suggest that the writing excerpted above was not meant to be boring would be to impute gross incompetence to the propaganda apparatus. Such articles conveyed their main message simply by filling a respectable amount of space: Thanks to the Leader, North Korea has its very own theoretical discourse, which the yawning, skimming reader would do well to leave to his betters.

"THE ERA OF THE SUBJECT": 1973-1981

Not that any amount of study could have made sense of the doctrine. It wasn't only that Kim Il Sung had singled out different ideas as its central point. ("Man is the master of all things," "The masses are the masters of revolution," "autonomy in politics, independence in the economy," etc, even "workers of the world unite": all had got a turn.) Sometimes the name *chuch'e sasang* was applied to the totality of Kim's thought, sometimes only to its core or essence. Sometimes it was claimed that the process of "coloring the country the one color of Subject Thought" had begun circa 1956; sometimes it was said to have begun in the colonial period.[19] The regime would later say the doctrine had been systematized by Kim Jong Il, who in turn would say his father had already systematized it.[20] Like *chuch'e sasang*'s dullness and abstraction from practice, its constant equivocation was meant to shake off even the most dogged readers, and thus to preclude judgment of Kim's performance by his own ostensible standards. There was and is very little a North Korean can say about *chuch'e sasang* without fear of making some grave mistake. This explains that snappishness which many tour guides manifest when pressed to explain it.[21]

In the 1970s Kim's ghostwriters added to *chuch'e sasang* in drips and drabs, usually for visitors' benefit. Nine out of ten of the doctrinal "talks" published after 1971 and anthologized (in Korean) in 1977 were addressed to foreigners.[22] A text supplied in his name to Australian journalists contained yet another nutshell version of the doctrine, according to which it

> is based on the philosophical principle that man is the master of all things and the decider of all things. . . . Man is a social being with independence. All man's activities are determined by his ideological consciousness. Because man has independent ideological consciousness he does not blindly yield to the external world but re-shapes it in a goal-oriented fashion according to his intentions and demands.[23]

And so on. Needless to say, there was nothing original here.[24] North Koreans must have intuited that if this stuff were vitally relevant to their own lives, their leader would not be keeping it under the counter for foreign visitors. The only message imparted with real propagandistic intent was that the world hung on Kim's lips.

The advent of what propaganda called the "Era of the Subject" (*chuch'e sidae*)[25] brought with it no political, social or cultural change assignable to the doctrine. As export-propagandistic, English-language boasts of "self-reliance" increased, so too did the country's foreign debt. Between 1970 and 1975 alone Pyongyang borrowed some $1.2 billion from the United Kingdom and other capitalist governments. (By the end of the Cold War, North Korea had received about $18 billion in aid and credits from around the world.)[26] In a tortuous effort to reconcile this with the Juche myth, an American scholar has asserted that, "Self-reliance required the strongest military one could muster."[27] The problem with that reasoning is obvious even without reference to the mutual defense treaties the DPRK had signed with China and the USSR. Pyongyang's habit of borrowing heavily from all and sundry, then brazenly defaulting on its debt, can be explained sufficiently well with reference to the unification-centric ultra-nationalism that had guided it since the 1940s. A special concern for self-reliance did not enter into things.

As for *chuch'e sasang*, its content had no great effect even on propaganda. Judging from the wall-posters reproduced in magazines and yearbooks, "man is the master of all things" did not even make it into the top thirty slogans. If anything, the long-standing effort to convince the masses that they were as helpless babies at the Parent Leader's breast became *more* extreme as the 1970s wore on. If they were to pay attention to Juche's human-centricity at all, it was only to understand that the regime was, to put things in American idiom, all about putting people first.

There was no equivalent in schools of the compendia of Mao's writings that were mandatory reading even in the lower grades in China.[28] Kim's fantasy biography was hammered home instead, with special emphasis on his childhood and youth. Whereas each Chinese family was supposed to have Mao's four-volume *Selected Works* at home,[29] most North Koreans saw their leader's already large oeuvre through a glass case in their farm or factory's sepulchral "study room." Lavishly bound, printed on smooth white paper with wide margins, and padded out with ceremonial miscellany, the imposing volumes were to be marveled at, not studied. Every now and then students or cadres might be called upon, as an endurance test if nothing else, to memorize certain speeches, but there seems to have been less of this sort of thing than there had been in the 1950s. At the core of party instruction were canonical novels and live-action movies about the Great Leader's guerrilla exploits.[30]

The only words of Kim's with which average citizens came into daily contact were one- or two-sentence statements quoted on interior walls or as lead-off quotes in media articles, usually without attribution to a particular text. Most were commonplaces extraneous to *chuch'e sasang*. Exhortations to do things well abounded: "To farm well, one must select and plant seeds well."[31] The

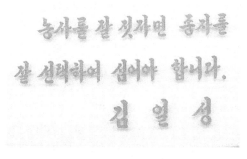

abundance of such truisms in writings on "Juche Agriculture," "Juche Art," "Juche Literature," etc, still encourages many observers to assert a strong connection between theory and daily life, as if North Koreans would not have thought of doing things well otherwise.[32] But such sayings of the leaders have never been meant to be taken as brilliant insight; their function is to reflect parental solicitude and a concern for all aspects of national life.

In short, this was the decade not of *chuch'e sasang* but of praise for it. The evening TV news began with reports of tributes sent from this or that country to the Great Leader. Hardly a week went by in which the *Rodong Sinmun* did not announce the opening of a new Juche conference, or the founding of a new research institute, usually in some African or South American capital. Little interest was shown in the concrete uses to which the Leader's wisdom was being put. Often the media did not even bother to identify the countries in question. This is from a report on an unnamed man in an unnamed state who had commemorated the Leader's sixty-second birthday:

> On this happy day he swore resolutely, before the portrait of the Leader which enjoyed pride of place in his home, that he would forever keep fighting in accordance with his teaching. Thus did he and his family set about studying the "Biography of Kim Il Sung" and the Leader's immortal works with even more diligence.
> And do you think this is only one family, in one country?[33]

The obvious mendacity of such reporting aside, we should not think the regime had given up on enhancing Kim's international stature. The great charm offensive continued throughout the decade, with ever more delegations sent abroad to, as a Hungarian diplomat in Pyongyang put it, "create suitable international conditions for the unification of the country, and the isolation of South Korea."[34] Joining the Non-Aligned Movement (NAM) in 1975, North Korea did all it could to prevent the rival state from following suit. Its obsessive effort to dominate the forum entailed bribery on a massive scale. According to an estimate then current among diplomats stationed in Pyongyang, the DPRK had by 1982 spent $100 million dollars on its lobbying drive.[35] This is not to say that Juche's content was beside the point. Had it not been such an airy affair of putting people first, and solving one's own problems when possible, it would have been harder for non-communist dignitaries to come out in support of the DPRK. The leader of Mali became one of many African blurb-providers, extolling the wisdom of the "Juche idea" on a visit to Pyongyang in 1976.[36] During Cuba's polarizing chairmanship of the NAM (1979-1983), the nationalist ruling party of Bangladesh expressed a hope that the North Koreans would take over instead.[37]

In these years, dozens of Juche texts were translated into English, Spanish, Japanese and other languages, and published in various formats, ranging from slender paperbacks to leatherette-bound tomes with Kim's profile stamped on the front. Edited more carefully than the first batch of export propaganda, they consisted of two main types. One was collections of writings published under Kim's name. These usually included parts of the speech to propagandists (1955), the Indonesia lecture (1965) and the *Mainichi* interview (1972). There was plenty of filler: "On the Orientation of the Compilation of an Encyclopedia and Maps," for example. Anything calling for a Korean approach to Korean problems was good enough. Some newly-forged speeches backdated to the 1930s were also included. The books were given titles like *On Juche in Our Revolution* (1975) so as to pass for records of a consistent theoretical discourse.[38]

Then there were articles and monographs by foreign admirers, who followed the official practice of alternating bold-print quotation with pseudo-exegetical panegyric. The very titles bespeak an effort to satisfy both the old-school communist and the ideology-shopper in search of something new: "Kim Il Sung — The Outstanding Marxist-Leninist of the Present Era who has Founded Great Kimilsungism."[39] The two isms' relationship had to be kept as murky as possible. On one page: "Kimilsungism is not a mere inheritance and development of Marxism-Leninism," but on another: "The Juche idea is the Marxism-Leninism of the present day, that has highly developed Marxist-Leninist theory."[40] The main difference between the domestic and the foreign-language Juche texts lay in the greater readability of the latter. Each paragraph at least carried the gist forward, as could not be said of the circular prose written for North Koreans to run a glazed eye over. These books were sent *gratis* to university libraries around the world. The shipping costs alone must have been immense.

In view of all this activity, one has to wonder why the South Korean opposition movement evinced so little awareness of *chuch'e sasang* until well into the 1980s. Draconian though it may have been, the ROK's National Security Law did not prevent generations of students from listening to Pyongyang's radio broadcasts. Whether or not one accepts North Korean migrants' assertions that KPA commandos played a leading role in the Kwangju Uprising of May 1980, radios in rebel-driven buses and jeeps were kept tuned to the Pyongyang station, and the banners strung along buildings were marked by a bloodthirsty idiom new to South Korean protest.[41] There were calls to "tear Chun Doo Hwan to pieces," to "grind [his] head against the concrete," and so on.[42] (Veterans of the uprising confess to having known nothing of such a villain beforehand; some wondered, as they gamely joined in the chants, if he was the Chŏn Tu-hwan who ran the local silkworm farm.)[43]

Yet despite a good deal of propagandistic infiltration, student protesters generally subscribed to old-school European Marxism-Leninism; Stalin's writings were studied well into the 1980s.[44] Although lectures on *chuch'e sasang* had been broadcast across the DMZ as early as 1972, the fact of such a doctrine's existence mattered far more than its content. Students in Seoul did not huddle around their short-wave radios to hear that "man is born with creativity"; they listened for inspiring myth-making about the guerrilla struggle, harsh anti-Park and anti-American invective, and guidelines (coded and uncoded) for fomenting rebellion.

Considering how many Juche research institutes were said to have been established around the world, it is telling that North Korea did not get one of its own until October 1979. As if to underscore its irrelevance to decision-making, it was set up in a farming area outside the capital. Predictably enough, the jet-setting Hwang Jang Yop was appointed its first director. Kim Jong Il told him the institute had to function as "the

party's international department," an organ for "externally-oriented ideological-theoretical work,"⁴⁵ in other words, for the management and organization of Juche-oriented institutes, seminars, etc, overseas. Hwang says, however, that he requested and received an opportunity to coach the members of the WP's Central Committee, who still had "no awareness" of the doctrine.⁴⁶

Meanwhile, ritual calls for *chuch'e-sasang-hwa* or the permeation of society in Subject Thought continued into the sixth congress of the Workers' Party in October 1980. The relevant passage in Kim Il Sung's report could have been taken from any number of magazine articles of the preceding years.

> Permeating the whole society in Subject Thought means regarding Subject Thought as the firm leading guide in revolution and construction, thoroughly implementing it, and building a communist society. . . . Subject Thought is the human-centered worldview according to which man is the center of all things, and that calls for service to man, and is a revolutionary theory for the realization of the working masses' autonomy. Only by regarding Subject Thought as a guide and thoroughly embodying it can all problems arising in connection with human-reshaping and social-reshaping, construction of the economy and construction of culture be solved.⁴⁷

Verbal style is no reliable indicator of truthfulness, but it does reflect how seriously someone wants to make a point. Whether or not Hitler believed what he said, there can be no doubt that he wanted to get it across. The same can be said of Kim's nationalist rhetoric — his praise for the homogeneity of the Korean race, for example. No sooner did he turn to *chuch'e sasang*, however, than he lapsed into tautologous verbiage which all but defied listeners to pay attention.

That no meta-ideological debate has taken place in the DPRK since the purported advent of the "Era of the Subject" is yet another indication of the sterility and fraudulence of doctrinal discussion. No theory can be applied in earnest without differences of interpretation becoming apparent and requiring resolution, which it was the main function of communist party congresses to provide. It was only logical for Kim Il Sung to conclude that the WP could henceforth do without congresses altogether.

"THE ERA OF THE SUBJECT": 1973-1981

1. *Hoegorok*, 211. The many observers who accept both Hwang's claim to authorship of Juche *and* the myth of the doctrine's authority must have a very low opinion of the ruling elite.
2. Ibid., 210.
3. Martin, *Cult and Canon*, 29.
4. Kim Il Sung, *Chosŏn hyŏngmyŏng ŭi chillo* (Pyongyang, 1978).
5. *Kim Il-sŏng sŏnjip* 9 (Pyongyang, 1980). 480.
6. "Tangsaŏp ŭl kaesŏn hamyŏ," *Kim Il-sŏng chŏjakchip* 21 (Pyongyang, 1983), 136-137.
7. Mao famously quoted this line (from *Foundations of Leninism*) in "On Practice." *Mao-Tse-tung: An Anthology of His Writings*, 210.
8. *Chongch'i sajŏn* (Pyongyang: 1973), 1055-1060.
9. See for example the article printed on Kim Jong Il's birthday: "Chuch'e sasang e kich'o han tang ŭi ch'ŏlt'ong kat'ŭn t'ongil tan'gyŏl ŭn uri hyŏngmyŏng kwa sahoejuŭi taegŏnsŏl chŏnt'u sŭngni ŭi hwakko han tambo," *Rodong Sinmun*, 16 February 1974. The term *tang chungang* was not new; it had been used in earlier decades to refer to the Central Committee, the party leadership, etc.
10. See for example, Kim Yŏng-nam, "Kyŏngae hanŭn suryŏng Kim Il-sŏng tongji ŭi yŏngsaeng pulmyŏl ŭi chuch'e sasang ŭn uri sidae ŭi widaehan segyejŏk sajo," *Kŭlloja*, April 1974, 27. Also: "The party center has scientifically formalized the Great Leader's revolutionary thought into a comprehensive system encompassing the thought, theory and methods of the subject . . . and put forth the fighting principle of painting the entire party and all of society in the one color of Subject Thought." O Chin-u, "Uri tang ŭn widaehan chuch'e sasang e ŭi hayŏ chido toenŭn hyŏngmyŏngjŏgin tang ida," *Kŭlloja*, October 1975, 30.
11. *Hoegorok*, 214. North Korea's own historiography prefers to claim that 1974 saw Kim Jong Il call for society's *chuch'e-sasang-hwa*, or "permeation in Subject Thought." In fact the slogan of the time had been "paint [society] in the one color of Subject Thought."

12. The Dear Leader's *Selected Works* (published in the 1990s) do indeed include a long speech on permeating society in "Kimilsungism" that was allegedly delivered to party propagandists on February 19, 1974. "On sahoe rŭl kimilsŏngjuŭihwa hagi wihan tang sasang saŏp ŭi tangmyŏn-han myŏt' kaji kwaŏp e taehayŏ," in *Kim Chŏng-il sŏnjip* (1994), 4:7-75. There is no reason to think it authentic, even though Hwang credibly asserts that on that date Kim Jong Il announced the existence of a comprehensive "Kimilsungism." Obviously phony is an article dated to 1976 which attempts to distance Kimilsungism from Marxism-Leninism: "Kimilsŏngjuŭi ŭi tokch'angsŏng ŭl olk'e insik halde taehayŏ," in *Kim Chŏng-il sŏnjip* (2011), 7:475-482. Many speeches in the "early" volumes of his works were fabricated in the early 1990s by Hwang and others. (See *Hoegorok*, 286.) Unfortunately most foreign scholars either take the pre-1980s dates on Kim Jong Il's published works at face value, or pretend to do so; this tendency is particularly conspicuous in research of North Korean art, literature and film.
13. Koh, "Ideology and North Korean Foreign Policy," 25.
14. We thus find an article in the September 18, 1977 issue of the *Rodong Sinmun* in which Yasui Kaoru is quoted as praising *Kimilsŏngjuŭi*.
15. Ra Tong-sik, "Widaehan suryŏngnim ŭi hyŏngmyong sasang ŭn kajang chŏnghwakhan kwahakchŏk kongsanjuŭi riron," *Ch'ŏllima*, November-December 1974, 17-19.
16. "Suryŏngnim kke kkŭt' ŏpsi ch'ungsŏng tahanŭn kŏs ŭn chuch'ehyŏng ŭi kongsanjuŭi hyŏngmyŏngga ŭi kajang kibonjŏgin p'umsŏng," *Kŭlloja*, May-June 1974, 8.
17. "Chuch'ehyŏng ŭi p'i ka kkŭllŭn simjangdŭl," *Ch'ŏllima*, July 1974, 33. "Kyŏngae hanŭn suryŏng Kim Il-sŏng tongji ŭi hyŏngmyŏng sasang ŭn chuch'e sidae ŭi yogu rŭl panyŏng hayŏ naon saeropko tokch'angjŏgin widaehan sasang," *Kŭlloja*, July 1974, 16.
18. Ch'oe Ch'ŏl-ung. "Chuch'e sasang ŭn hyŏngmyŏng kwa kŏnsŏl ŭi chuin ŭn inmin taejungimyŏ kŭ gŏs ŭl ch'udonghanŭn him to inmin taejung ege ittanŭn sasang," *Ch'ŏllima*, June 1974, 13.
19. "Widaehan chuch'e sasang ŭro on sahoe rŭl ilsaekhwa haja," *Ch'ŏllima*, July 1974, 29.

20. "Maksŭ-reninjuŭi wa chuch'e sasang ŭi kich'i rŭl nop'i tŭlgo naagaja," *Kŭlloja*, May 1983, 6.
21. I would like to thank those readers of *The Cleanest Race* who have shared with me relevant anecdotes of their visits to Pyongyang. I should add that the idea for a book on the Juche myth came to me during a bus tour to Kaesong in spring 2008. While my Australian friend was in the gift shop with the other (South Korean) travelers, I stood out in the parking lot engaging some curious middle-aged minders in Korean conversation. They were thrilled to learn I was reading the Great Leader's work. Their smiles faded, however, when I started asking very basic and respectful questions about it. As in: Which speeches did every North Korean know? When I mentioned the ones I had been reading, their eyes narrowed; they seemed to suspect me of inventing titles as a test. Although already a Juche skeptic, I had expected to encounter more knowledge of the leaders' writings. "Isn't it time for you to get back on the bus?" I was finally asked.
22. Kim Il Sung, *Chuch'e sasang e taehayŏ* (Pyongyang, 1977).
23. Kim Il Sung, "Osŭt'ŭrallia kija-dŭl i chegi han chilmun e taehan taedap (1974-nyŏn 11-wŏl 4-il)," *Chuch'e sasang e taehayŏ*, 564-565. Kim told the Australians, sans examples, that some aspects of Juche as practiced in the DPRK might not be suited for other countries, which should thus be careful to adjust it to their own conditions.
24. The trite emphasis on man as a socially-connected being recalls the Japanese Marxism of the 1930s. William Miles Fletcher III, *Search for a New Order* (Chapel Hill, NC, 1982), 18-19.
25. Ri Sang-gŏn, "Chuch'e ŭi sae sidae ga yŏllyŏtta," *Chosŏn Munhak*, April 1974, 36; "Kyŏngaehanŭn suryŏng Kim Il-sŏng tongji ŭi hyŏngmyŏng sasang ŭn chuch'e sidae ŭi yogu rŭl panyŏng hayŏ naon saeropko tokch'angjŏgin widaehan sasang," *Kŭlloja*, July 1974, 9.
26. Selig Harrison, *Korean Endgame*, xiv.
27. Cha, *The Impossible State*, 116-117.
28. Martin, *Cult and Canon*, 23.
29. Ibid., 14.
30. Hwang, *Ŏdum ŭi p'yŏn i toen haetbyŏt'*, 40.

31. In 2011 I noted this statement, and took the accompanying photograph, at the little museum run by a model farm near Sariwon, one of the requisite stops for foreign tourists.
32. It is a shame how much time and energy young academics expend on this sort of research, examples of which, in the form of doctoral theses and journal submissions, I am occasionally asked to look at. Let's say Joe wants to write the history of North Korean pottery. (I hope this is still a purely hypothetical example.) First he makes a beeline for the leaders' collected works. There he finds a speech by Kim Jong Il entitled, say, "Juche Ceramics Theory." Unaware that it was ghostwritten in the 1990s and merely back-dated to 1971, he accepts it as a formative influence on pottery in the 1970s. (One would think the world had seen enough of Kim Jong Il during his rule to know that he was no theoretician and never had been, but intuition counts for little in the so-called social sciences; Western academics seem to accept even more of his mytho-biography than of his father's.) Alas, the pages Joe has photocopied are easily reduced to one message: "Pottery must be made correctly; otherwise it will be bad and the masses will reject it." Our scholar tries gamely to read something of significance into this. Finally he spins out a few pages about how correctness is defined by the regime, as if potters would not have known this already.
33. Ri Sang-gŏn, "Chuch'e ŭi saesidae ga yŏllyŏtta!", *Chosŏn Munhak*, April 1974, 37.
34. "Hungarian Embassy in the DPRK, Report, 27 September 1973. Subject: The DPRK and the Non-Aligned Summit in Algiers," translated by Balazs Szalontai, DA/WWC.
35. "Hungarian Embassy in the DPRK, Report, 11 March 1982. Subject: North Korean Activities in the Non-Aligned Movement," translated by Balazs Szalontai, DA/WWC.
36. "Hungarian Embassy in the DPRK, Telegram, 2 June 1976. Subject: Visit of the President of Mali in the DPRK," translated by Balazs Szalontai, DA/WWC.
37. "Hungarian Embassy in Bangladesh, Telegram, 28 December 1981. Subject: DPRK-Bangladesh Relations," translated by Balazs Szalontai, DA/WWC.

38. Kim Il Sung, *On Juche in our Revolution* (Pyongyang, 1975).
39. "Warm Greetings to the Sixty-Second Birthday of President Kim Il Sung — The Outstanding Marxist-Leninist of the Present Era who has Founded Great Kimilsungism," in *The World Historic Significance of the Juche Idea: Essays and Articles* (Pyongyang, 1975), 1.
40. "Warm Greetings to the Sixty-Second Birthday," 4; Kuriki Yasunobu, "World Historic Significance of the Juche Idea," in *The World Historic Significance of the Juche Idea*, 9.
41. Kim Tae-ryŏng, *Yŏksa ro sŏ ŭi 5.18*, 1:324-329.
42. Ibid., 1:346.
43. Ibid., 1:37-69.
44. Ryu Kŭn-il, Hong Chin-p'yo, *Chisŏng kwa pan chisŏng* (Seoul, 2004), 74.
45. Hwang, *Hoegorok*, 227.
46. Ibid., 231.
47. Kim Il Sung, "Chosŏn rodongdang che 6-ch'a taehoe esŏ han chungang wiwŏnhoe ch'onghwa pogo," in *Kim Il-sŏng chŏjakchip* 35 (Pyongyang, 1987), 313.

8

A FATHER AND SON AFFAIR: 1982-1994

SINCE THE LATE 1960s North Korean media had compared *chuch'e sasang* to a torch lighting the world to a better future.[1] The metaphor took on more substantial form on April 15, 1982, Kim Il Sung's seventieth birthday, when the regime unveiled a tower on the bank of the Taedong River, complete with a flame-shaped light on top that burned red at night. In a niche built into the back of this Tower of the Juche Idea, as the *chuch'e sasang t'ap* was called in English, were "friendship plaques" allegedly donated by foreign study societies. Many of them referred to Kimilsungism. As if to make extra sure that thought and thinker were never uncoupled, the monument was said to consist of 25,550 granite blocks: one for every day of Kim Il Sung's seventy years.[2]

In March 1982 the third and final volume of *The Great Victory of Subject Thought* (*Chuch'e sasang ŭi widaehan sŭngni*) appeared. A numbingly vague history of the doctrine's shaping of the republic, it made no reference to Kim Jong Il even in sections on art and literature.[3] This suggests that although the burgeoning of the heir's cult had almost certainly been planned well in advance, his public pose as a seasoned generator of Juche theory had not, which is all the more reason for us to be skeptical of his hagiographers' retrospective accounts of the 1970s.

Be all that as it may, a text entitled *On Subject Thought* (*Chuch'e sasang e taehayŏ*) appeared under his name in April 1982.[4] The subtitle, dating it to the last day of the previous month, describes it as having been sent to the "National Subject Thought Forum" then underway.[5] That it was probably ghostwritten goes without saying.

At first glance, the paper's lack of any bold-print quotes from the Great Leader suggests plenty of original content. In fact the main points were all familiar: the masses are the subject of history, whose independent ideological consciousness plays a decisive role in their struggle for independence, and so on. Even the few new elements in it were treated as having come from Kim Il Sung. Evidently the propaganda apparatus wanted to impart more substance to the doctrine without straying too obviously from what had already been printed. In the 1970s the Great Leader or his ghostwriter had described man as a social creature with independence. He had also asserted the need for a creative position and for proper consciousness. These remarks were now treated as a purportedly original insight that independence, creativity and consciousness constitute the basic nature of man.[6] Everything was spun out in the usual tautological style.

> To man, who is a social being, independence is life. When we say that independence is life to man, we are referring to socio-political life. Man has both physical life and socio-political life. If physical life is life to man as a biological organism, then socio-political life is life to man as a social being.[7]

A FATHER AND SON AFFAIR: 1982-1994

That someone being touted for unparalleled insight into his father's thought should have debuted with such pap only underscores its distance from the *de facto* ideology — then as now a thing expressed in more urgent prose. Clearly, the paper's main function was to fit out the heir with a record of intellectual service. By putting his name on this first authoritative monograph of *chuch'e sasang*, the regime also made it harder for anyone to challenge the hereditary succession on doctrinal grounds. The text could serve these functions merely by being printed, and praised in the press. Had the regime expected it to be read attentively, it would have done more to justify the claims made for it. But *On Subject Thought* was at least the first comprehensive collation of points that had hitherto been scattered across Kim Il Sung's ghost-written works. It quickly became the most often-cited source on the doctrine.

Meanwhile the regime was putting its public-diplomacy budget to subtler uses than before. Foreign academics were invited to attend Juche courses in the DPRK. In 1982, Alfred Pfabigan and three other philosophy scholars from the University of Vienna accepted an invitation to study for a few weeks, all expenses paid, at the so-called Juche Institute outside the capital. In his book about the experience, Pfabigan says that the building also went by the names of the Academy of Social Sciences and Association of Korean Social Scientists.[8] It may well have become the Juche Institute only when guests were there, which was evidently not all that often; the Austrians encountered no other students.

Here Pfabigan recounts the instruction given by one Professor Pak Chang-gon (in tandem with an interpreter) for roughly six hours a day.

"Marx made no contribution to the re-shaping of the world.... the destiny of mankind was not so important to him... Marxism-Leninism cannot give an answer to questions of our own time. Juche knows what man is and what comprises the goal of his existence. The important thing is whether an ideology has brought happiness to man. This is why there was great reflection about the task of philosophy. Our beloved and respected leader, Comrade Kim Il Sung, found the solution: Philosophy must expose man's fate and legitimate development." What was I supposed to do with that? My teacher's lecture, which sounds very simple, is part fragment, part wrong, part irrelevant. But is this impression correct?... Can one understand Juche at all, without being a Korean?... If we want to assume that our teacher is no idiot or liar, it must be the translation's fault; for us, Juche is a content-less mush that endlessly repeats itself.[9]

Such cautious responses to Juche were common. Westerners are reluctant to trust their intellectual instincts in regard to something from the Far East, the source of so much wisdom which may at first appear trite or incoherent. But we see here that North Koreans were more dismissive of Marx in the presence of non-aligned visitors than they would have dared to be around East Europeans. More diplomatic were writings published under the leaders' names. In May 1983 Kim Jong Il or his ghostwriter celebrated Marx's 165th birthday with a piece entitled "Forward, holding high the banner of Marxism-Leninism and Subject Thought."

> Only by correctly applying Marxism-Leninism from a subjective standpoint can one highly enhance its power and create new revolutionary theory, thus adding to the abundance of Marxism-Leninism's store of treasure. . . . [In] Subject Thought is concentrated the new practical thought and theory derived from, and developed and enriched in, the process of fighting the revolutionary struggle under the banner of Marxism-Leninism.[10]

In the outer track, then, the relationship between communist orthodoxy and *chuch'e sasang* was still being presented, 1960s-style, as that between a "pure" ideology and the practical, country-specific thought governing its application.

The Austrians were also subjected to plenty of talk, unpleasant to them for obvious reasons, about every people's need for a strong leader. This so-called "leader theory" (*suryŏngnon*) featured occasionally in texts published under Kim Jong Il's name. In the article just mentioned, for example, Marx is described as the "first leader of the working class," without whom it would have "continued to wander in darkness." Had Lenin not proclaimed Leninism, the USSR would not have come into being. Kim Il Sung, for his part, had shown the way to joint victory for the communist and national-liberation movements on the peninsula.[11] Talk of the decisive role of leaders was hardly new to North Korea, but it was new to *chuch'e sasang* proper, the regime having naturally been reluctant to have the Great Leader assert his own indispensability. As trite as it was, therefore, "leader theory" can be regarded as an addition to the points Kim Il Sung

had made in 1972. Hostile South Korean observers err, however, in regarding it as a concept central to *chuch'e sasang*.[12]

Pfabigan's book charts his intellectual journey from curiosity to puzzlement to a realization of the doctrine's emptiness. Like Helmut Martin before him, he identified the country's true canon: "all information that my minders give me, all memorial sites that I visit, all the teachings that are conveyed to me, are contained in the leader's biography."[13] Regardless of the internationalism preached in their daily classes, the Austrians were treated in accordance with the *de facto* ideology; an unauthorized stroll to a nearby village ended in angry detention by local security forces.[14]

In 1983, not long after returning to Austria, Pfabigan attended a so-called Juche conference in Innsbruck. The DPRK's embassy in Vienna assumed the costs for the speakers, as well as expenses for attendees from across the local political spectrum. Among those present were members of a "Juche study group," who were excited about a trip to Pyongyang they had recently taken — that too, it seems safe to assume, on Kim Il Sung's dime. "The comfortable hotel and the good food" were "indeed a factor holding the Innsbruck coalition together," Pfabigan noted drily. *No speaker lectured on Juche itself.* Instead the ostensible theme of the conference served as a springboard for general pro-Pyongyang speechifying, and from none too left-wing a perspective either. During a recess, one Professor Hans Klecatsky from the University of Innsbruck confessed to Pfabigan that what had attracted him to Juche was its "consistent anti-Marxism."[15] Klecatsky then took the podium to complain about the subversion of Western democracy by vested interests — including trade unions.

> Now, in its concluding sentences, the tenets of Juche are alluded to for the first time: Humanism unites Kim Il Sung and Hans Klecatsky ("Man is the most important being on earth"), creative capacities are celebrated, as are trust in one's own power and Kim Il Sung's opposition to dogmatism and flunkeyism. In Austria

there is too much flunkeyism, Klecatsky says, and the audience rejoices in this little fouling of the nest. . . . Understood in this way, [Pfabigan concludes] Juche really is a universal ideology in the sense of its creators. The lack of content, yes, the randomness of its formulae . . . yields unsuspected advantages.[16]

More insight is expressed in that last part than in all the North Korea scholarship of the day. In an influential article published in 1982, the American political scientist Bruce Cumings made the first of several efforts to stylize the word *chuch'e* into an *arcanum*, a mystery inaccessible to the foreign mind.

The North Koreans say things like "everyone must have *chuch'e* firm in mind and spirit"; "only when *chuch'e* is firmly implanted can we be happy". . . . The closer one gets to its meaning, the more its meaning recedes. It is the opaque core of Korean national solipsism.[17]

Overlooking the banal content of the doctrine in order to puzzle respectfully over its name has been the academic custom ever since. I remind my reader that the term *chuch'e sasang* (or *chuch'e ŭi sasang*) was coined in 1962 to denote the WP's own or subjective body of practical thought; there is nothing opaque about it. (A word can be vague or ambiguous — like *ideology* — without defying understanding.) As for the formulations Cumings quotes or seems to quote — no citation is given —, they are hardly typical.[18] In any case we can easily understand them according to the word's standard pan-Korean definition, though a literate South Korean would have talked of *chuch'esŏng* (subjectivity) instead. Cumings, however, jumps from the obvious wrongness of the translation to the conclusion that *chuch'e* means much *more* than self-reliance — more, indeed, than the Westerner can hope to grasp. Samuel Johnson was right: "Sometimes things may be made darker by definition."[19]

Pyongyang had been lobbying the world hard, but by 1980 the rival state was outspending it. The Non-Aligned Movement's deradicalization was such that it would probably have drifted out of sympathy with the DPRK anyway. The International Olympic Committee's decision to award the 1988 games to Seoul was a great blow to Kim Il Sung. Desperate to restore face by winning the right to host the NAM's eighth summit in 1986, he stepped up efforts to promote the supremely unobjectionable "Juche idea" as a unifying credo for its disparate members.[20] In August 1983, according to the Hungarian embassy, culture and education ministers from NAM countries attending a conference in Pyongyang were "forcefully pressured" to praise both the wisdom of the two Kims and the "international applicability of Juche" in their presentations. While the Cubans and Indians refused, "delegates of a number of African countries were particularly willing to assume the aforesaid role, a fact that one might also attribute to the apparently effective bribery conducted by the Koreans."[21]

This was the last strong push to influence the NAM. The North Korean bomb attack on the ROK president's delegation in Burma in October 1983 showed that if the Great Leader had ever seriously wanted to win non-aligned friends, it was only in order to expedite unification.

Yet the myth of the doctrine still had important domestic work to do. Preparation for the succession necessitated due fuss over Kim Jong Il's contributions to *chuch'e sasang*. In 1985 the regime published a Korean-language handbook on it which is still sold in bookstores.[22] The heir's statements were quoted in the same bold print as his father's, and with roughly the same frequency, so that any random page would show *chuch'e sasang* to be the product of not one but two geniuses. A representative excerpt:

> So how does one go about doing the work of revolution and construction in accordance with actual conditions?

Subject Thought reveals that in order to do the work of revolution and construction in accordance with actual conditions, it is necessary to figure out concrete conditions well, and to define a political line, policies and strategies that are suited to them.

The Dear Leader Comrade Kim Jong Il has instructed as follows.

"To carry out the revolutionary struggle in accordance with actual conditions, it is necessary to figure out the subjective and objective conditions of one's country's revolution, and define a political line, policies and strategies that are suited to them."

If one is to achieve victory and good results in revolution and construction, there must be, more than anything else, a correct line, policies and strategies. This having been already discussed above, it is not necessary to repeat it again.

So the question is, how does one establish the correct line, policies and strategies?

As Subject Thought reveals, to establish the correct line, policies and strategies, it is necessary to make a scientific analysis of the subjective and objective conditions of one's country's revolution.[23]

The giveaway of the doctrine's true function is that for all its self-evident talk of focusing on local conditions, it does no focusing of its own, instead speaking in the most universal terms possible. Had foreign observers bothered to read any of these books through, if only in English, they would surely have understood what game was being played.

It is heartening to see that not everyone was taken in. In a report on his visit to Pyongyang in 1985, *The New York Times*' John F. Burns sounded a skeptical note.

When asked to define the doctrine officials become terse, saying that its essence lies in the idea that the destiny of mankind rests with the masses. . . . To an outsider there is a numbing quality in the millions of words that the Pyongyang presses have poured forth on the *juche* idea, also known as Kimilsungism. . . . "The *juche* idea," [a] book says, "is an idea of taking the attitude of a master, an independent and creative stand, toward the revolution and construction. To take the attitude of a master toward revolution and construction is a basic requirement of the *juche* idea. The attitude of the master finds its expression in the independent and creative stand. The independent and creative stand is essential to the establishment of *juche*."[24]

So the cadres whose ostensible duty was to promulgate the doctrine did not want to discuss it. By writing that Juche was numbing "to an outsider," Burns seemed to qualify his implicit suspicions, but his report ended pointedly with a description of a North Korean sleeping on a pile of books.

The forgery-ridden *Selected* and *Collected Works* of Kim Jong Il, both of which sets were published in later decades, try to convey the impression that he spent the 1980s contributing tirelessly to the Juche discourse. In fact it was not uncommon for several months to go by without a doctrinal word from him.[25] Most of what did appear was dated to a significantly earlier time. For example, "On a Few Problems in Understanding Subject Philosophy," which appeared in 1984, was dated to 1974.[26] (In a transparent effort to explain why it had caused no ripples then, the backdating ghostwriter has Kim Jong Il ask his hearers "not to convey my words yet.")[27] A talk on the doctrine's view of revolution, supposedly given in October 1987, did not make it into print until 14 months later.[28] These unexplained delays make clear that the regime did not want citizens awaiting such writings as advancements of a guiding line.[29]

But it would not do to exaggerate the Juche discourse's importance to the Kims' personality cults either. It never loomed as large in the older man's legend as his liberation of the country, his down-to-earth benevolence and his life of self-denial. (None of the North Korean citizens and migrants who have praised him almost tearfully in my presence has thought to mention Juche.) Propaganda about Kim Jong Il dealt just as heavily in emotionally-appealing themes: his motherless childhood, his lifelong refusal of special treatment, and his loving care for his father. It is therefore unlikely that the average cadre

felt the need to study many of the publications that my argument forces me to discuss. American reporters visiting Pyongyang in 1992, ten years after Kim Jong Il's public debut as a Juche theorist, found most officials at a loss to explain what he had done for the country.[30]

Let us turn now to relevant developments south of the DMZ. Until the mid-1980s, *chuch'e sasang* played no significant role there. The pro-Pyongyang left hewed to old-school Marxism-Leninism instead. But by 1985, Kim Young-hwan, a student activist at Seoul National University, had lost patience with the left's reluctance to address what he saw as the central problem of national autonomy.[31] By infusing harsh anti-Americanism into campus protests he struck a chord with the student population and even much of the middle-class. Soon left-wing student groups across the ROK had coalesced into one broad movement under his leadership.

Searching for a theory with which to guide it, he and other activists arrived during the winter vacation of 1985-1986 at *chuch'e sasang*, which they read about in texts published in Seoul for local Pyongyang watchers. Anti-Americanism and admiration for North Korea thus led to interest in the dictator's thought, and not vice versa. Kim Young-hwan seems to have approached *chuch'e sasang* with a determination to like it, on un-intellectual grounds if necessary: its "human-oriented" talk made it seem less "sardonic" than Marxism-Leninism, more suited to the Korean temperament, and so on. Irony of ironies, he now traces the keyword's emotive power back to his upbringing on Park Chung Hee's talk of "the national subject" (*minjok chuch'e*).[32] The same unconscious associations probably influenced the movement as a whole. Park and his ministers had publicly expressed themselves in far more nationalist tones than the North Korean regime had done in the outer track.[33]

Having attended language classes at Yonsei University in 1986, a time when tear-gas would occasionally waft in through the windows, I can attest to the sympathy for the DPRK then prevailing among South Korea's college students.[34] *Chuch'e sasang*'s vagueness enabled them to project onto it whatever relationship to Marxism-Leninism, whatever degree of nationalism they liked.[35] Best of all, they needed only a few minutes to get the basic drift. Where Western academia equated Juche with self-reliance, the South Koreans reduced it more correctly to autonomy or independence instead.

Hong Chin-p'yo, a former member of the movement, recalls:

Actually Marxism is a little difficult to study. You . . . can hardly look into *Das Kapital* without getting a headache. With Subject Thought, on the other hand, all you need to do is shout "autonomy!" [*chajusŏng*] Since nationalism was a strong force in our society to begin with, you don't need to engage in any special study. And it's because the student movement was grounded in nationalism that it could maintain its momentum into the 1990s, despite the collapse of the USSR and the East Bloc, and the rapid progress of democratization.[36]

But for Pyongyang, the good tidings from South Korea were balanced out by bad news from the communist camp. Ceauşescu's downfall in 1989 hit Kim Il Sung hard, Germany's unification the following year even harder. The outer track inveighed against these developments without criticizing Gorbachev by name. Instead of underscoring the difference between *chuch'e sasang* and Marxism-Leninism, as one might have expected, the regime continued posing as a guardian of the orthodox communist flame. In a speech attributed to Kim Jong Il and dated to May 30, 1990, issue was taken with the idea that there was anything wrong with Marxism-Leninism itself; responsibility rested with communist parties that had lapsed into preaching "revisionism" and "humanist, democratic socialism."[37] This was rich coming from a regime which had spent eighteen years claiming, albeit through a fog of equivocation, to have subjected the Soviet orthodoxy to human-centered improvement.

The regime knew that if it was going to foment an uprising south of the DMZ, it had to do so quickly, before the inevitable collapse of its aid-addicted economy. In 1991, it summoned the South Korean activist Kim Young-hwan, whose writings were still being widely read on campuses. By this time he had already been recruited into outright espionage by an operative who assured him that the Great Leader enjoyed his work (in enlarged photocopies, due to failing eyesight). The young man followed coded instructions to wait on an island off the ROK's west coast, whence he was taken by semi-submarine to the North Korean port of Haeju, and then by helicopter to Pyongyang. There he met with officials to discuss how to destabilize the ROK's fledgling democracy.

The visitor was granted the special honor of two audiences with the almost eighty-year-old Kim Il Sung at his retreat in the Myohyang mountains. For a combined total of five hours the older man held forth. "I tried to steer the conversation toward *chuch'e sasang*," Kim Young-hwan later recalled, "but it soon became clear to me that he didn't know about it."[38] He explains:

> Subject Thought can be divided into three parts. One is the national communism that Kim Il Sung came up with. It's not original, just Stalinism with a light coating of nationalist language, like autonomy, self-defense. The second part is the Subject Philosophy of Mr Hwang Jang Yop. This is the core of Subject Thought. The other part is the leader theory conceived by people in North Korea's propaganda apparatus ... which just says "be loyal".... All Kim Il Sung talked about was his national communism.[39]

The former dissident has since said in another interview, "[Kim] was not interested in what had been put out under his name. I felt an indescribable disappointment that he was incapable even of a minimum of theoretical discussion."[40] Yet the dictator expressed hope that the doctrine's spread in the ROK would lead to an uprising, much as the rise of Islamism had toppled the Shah of Iran.[41]

This was not as far-fetched a goal as all that. The North Korean defector who famously said that the first adherents of *chuch'e sasang* he ever saw were in Seoul was making a serious point.[42] In the early 1990s almost half the student-body presidents at South Korean universities belonged to the pro-North movement, a fact of significance when one considers the influence the student population exerted on society as a whole.[43] Several professors belonged too, and made financial donations to Pyongyang, as did many well-placed leftists in labor, religious and cultural circles.[44] Had the movement maintained the same rate of growth, the Great Leader's dream might have come to fruition by the turn of the millennium. But despite the vanguard's fervor, the rank and file began dropping out in response to the expansion of civil rights in the ROK, the critical post-mortems being performed on the communist bloc, and news of the DPRK's economic ruin. Although the famine had not yet begun in earnest, news of the North Korean logging camps in the Russian Far East was disillusioning enough to the South Korean left.

The regime in Pyongyang sought to bolster its standing on both sides of the DMZ by distancing itself from communism. Where it had once pretended to an internationally-applicable, humanist development of Marxism-Leninism, it now emphasized the slogan "our style of socialism" in a tone that implied defiance of the world.[45] With the USSR gone, and Beijing cozying up to Seoul, the regime had little to lose, but it remained careful not to reveal the full virulence of its race-nationalism. In a paper released on January 3, 1992 under Kim Jong Il's name, Marxism-Leninism was faulted for failing to offer "the correct answer to the problem of how to build communist society." The Great Leader's insights would protect the DPRK from the troubles that had brought down its allies.[46]

In April 1992 the regime issued a revision of the so-called socialist constitution of 1972. The official ideology was now defined in strikingly innocuous terms: "The DPRK is guided in its activities by Subject Thought, a world outlook centered on people, a revolutionary ideology for achieving the independence of the masses of people."[47] The old reference to Marxist-Leninist internationalism was replaced with a profession of commitment to "peace and friendship." There was one passing mention of communism, but no reference to Marxism-Leninism. This raises obvious questions about how *chuch'e sasang*'s nature and scope were henceforth to be understood. It was as if the Pope suddenly spoke only of theology, without mentioning the Bible. One wonders why the regime did not take this opportunity to enshrine Kimilsungism instead, the suffix of which would have better signaled a stand-alone ideology. The likely answer is that this might have been interpreted by China as a too dramatic break with tradition.

Outside scholars look back on the constitution of 1992 as the culmination of Juche's long campaign of conquests, its final elevation "to the status of a kind of religious and moral system."[48] In fact, little attention was paid to the event inside the DPRK; the regime had no interest in alerting its citizens either to the undignified jettisoning of Marxism-Leninism or to that line about "peace and friendship." Ideology continued to be carried by biography. The first instalments of Kim Il Sung's purported memoirs, which ghostwriters had spun out of canonical movies and novels, were made required reading inside the party.[49] The 1992 constitution therefore appears to have been conceived primarily to assuage South Korean fears of a communizing North, not least in order to bolster Kim Dae Jung's chances of winning the presidency that autumn.

Important North Korean trends have always surfaced in the inner track first. The sharp increase in bellicose rhetoric was no exception, beginning a good five years before the term "Military-First" (sŏn'gun) was sloganized in the outer track in 1997-1998.[50] At work was the perception not of any increased American threat, but of the need to adjust official myth to the new realities. With the East Bloc gone, militarism could play a more prominent role — as indeed it had to. The old opposition of the North's "heaven on earth" to the South's "living hell" having outlived its usefulness, the regime that had once boasted equally of the state's prosperity and strength now acted as if economic matters were beyond its purview. Although Kim Jong Il had been glorified throughout the 1980s as an all-round genius, he now appeared primarily as a military man, if not quite a martial one. In December 1992 he assumed formal command of the armed forces. In March 1993 he put the country on war alert before announcing that it would leave the Nuclear Non-Proliferation Treaty. A tense standoff with the USA ensued. In April he assumed chairmanship of the National Defense Council.

The word chuch'e was now functioning more than ever as a mere glittering generality, as when media talked of "the great endeavor of the Subject Revolution," or of the "Subject Bloodline" that Kim Jong Il vowed to carry on "in all its purity."[51] Hwang Jang Yop's stature declined accordingly.[52] Although he held on to the post of the party's secretary for chuch'e sasang, his so-called research institute was subsumed into the WP's international division, which focused exclusively on South Koreans and foreigners.[53] To judge from Hwang's memoirs, the main goal of his overseas activities was to earn hard currency for his boss.[54]

But North Korea could not stop paying lip service to chuch'e sasang altogether, nor could it cease financing a minimum of conferences and study groups overseas. Too clean a break with the past would have implied criticism of the Great Leader himself, and thus undermined the myth paving the way for the hereditary succession. It would also have gone down badly with the regime's sympathizers across the DMZ, who expected some show of left-theoretical governance. (Even those South Koreans who admired the DPRK mainly for its intransigence and militarism needed to perceive themselves as progressive.)[55] Third, the Juche myth had a significant role to play in keeping the nuclear crisis from tipping into outright conflict with the United States.

The Clinton administration's main consultants on North Korean politics were Han S. Park and Tony Namkung, two Korean Americans given to Juche-themed mystification. No doubt this is one reason why they were consulted; the more importance an expert attributes to something beyond the layman's knowing, the more invaluable he makes himself. Park's commitment to the Juche myth is clear from his published writings on North Korea.[56] He even treats the pseudo-concepts teased out of the dictator's speeches by "Juche theoreticians" in the 1970s and 1980s as forces in actual policy-making. The myth predisposed him to an apologetic view of Pyongyang's nuclear program: "North Korea has fostered military preparedness, mainly because of the uncompromising doctrine of self-defense called for by the Juche ideology."[57] This was not just one of many academics invited (as I have been) to the occasional government conference. Park did so much consulting and Track 2 service for the State Department that Donald Gregg, the former US ambassador to Seoul (1989-1993), approvingly referred to him as "the architect of US-DPRK relations."[58]

Tony Namkung, for his part, conflated Juche and the personality cult into one quasi-religion reflective of the regime's deep spirituality. Here (he allegedly said) was something Washington and Pyongyang could bond over — but only if America sent the right emissaries. The North Koreans "do not like talking to secular, 'modern' Westerners. They do not know how to deal with the deep cynicism that pertains to matters of the 'spirit' or the metaphysical."[59] This sort of talk did not even raise doubts about the communist model of the country; Juche was optimistically thought to unite Marx and God. The evangelist Billy Graham, having already been charmed by Kim Il Sung in Pyongyang, fell hard for Namkung's spiel. In a memorandum to Jimmy Carter before the latter's trip to the DPRK, he faulted the Clinton administration for not understanding Juche well enough.[60]

Did the myth encourage the hope that the North would give up nuclear weapons in return for its own energy supply? Perhaps; but I do not believe things would have been very different even if the Americans had never heard of Juche. They would still have chosen to negotiate with this moribund communist straggler, as they saw the DPRK, before resorting to measures that might have led to war. Their own ideology — then finding expression in the slogan, "It's the economy, stupid" — prevented them from acknowledging, let alone understanding, the growth of the North's popularity among South Koreans. Proper awareness of this development, which was more relevant to Kim's top priority than the decline in his own people's living standards, might have made more American observers realize that the nuclear program was no mere "bargaining chip" after all.[61]

But if the Juche fallacy did not define perception of the nuclear crisis, it played an important auxiliary role. For one thing, it helped the Clinton administration assure itself that this Kim Il Sung was very different from the one who had started a war of unification in 1950 — that by declaring a new ideology in 1955, he had set the DPRK's sights on a more benign goal. Conversely, of course, we can assume that a proper understanding of Juche's true function would have made the Americans pay more attention to inner-track propaganda.

They might then have been less naïve about what was said in the outer and export tracks. We know from one American source, which passes on the story in admiring tones, that US intelligence interpreted some KCNA reports as indications of "open bureaucratic warfare between the army and the Foreign Ministry."[62] Granted, this was before Hwang Jang Yop divulged the news agency's key role in ye olde hawks-and-doves ruse.[63] But how could anyone think the regime would publicize real disunity at such a dangerous time?

1. Ri Ho-il, "Chuch'e ŭi choguk, manse!" *Chosŏn Munhak*, August-September 1971, 12.
2. "Past News," KCNA, 15 March 2000. As far as I can see, the claim was not made right away. One is reminded of the Chinese habit of making Mao statues exactly 12.26 meters high, the Great Helmsman's birthday being December 26.
3. *Chuch'e sasang ŭi widaehan sŭngni* 3 (Pyongyang, 1982), 93-130.
4. Kim Jong Il, *Chuch'e sasang e taehayŏ* (Pyongyang, 1982).
5. "Widaehan suryŏng Kim Il-sŏng tongji t'ansaeng 70-tol ki'nyŏm," *Rodong Sinmun*, 26 March 1982.
6. Kim Jong Il, "Chuch'e sasang e taehayŏ," in *Kim Chŏng-il sŏnjip* (Pyongyang, 2011), 436.
7. Ibid.
8. By his own account Pfabigan met only the deputy chairman of the institute, not Hwang. *Schlaflos in Pjöngjang*, 20, 83.
9. Ibid., 86-87.
10. "Maksŭ-reninjuŭi wa chuch'e sasang ŭi kich'i rŭl nop'i tŭlgo naagaja," *Kŭlloja*, May 1983, 6.
11. Ibid., 4.
12. Sin Il-ch'ŏl, *Chuch'e sasang ŭi hyŏngsŏng kwa soet'oe*, 161-164. In a 411-page monograph plainly conceived to incorporate as much of Kim Jong Il's Juche writing as possible, only 9 pages — under a sub-sub-subheading — center on the masses' need for leadership. Kim Hyŏn-suk, *Pulmyŏl ŭi chuch'e sasang* (Pyongyang, 1985), 192-207.
13. *Schlaflos in Pjöngjang*, 58.
14. Ibid., 152-156
15. Ibid., 245.
16. Ibid., 247.
17. Cumings, "Corporatism in North Korea," 289. Apparently unaware of *shutai*, Cumings asserted that *chuch'e*'s nearest Japanese equivalent was the word *kokutai* (national body). He later corrected that error, yet stuck to his original assertion of *chuch'e*'s unique impenetrability: "The term is really

untranslatable; for a foreigner its meaning is ever receding, into a pool of everything that makes Koreans Korean, and therefore ultimately inaccessible to the non-Korean." ("The Corporate State in North Korea," 214.)

18. Which reminds me: It is time to retire the oft-cited claim, made sans citations in Cumings' *Korea's Place in the Sun* (420), that the personality cult's alleged use of the term *urŏrŏ patta,* literally "to look up and receive," reflects a perhaps conscious imitation of Christianity. (See for example Andy Morimoto, "The Sources of North Korean Conduct," *The Diplomat*, 1 February 2015.) While I cannot guarantee that *urŏrŏ patta* was never used in the Kim cult, it has certainly never been common. I suspect there has been a mix-up with *pattŭlda,* or venerate, a verb that far more colonial Koreans came across in Japanese-imperial than in Christian contexts.
19. Quoted by James Boswell in *Life of Johnson*, ed. R. W. Chapman (Oxford, 1998), 911.
20. "Hungarian Embassy in the DPRK, Report, 17 November 1982. Subject: The Visit of Pakistani President Zia Ul-Haq in the DPRK," translated by Balazs Szalontai, DA/WWC.
21. "Hungarian Embassy in the DPRK, Ciphered Telegram, 15 August 1983," translated by Balazs Szalontai, DA/WWC.
22. Kim Ch'ang-ha, *Pulmyŏl ŭi chuch'e sasang* (Pyongyang, 1985).
23. Ibid., 382-383.
24. "The Kim Dynasty's North Korea," *The New York Times*, 9 July 1985.
25. For example, nothing of Kim Jong Il's was published in the journal from January to May 1987, or from January to June 1988.
26. "Chuch'e ch'ŏrhak ŭi rihae esŏ chegi toenŭn myŏt' kaji munje e taehayŏ," *Kŭlloja*, 1 April 1984, 2.
27. Ibid., 6.
28. "Chuch'e ŭi hyŏngmyŏnggwan ŭl t'ŭnt'ŭnhi seulde e tae hayŏ," *Kŭlloja*, December 1988, 3-16.
29. Kim Jong Il's writings on the arts were backdated too. A paper on moviemaking published in *Kŭlloja* in 1984 was dated to 1970. In contrast, an article under his name on improving labor administration, dated to 27 November

1989, came out in a matter of days. "Rodong haengjŏng saŏp ŭl tŏuk kaesŏn kanghwa halde e taehayŏ," *Kŭlloja*, December 1989, 3-25.
30. David E. Sanger, "Journey to Isolation," *New York Times*, 15 November 1992.
31. Except where otherwise indicated, this account is based on my own interview with Kim Young-hwan in Seoul on November 7, 2013.
32. Pak Wŏn-sik, "Kim Yŏng-hwan ŭn nugu in'ga," Commentary.co.kr, 6 December 2012.
33. In an article entitled "Key is Self-Reliance," Sam Jameson, a correspondent for the *Los Angeles Times*, reported on July 20, 1976 on South Korea's latest "purification" drive. Korea's culture, Park Chung Hee had recently said, was not to be "polluted" by foreign influence. "I don't think there will be any role for foreign influence in our culture in the future," Culture Minister Kim Seong Jin is quoted as saying. I thank Jacco Zwetsloot for sending me this article.
34. They were a remarkably sequacious lot for all their rebellious rhetoric. Before the various protest groups coalesced, each university department's students would monolithically support the one chosen by their department's student president. The French majors would be for Group X, the German majors for Group Y, and so on.
35. Its main though smaller rival remained the PD or People's Democracy movement, which adhered more closely to Marxism-Leninism.
36. Hong Chin-p'yo, in conversation with Ryu Kŭn-il in *Chisŏng kwa pan chisŏng* (Seoul, 2005), 39.
37. "Sahoejuŭi sasangjŏk kich'o e kwanhan myŏt' kaji munje e taehayŏ," *Kim Chŏng-il sŏnjip* 10 (Pyongyang, 1997), 109.
38. Interview with the author, Seoul, 7 November 2013.
39. "Kim Il-sŏng tubŏn mannatchiman chuch'e sasang morŭdŏra," *Munhwa Ilbo*, 3 August 2012.
40. Yi Hyŏn-o, "Myohyang san esŏ Kim Il-sŏng 5 sigan mannassŭmnida," Konas.net.
41. Ibid.

42. The defector: Kim Yŏng-sŏng. Pak Hong, *Redŭ bairŏsŭ*, 127.
43. Ibid.
44. Ibid., 128.
45. Although it had been used occasionally in earlier decades, when the greater exoteric context gave it less of a nationalist ring, it was vigorously sloganized in the winter of 1990-1991. See for example Ch'oe Yŏng-nim, "Uri sik ŭi tokt'ŭk han sahoejuŭi rŭl pit'naeyŏ naganŭn tang," *Kŭlloja*, February 1991, 17-22.
46. "Sahoejuŭi kŏnsŏl ŭi ryŏksajŏk kyohun kwa uri tang ŭi ch'ongnosŏn," in *Kim Chŏng-il sŏnjip* 12 (Pyongyang, 1997), 279.
47. Dae-Kyu Yoon, "The Constitution of North Korea," Vol. 27 (2003), 1298.
48. Young Soo Park, "Policies and Ideologies of the Kim Jong-un Regime," 6.
49. Hwang, *Ŏdum ŭi p'yŏn i toen haetbyŏt'*, 41.
50. The same scholars who project Juche's emergence back to 1955 or earlier tend to posit the advent of Military-First Politics as late as possible, the better to present it as a reaction to the Clinton administration's alleged violations of the Agreed Framework, or even to George W. Bush's "axis of evil" speech of 2002. See for example O Il-hwan, "Pukhan ŭi sŏn'gun chŏngch'i ŭi hyŏnhwang kwa chaengjŏm punsŏk," *At'ae chaengjŏm kwa yŏn'gu*, Spring 2006, 95-118.
51. In Korean: *chuch'e hyŏngmyŏng wiŏp* and *chuch'e hyŏlt'ong* respectively. See "Chuch'e ŭi p'ilbong ŭro uri tang ŭl ongwi haja," *Ch'ŏllima*, December 1993, 56; "Chuch'e ŭi hyŏlt'ong ŭl pit'naerisiryŏgo," *Ch'ŏllima*, May 1992, 38; "Chuch'e ŭi hyŏlt'ong ŭl pit'naerinŭn uri tang," *Ch'ŏllima*, November 1992, 16.
52. *Hoegorok*, 310.
53. Ibid.
54. Together with his aide he established a trading company in Beijing. He seems to want us to think that he made over half a million dollars by exporting a more appealing line of Juche texts. *Hoegorok*, 320.
55. http://www.minjokcorea.co.kr/sub_read.html?uid=9996
56. At the time of the nuclear crisis he must have been writing *North Korea: Ideology, Politics, Economy*, which came out in 1995.

57. *The Politics of Unconventional Wisdom*, 92.
58. http://hanpark.myweb.uga.edu/biosketch.html
59. Quoted (without critical comment) by Leon Sigal in *Disarming Strangers*, 149.
60. Ibid., 148. Stephen Linton was another who believed that the great oppressor of Korean Christianity felt a special connection to Christian foreigners. (*Credo quia absurdum*?) See "Life After Death in North Korea," in *Korea Briefing: Towards Reunification*, edited by Donald McCann, 89.
61. See for example Oberdorfer, *The Two Koreas*, 305.
62. Ibid., 354. As for export propaganda, Oberdorfer gives a wide-eyed account of how Kim Il Sung and Kang Sok Ju enacted a little dog-and-pony show for Jimmy Carter's benefit. This was, the author tells us, "one of the few times when outsiders witnessed policy actually being made in North Korea" (ibid., 328). American innocence: It would be endearing if not for its knack of making wars more likely in the long run.
63. *Pukhan ŭi chinsil kwa hŏwi* (Seoul, 1998), 65. Despite these warnings, American scholars continued citing KCNA reports as evidence of pluralism under Kim Jong Il's rule; McEachern's *Inside the Red Box* (New York, 2011), for example, draws heavily from such material.

9

THE MYTH IN DECLINE: 1994-2011

On July 8, 1994, only weeks after Jimmy Carter's departure, Kim Il Sung died at his mountain resort. A long mourning period ensued, which reduced the harvest and hastened the country's decline into famine. Newspaper pictorials of the Great Leader's life-work naturally focused more on his military exploits and "on-the-spot guidance" visits than on his theoretical attainments, though there was talk of the grief expressed by Juche devotees around the world.

When Kim Jong Il finally emerged from mourning, it was in order to continue spurring on the militarization of society. Most of his time in the public eye was spent inspecting army bases.[1] Hwang Jang Yop's main function in these years, apart from earning hard currency, was to divert foreign attention away from the increasingly martial mood. In February 1996 the DPRK embassy in Moscow hosted a so-called Juche conference, an event that would have been unthinkable in Soviet times. Hwang says he took some teenage girls with him to display his country's "educational and cultural level." At least he himself talked on Juche proper, describing it as a development of Marxism-Leninism.[2]

This point had been made often during the Cold War, but was now interpreted in Pyongyang as a "serious doctrinal error."[3] Upon returning home, Hwang was rebuked by the Dear Leader, who ordered him to ghost-write a corrective essay so that he, Kim, would appear to be setting the record straight. It appeared on July 26, 1996.[4] Certain people, the essay conceded in extenuation, might have overstated *chuch'e sasang*'s debt to Marxism for the purpose of overseas propaganda, but current events made proper illumination of its originality more necessary than ever. While social scientists still needed to know Marxism-Leninism in addition to the Great Leader's thought, it was wrong to claim that the latter's essence lay in its development of the former. It was a fundamentally original philosophy, the first to explain man's basic nature and place in the world. Social scientists were to propagandize it accordingly.[5]

Hwang's detractors had probably riled the dictator up for their own careerist reasons, but they had a point: It was folly to pander to a few USSR-nostalgists in Moscow when a far more important constituency beyond the DMZ wanted to hear how Korean the doctrine was. Since Hwang had committed no error of actual ideological importance — it was only Juche, after all — he was soon back on the international circuit. In February 1997 he presided over another conference, this time in Tokyo. Michael Lev of *The Chicago Tribune* reported that discussions were quick to veer off the topic of Juche, which he described as "an intense blend of Communist-style propaganda and psychological jargon appropriate to self-help books." The speakers showed more interest in calling on Japan to recognize the DPRK and pay war reparations.[6]

Afterwards Hwang flew to Beijing, where he usually changed planes on his way home. This time, for reasons we need not speculate about, he sought asylum at the ROK embassy instead.[7] Several weeks later he

THE MYTH IN DECLINE: 1994-2011

arrived in Seoul via the Philippines. The welcome accorded him by local conservatives was matched only by the fury of the left.[8] Hwang threw himself into public criticism of the regime in Pyongyang while continuing to attribute world-improving potential to "Subject Philosophy" (*chuch'e ch'ŏrhak*), which he claimed to have conceived in good faith.[9]

Shortly after Hwang's defection, the KCNA quoted the Dear Leader as having invoked a line from an old propaganda song: "Cowards, leave if you want to. We will defend the red flag of revolution to the end."[10] This statement encouraged the rise in the late 1990s of the slogan "Red Banner Thought" (*pulgŭn ki sasang*), which was vaguely defined as "traditional revolutionary thought." I take issue with the assertion of some Pyongyang watchers that it was a distinct ideology subsidiary to Juche.[11] A political ideology is a worldview; one cannot hold two at the same time. The slogans of "our style of socialism," "Red Banner Thought" and "Subject Thought" were thus bandied about in much the same vague sense. In contrast to foreigners, whose attention was diverted to Juche texts, the local masses were to perceive the ruling ideology as having been embodied in the entirety of both leaders' lives. In case of internal contradiction, precedence was to be given to whatever the current leader was saying and doing at the moment.

Nevertheless, the regime's claim to be discharging Kim Il Sung's  legacy required the publication of what were purported to be his last writings. Predictably enough, the media highlighted the parts which urged unconditional obedience to his son. The rest, apart from his serially published "memoirs," went virtually unnoticed; even the *Selected Works* were already too long and costly to be used in group study, the only kind the regime felt safe in encouraging. As for the *Collected Works*, they were unfit to any propaganda purpose except to lead awed schoolchildren past. Even in a society with a better electricity supply and more leisure time, a 20- or 30-volume canon would have defeated its own purpose, to say

— 187 —

nothing of the 100 volumes which the Great Leader's editors were on their way to filling. New instalments of Kim Jong Il's *Selected Works* were being added too, albeit in an odd sequence that reflected both the time needed to cook up the "earlier" volumes, and the rather low priority the regime attached to the project.

The absence of portable compendia has long resulted in faintly ridiculous posters of men clutching a volume from one of the two leaders' works. Are we to believe they have the full set at home? Or that they made off with a topically relevant volume from the factory study-room? Visible on the concave frieze of the Workers' Party monument in Pyongyang is the alternative practice: putting the title of some speech or another on the cover while giving the spine a wildly disproportionate width.

Outsiders nonetheless take the largeness of the two dead Kims' oeuvres as evidence of the canonicity of their every recorded word. Foreign governments think it clever to remind the current leader of his grandfather's call for denuclearization. There have been miscalculations in the business sphere as well. In his memoirs the former South Korean president Lee Myung Bak writes that in the 1990s, a seasoned traveler to Pyongyang assured him the Unification Church would get the contract to manage the Kŭmgangsan tourist resort. Had not the Great Leader issued a written promise to that effect just before his death? Lee predicted the deal would go to Hyundai, which was offering better terms. The frequent Air

Koryo flyer scoffed at this ignorance of North Korean culture. Lee turned out to be right.[12]

The hollowing out of the doctrine's name reached a new stage in September 1997 with the advent of a so-called *chuch'e* calendar. Year One was not 1972, when the Great Leader made his historic declaration to foreign journalists. Nor was it 1955, the year of his first mention of "the subject." Nor was it 1930, when he had purportedly declared his "subjective" line to fellow revolutionaries in Manchuria. No, the Subject Era was said to have begun in 1912, the year of his *birth*.

Meanwhile the pro-North movement had passed its peak in Seoul. Even on the left *chuch'e sasang* was coming under fire as a mere tool with which to legitimize the succession.[13] Pyongyang's attempts to reconcile the "man is master of all things" line with the personality cult by invoking "leader theory" did more harm than good; South Koreans had had their fill of that sort of thing under Park Chung Hee. Even the movement's core was having doubts. Yi Myŏng-jun, a former member, relates the problems he had with Kim Jong Il's *On Subject Thought* (1982):

> It starts right off with the declaration that "Man is the master of all things and decides all things." And it asserts that [Subject Thought] overcame the opposition of mind versus material in favor of a human-centered worldview of man versus exterior world. But no logical explanation is given as to why Marxism had to give way to Subject Thought. At most there is the assertion that "after Marx the world-historical state of affairs changed, and Subject Thought was created in accordance with the practical demands of the Korean revolution under those historical conditions." From then on it keeps repeating similar things. One can say that it's closer to scripture than to philosophy.[14]

Yi recalls that older students were at a loss to explain things; after a while he "just nodded and let things pass." The vague triteness that had initially helped unite students under the doctrine's banner was quick to pall. Yi:

> [T]here is nothing special in Subject Thought. It's just nice and obvious things told in formal language. "Man is a social being with autonomy, creativity and consciousness" is quite a good thing to say, but is it so original as to have the name Subject Thought applied to it? And the assertion that Kim Il Sung must have been one very great personage to have conceived it gives rise to one doubt after another.[15]

In the West, however, Juche was being taken ever more seriously as a shaper of North Korean life. The fallacy made its way into most analyses of the famine. In part this reflected academia's effort to maintain its authority over North Korea commentary after decades of overestimating the country's economic health.[16] Plenty of African dictators had starved their people in comparable fashion, but this famine, in contrast, was explained as the consequence of an *excess* of principle, a too radical commitment to self-sufficiency.[17] Self-sufficiency, in a country with so little arable land! Again the leadership benefited from foreigners' underestimation of its savvy; it is better to be thought impractical than heartless. There was plenty of talk in the Western media (which must have elicited chuckles in Moscow and Beijing) about how hard it was for these high-souled self-providers to have to ask for help. Nevertheless, the communist camp's demise was cited as an equally important cause of the famine, often in the same breath: "The economy of isolationist North Korea, based on a bizarre self-reliant socialism known as *juche*, lost what shaky props it still had when the Soviet bloc disintegrated."[18]

Thus were the world's purse-strings loosened at a time when Kim Jong Il was spending hundreds of millions of dollars on the construction (with imported materials) of new monuments and palaces.[19] The aid poured in even after it became clear that the regime was reducing its own spending on food accordingly.[20] One American at a well-endowed foundation recommended that North Korea and the West join as "unlikely partners in the quest for *juche*," trying "to reinterpret [it] so that it can be the basis for authentic self-reliant, but also participatory and liberating, human development."[21] The doctrine thus maintained its aura of intellectual respectability even while being wrongly blamed for the famine.

Helpful though the Juche myth continued to be overseas, the domestic public could be expected to overlook only so wide a gap between the two propaganda tracks. Besides, world-defying slogans sound hollow unless spoken in the world's hearing. North Korean militarism went fully exoteric in October 1997, when the news agency reported the Dear Leader's declaration that "however big a burden the state of the economy becomes, we must put the military first, then the working class."[22] The relevant compound: *sŏn'gun-huro*, or "first-military-then-labor." That literal translation bears lingering over. No takeover by the military had occurred or was implied. It was ostensibly the WP, though in reality the regime far above it, which was putting the military's needs first. The message was strengthened on April 25, 1998, Armed Forces Day, when an editorial looked back on Kim Il Sung's "Military-First Revolutionary Thought."[23]

This new construct was clearly to be seen as separate from, yet roughly equal in stature to, Subject Thought. Both were to be regarded as constituents of one ideology: Kim Il Sung's thought. The regime wanted it believed that he had himself practiced Military-First leadership — distinct, in some nebulous way, from *chuch'e* leadership — in the 1930s. Since the dead man's legend remained the regime's main source of pride, the only way to legitimize the new dispensation was to pretend it was not new at all. The odd result, however, was that Military-First Thought now rivaled Subject Thought even in terms of purported age, thus depriving the latter of much of the credit it had enjoyed since the 1960s for the shining victories over Japan and America.

True to form, the regime equivocated by claiming that Military First Thought "has its roots in Subject Thought."²⁴ There is no refuting this, of course. What line *cannot* be said to derive from the idea that a country's policies must suit its conditions? But there is no significant connection between the universal-humanist  cant of *chuch'e sasang* and the bellicose, strenuously Korea-specific content of Military-First Thought.

The Juche myth played no important role in the superficial improvement of Seoul-Pyongyang relations that began in the late 1990s. Kim Dae Jung's ascension to the presidency was followed by the arrest of several leading members of South Korea's Juche movement. By that time it was already in steep decline anyway. From then on neither government on the peninsula had an interest in reminding middle-class South Koreans of a doctrine they associated with a treasonous underground. Although the Sunshine Policy engendered a boom in apologetic research of the North's system, its ideology included, the term *chuch'e sasang* still carries a more negative ring in the ROK than the word Juche does in the West.²⁵

The North-South summit of June 2000 afforded a classic demonstration of multi-track propaganda. "It's you they are cheering," Kim Jong Il said to Kim Dae Jung as they drove down the crowd-lined streets of Pyongyang. Meanwhile the official news media treated the summit as a showcase for the host's wonderfulness; the South Korean's presence was acknowledged in civil terms but without biographical information. The inner track, for its part, mocked the visitor as a limping lackey of the Yankees who had come to negotiate in bad faith.²⁶ To Kim Dae Jung and his many American admirers, however, the chummy discussion at the summit was the only discourse that really mattered.[27]

Hardly had the summit ended than even the outer track reverted to Military-First mode. The truculent TV news, interspersed with music-videos of soldiers hurtling through smoky forests, conveyed the impression of a nation itching for war. The only graphic symbol more common than the bayonet was the Supreme Commander's standard, a five-pointed star inside another one, against a red background. In  wall posters it flew not only above the Juche Tower, but above the flags of the party and state as well.

There is no reason to believe all this did not go down well with the public. Military-First Thought was a far more appealing construct than Subject Thought, the prestige of which, such as it was, had derived from fraudulent tales of its international renown. The commencement of Six Party Talks in 2003 came as a great fillip to the country's pride. As nice as it had been to hear of Juche study groups in Brazzaville and Quito, it was more gratifying to know that Military-First Thought had brought the Yankees crawling back to the negotiating table.

The amount of lip service paid to *chuch'e sasang* declined steadily throughout the 2000s. The entry for it in the nineteenth volume of the encyclopedia published in 2001 ran to a little over one full page, the tautologous text yielding only a few lines of paraphrasable sense. (Twice as much space was given to the tower bearing its name.)[28] Kim Il Sung's teenage conception of the doctrine earned only a few paragraphs in schoolbooks devoted to revolutionary history.[29] According to migrant testimony, the regime became downright averse to mentioning *chuch'e sasang* in internal communication; in 2002, local WP organizations were ordered to speak always of "Military-First Politics" instead.[30] I assume that "Military-First Thought" was all right too, but evidently the word "politics" was (contrary to its connotations in English) meant to suggest something more straightforward and forceful. Where Subject Thought had been likened to a torch, Military-First Politics was a *pogŏm* or "precious sword."³¹ The official media explained the term in April 2003 as a commitment to the race or *minjok* above all else.

> The vitality and legitimacy of a political method lies in its firm guarantee of the autonomy of country [*nara*] and race [*minjok*]. The race is above class and social stratum, the homeland above ideology [*sasang*] and doctrine [*rinyŏm*].³²

A former North Korean diplomat stated that reference to *chuch'e sasang* had been "completely replaced" in (Foreign Ministry) communication by 2007.³³

In April 2009, after responding to the new Obama administration's peace overtures with a spate of missile launches, North Korea issued a new version of its constitution. The DPRK was now said to be "guided in its activity by Subject Thought *and Military-First Thought*, a human-centered worldview and revolutionary ideology for achieving the people's independence." (My italics indicate the new part.) I have translated *sasang* in its first two appearances as "Thought," and in its third as "ideology," because Subject Thought and Military-First Thought are clearly to be understood as parts of one unnamed whole. (This in contrast to some observers' notions of two ideologies ruling in tandem.)³⁴ Now as always since 1967, the regime prides itself on a "monolithic ideological system."

The revision of the constitution appears to have been conceived as export propaganda, with the goal of impressing on the world the permanence of the regime's commitment to nuclearization. To be sure, Kim Jong Il had benefited greatly from many Americans' assumption that he was spending billions on nukes in order to trade them in for an aid deal of even bigger proportions. Some, taking America-centricity to a new height, suggested he would settle for a peace treaty and a US embassy. The problem was that all this wishful thinking, combined with the habituating effect of North Korean saber-rattling, made the enemy take the threat too lightly even for the regime's own purposes. The Obama administration joined cartoonists in likening the DPRK's behavior to a child's tantrums.[35] The worst the Americans could imagine was that Kim Jong Il might someday sell nuclear material to people capable of using it.

With every year, therefore, it became harder for Pyongyang to intimidate Washington and Seoul into paying the appeasement-motivated tributes — economic and symbolic, e.g. summit meetings — that it had come to rely on. (Eberstadt talks of revenue derived from "exporting strategic insecurity.")[36] By announcing that Military-First Thought was no mere campaign, but an integral part of the DPRK's ideological makeup, Kim Jong Il meant to make the enemy's refusal to negotiate on his terms look unconscionably reckless. The omission from the constitution of all mention of communism, a word which had taken on a reassuring ring since the East Bloc's peaceful demise, served the same end.

By this time observers should have realized that if North Korea had ever been a Stalinist state, it was one no longer, but they remained reluctant to see beyond the hammer and sickle on the WP standard. More was at work here than intellectual inertia. The main geopolitical players all had a strong interest in sticking to the communist model of the DPRK. This gave their intelligence-providers, in-house and external, an interest in it too.[37] If Beijing was to keep justifying to its people the aid it sent Pyongyang; if Seoul and Washington were to keep persuading US taxpayers to fund the South's defense; if Western collaborators with the Kim dictatorship were to pass themselves off as forces for trust-building and reform — if these and many other games were to go on, the DPRK had to be seen as red, no matter how little effort it put into the masquerade itself. Here too, the Juche myth had a significant role to play. The prevailing model of the country would have had a harder time had it not been wrapped in the thick fog of a doctrine which somehow managed to be communist even while "turning Marx on his head."[38]

For decades, selected Westerners had been invited to Pyongyang for status-enhancing tours and meetings with officials. The regime had allowed others in for business or humanitarian purposes, knowing they too would end up pleading for an accomodationist approach to the North, if only to rationalize their own activity. As John Everard has written, "The DPRK is expert at using such people, and especially at flattering them into believing that they are contributing to a resolution of tensions."[39] In this way it had helped school the people to whom governments and media outlets now turned for information. Entrepreneurs, charitocrats, aid workers, organizers of tours and exchanges, former diplomats — by 2010 they were setting the tone even of academic discussion of the DPRK. They sat on conference panels, and on the editorial boards of journals; they wrote op-ed pieces for the *Washington Post* and *New York Times*. All had a vested interest in exaggerating the significance of things said to them personally, so that the actual hierarchy of ideological sincerity tended to be misrepresented as its inverse: export propaganda on top, then the outer track, and the inner track (when it was acknowledged at all) on the bottom.[40] These people genuinely believed that by dint of their patience, charm and cultural sensitivity, they had gained access to a strategic big picture the regime withheld from its own citizens. Almost to a man, they preached the fine-line message Kim Jong Il wanted preached: The DPRK was now too dangerous not to be talked to on its own terms, yet not so dangerous as to merit anyone's hostility. A natural concomitant was the marginalization of more critical voices.

The Juche myth was not central to all this, but without its disinhibiting influence a few might have thought twice about posing as experts at all. Perhaps the easiest way to explain this point is by way of a digression. Sometimes I feel an urge to play the China hand, having worked in that country for a German car company in the 1990s. Heaven knows I visited enough remote areas, and dined with enough officials; the same background, *mutatis mutandis*, would make one a sought-after panelist at North Korea conferences. What daunts me is the awareness of how much political-cultural context lies beyond the reach of my survival Mandarin. If only all that stuff could be reduced to one slogan, as in: "The Chinese are committed to *zili gengsheng*, which is usually translated as self-reliance,

THE MYTH IN DECLINE: 1994-2011

but means a lot more. Car imports are therefore highly taxed . . ." Once I got my bearings, I could venture into other issues. China's arms build-up? Military self-reliance. And so on. I am not joking as broadly as all that. This is the level on which North Korean ideology is all too often discussed.

A concise example, from a book published in 2007:

> The North Korean population might decide that the nationalist Korean project that is the essential foundation of the "Juche" philosophy of self-reliance could easily be satisfied by integration with South Korea. War is not therefore an option for the DPRK government.[41]

I'm not sure why the first sentence does not lead to the opposite conclusion, but let that go. Does any other branch of Asian studies make the discussion of crucial ideological matters this easy for itself? One may jump on and off the topic of Juche in a sentence or two, because it is considered beyond analysis anyway. The less reading of relevant primary materials the scholar has done (or is capable of doing), the breezier the pronouncements tend to be.[42] Of course, a double standard is in force here too; if that first sentence *had* led to the opposite conclusion, the author's claim to speak with authority would promptly have been called into question.

The need for fairness dictates I quote from a longer attempt at discussing Juche. This is from a former US official's manual on how to negotiate with Pyongyang.

> The North Korean philosophy of self-reliance (Juche) is inseparable from North Korean culture and behavior. This guiding framework of thought provides the equivalent of an entire worldview from which North Koreans operate. . . . [T]hose who negotiate with North Korea should strive to understand it. . . . Juche is an ideology centered on man as the master of his universe. . . . The imperative of the nation is to attain independence and preserve national sovereignty. . . . Under the auspices of Juche, North Korea will never allow itself to appear subservient to a foreign power.[43]

The uncorroborated assertion of Juche's importance is typical. If a personality cult says the Leader's teachings provide the "guiding framework" for his people, that's good enough for most Pyongyang watchers. Also typical is the effort to make Juche's innocuous content sound both exotic and extreme.[44] When I ask what country does *not* want to avoid domination, I tend to get this sort of response: "Yes, but the North Koreans' idea of sovereignty is so radical; look how they lash out when they feel threatened." But this means using the regime's behavior to give meaning to Juche, instead of the other way around. The general effect of the self-confusion is a more indulgent view. One starts to see the North's nuclear and ballistic events as *ad hoc* manifestations of a Juche-induced touchiness, in contrast to how the regime presents them to its own citizens, i.e., as carefully planned, linear stations on the road to "final victory."

Few Westerners had expected the North Korean system to survive the famine. To see the country bear down on 2010 with a stable and even growing population was even more surprising. There was little mystery here if one understood that the leadership was giving the people what they expected from it, i.e., the impression that their state was feared and respected around the world, and was making steady progress toward full national liberation. Though not unimportant, the economy had and still has no direct bearing on the regime's legitimacy or popularity. The proclamation of Military-First Thought had de-ideologized the economic sphere, turning even nominally illegal transactions into *adiaphora*. Growing awareness of the ROK's prosperity posed a challenge all right, but the regime argued that its own policies deserved credit for it, having deterred the Yankees from another devastating war. It was therefore possible for propaganda to continue talking of prosperity — and a very modestly-imagined prosperity at that — as something to be realized in the future.

But with nothing but the Cold War to extrapolate from, the orthodox Pyongyang watcher was left scratching his head. How could a state committed to self-reliant communism maintain mass support in the face of such a huge rich-poor gap, and so heavy a dependence on foreign aid? The standard softline explanation, to which I have already referred, was that the DPRK had done uniquely well in adapting communism to indigenous traditions. Much was made of how it had allegedly tapped into Confucianism in particular, the assumption being that this had gone down so well with the masses as to hold the state together even in hard times.[45] But I have talked about that already too. Suffice to say here that anyone who considers the infantilizing, militarist, emotionalist, race-obsessed DPRK to be Korean-Confucian in essential spirit has failed to feel his way into at least one of those two cultures.

The more conservative observers, for their part, concluded that signs of marketization could only be superficial and misleading, like light from a dead star; the regime *must* have already begun turning the clock back. Depending on which half of the communist-Juche model they took more seriously, they spoke of a "re-Stalinizing" process or of "neojuche revivalism."[46] These assertions were accepted even by many softliners, who, proceeding from their old fantasy of turf-wars on the Taedong, assumed that the hawks or ideologues had taken advantage of Kim Jong Il's infirmity to put the pragmatists on the defensive. All the more reason for America to strengthen the good guys with development assistance.[47] No one bothered to square the talk of ideologues with *chuch'e sasang*, which, true to its public-diplomatic function, had always stressed the need for economic and other policies to fit their time and place.[48]

The most hardline interpretation of events, which one often heard from human-rights NGOs and right-wing journalists, was that the regime survived through sheer repressiveness. As if Kim Jong Il could have done a more effective job of surveillance and coercion than Erich Honecker had![49] He lacked the resources even to seal off the northern border, let alone to spy on a population much larger than East Germany's. To this day the regime knows far less about the average North Korean than the US government knows about its obligingly self-surveilling citizens. Undercover footage exists of sidewalk vendors in Pyongyang talking back to police, something I for one would never try in Washington, DC.[50] This is not to deny the regime's brutality, only to assert that the degree and kind of it do not yet reflect great worry about the mainstream's loyalty to the state.

Meanwhile Kim Jong Il's worsening health had forced him to begin preparing the succession in earnest.[51] Knowing how problematic his son's past was, he sought to put the new personality cult on a firm footing at home before moving it into the outer track. In 2008 the "young Four-Star General" began to be praised at farms and factories. Citizens in some towns heard of his technological research abroad, while others heard stories of shock-brigade exploits on the construction front. Although unable to ignore the growing hyperbole completely, the outer track went no further than references — decoded, no doubt, in workplace study sessions — to Mount Paektu bloodlines and the like. Foreign visitors who had always prided themselves on their rapport with the locals learned no more about the putative successor than they had learned about his flamboyant mother's appearances with Kim Jong Il. We see once again that the term esoteric propaganda is no oxymoron; the country can keep important news to itself for months on end.[52]

Soon enough, however, border-crossers began selling the truth to South Korean journalists in China, who were quick to tell the world. In summer 2009, a Taiwanese tourist photographed a wall-poster that praised Kim Jong Un by name. At a WP conference on September 28, 2010 the young man finally made his debut before the cameras. The day before, the party had announced his formal promotion to the military rank he had enjoyed in propaganda for years. He then began appearing with his father in photographs and broadcasts, at first without captions or voice-overs drawing special attention to him. Although his face and name had gone outer-track, his cult was still an inner-track affair. That it was in full swing was clear from the excitement of people filmed in his presence.

The pending succession gave Pyongyang watchers something relatively reassuring to which they could chalk up the torpedoing of a ROK naval vessel in March 2010, which resulted in the deaths of 46 sailors.[53] It was speculated, with no evidence, that Kim Jong Il needed to placate his generals so that they would sign off on the power transfer. The implication: Everything would quiet down once the "Swiss-educated" young man was ensconced on the throne, whereupon he would break with his father's style of rule and focus on the economy.

THE MYTH IN DECLINE: 1994-2011

But the Juche myth featured in commentary too. The upshot of the usual op-ed piece, in my own words: "The sinking of the *Cheonan* underscores the folly of our refusal to accord the DPRK the respect it craves. The country is far too dangerous to keep ignoring, but only because the combination of high-tech weaponry and ideologically-induced irascibility is such a volatile mix, not because the regime means anyone any harm." One article, bearing the *Onion*-worthy title "Retaliate with Diplomacy," ended with the sentence: "The last thing we want is a country with nothing to lose and plenty of weapons to go out in a blaze of *juche*."[54]

A blaze of sorts came a half-year later, on November 23, 2010, when the DPRK shelled the South Korean island of Yeonpyeong, killing four people. The ruins were still smoldering when Jimmy Carter weighed in.

> No one can completely understand the motivations of the North Koreans, but it is entirely possible that . . . Pyongyang's shelling of a South Korean island on Tuesday [was] designed to remind the world that they deserve respect in negotiations. . . . We know that the state religion of this secretive society is "juche," which means self-reliance and avoidance of domination by others.[55]

Note how the exotic word can be stretched to do whatever service the writer requires. The subtext here: Being both heightened and dignified by quasi-religious dogma, the North Koreans' desire for respect should be satisfied no matter how barbarously they express it. The same reasoning is exercised in the West's appeasement of Islam: Because the more rational side in any conflict has the greater leeway, it must always be the one to yield.

The Obama administration was not unaffected by the general tenor of commentary. When South Korea's president Lee Myung Bak announced that ROK forces would promptly rehearse responses to a future attack, the US ambassador and the commander of US troops in the ROK warned that doing so would raise the likelihood of more trouble. Worse, they did so on the front page of local newspapers, thereby ruining the impression of allied resolve Lee had sought to convey with his decision — which, once announced, he had to carry out anyway.[56] Had the Americans properly grasped the DPRK as a far-right state, they would have agreed with him that *not* making a speedy show of resolve was the more dangerous course of action. (In the event, the North Koreans did nothing.) The DPRK's constitutional revision of spring 2009 had not stopped Washington from regarding the country's "provocations" as counter-productive pleas for respect and security.

THE MYTH IN DECLINE: 1994-2011

1. B.C. Koh, "The North Korean Political System Under Kim Jong Il," 36.
2. *Hoegorok*, 332. Another version of events, which may have come from Hwang too, is that he took the occasion to express pacifist views as well as support for Chinese-style market reforms. (Oberdorfer, *The Two Koreas*, 314-315.) But had he offended his boss with such remarks, the "corrective" article later published would have alluded to them in some way.
3. Andrew Pollack, "To Outsiders Who Have Met Him, the Thinking Man's Communist Ideologist," *New York Times*, 19 March 1997.
4. *Hoegorok*, 338. Oberdorfer implies that Hwang did not pen this article and was perhaps frightened to see it in print. (*The Two Koreas*, 315.) This may well have been one of Hwang's versions of events, but I find the one in his memoirs more credible, especially considering that it makes him less of a victim. In any case, this had long since ceased to be a country where a purge had to be preceded by a press campaign. Had Hwang fallen out of favor, he would not have been allowed to keep flying abroad.
5. "Chuch'e ch'ŏrhak ŭn tokch'angjŏgin hyŏngmyŏng ch'ŏrhagida," *Kim Chŏng-il sŏnjip* 14 (Pyongyang, 2000), 189-202.
6. Michael Lev, "N. Koreans Export Idea That's Doing Them In," *Chicago Tribune*, 10 February 1997.
7. The South Korean media have reported that Hwang and Kim Jong Il's uncle Chang Sŏng-t'aek plotted to assassinate the dictator in 1996, and that Hwang fled upon suspecting they had been found out. (Chang Se-jeong, Ser Myo-ja, "Jang plotted 1996 coup with Hwang Jang-yop," *Joongang Daily*, 16 December 2013.) Even if we assume that Kim learned of the plot without finding out about his uncle's involvement, which is improbable enough, we must still believe that the ROK intelligence service kept this secret from Pyongyang even through the Kim Dae Jung and Roh Moo Hyun administrations. I am skeptical.
8. Kim Hak-joon, op.cit., 458.
9. This won him the ridicule of South Korean conservatives, who regarded the "man is the master of all things" line as a statement of the obvious. Pak Hong, *Redŭ bairŏsŭ*, 92.

10. Andrew Pollack, "North Korea's Leader Says 'Cowards' Are Welcome to Leave," *New York Times*, 19 February 1997. This was a line Kim Il Sung had quoted in the early 1960s when siding with Mao against Khrushchev. See "Tang chojik saŏp kwa sasang saŏp ŭl kaesŏn kanghwa hanŭnde taehayŏ," in *Kim Il-sŏng chŏjak sŏnjip* 3 (Pyongyang, 1968), 326.
11. See for example, B.C.Koh, "The North Korean Political System under Kim Jong Il," 50-51.
12. Yi Myŏng-bak (Lee Myung Bak), *Taet'ongnyŏng ŭi sigan* (Seoul, 2015), 313-314.
13. Kim Hakjoon, *The Domestic Politics of Korean Unification*, 336-342, 354-355.
14. Yi Myŏng-jun, *Kŭdŭl ŭn ŏttŏk'e chusap'a ga toeŏttnŭn'ga* (Seoul, 2012), 204.
15. Ibid., 204-205. None of this prevented the North from continuing to tout Juche's popularity south of the DMZ. "Chuch'e ŭi pit'pal ŭl ttarŭnŭn namny'ŏk'," *Ch'ŏllima*, January 1993, 80-82.
16. "North Korea offers the best example in the postcolonial developing world of a . . . serious attempt to construct an independent, self-contained economy. As a result, it is the most autarkic industrial economy in the world. Unlike Albania in the socialist world and Burma in the 'free world' . . . North Korea never idled but always raced. This was withdrawal with development, withdrawal for development." Cumings, *Korea's Place in the Sun* (1997), 419-420. In fact it was withdrawal with massive foreign aid, followed by a quick slide into famine when that aid was reduced, as should have been clear even to the most apologetic observer by 1996 at the latest. It says a lot about the field that it considers the greater blunder in the Pyongyang-watching of the time to have been the prediction of regime collapse made by out-group scholars, journalists and politicians.
17. Andrew S. Natsios, *The Great North Korean Famine* (Washington, DC, 2001), 6.
18. Barbara Crossette, "Korean Famine Toll: More than Two Million," *New York Times*, 20 August 1999.
19. B.C. Koh, "The North Korean Political System under Kim Jong Il," 33.

20. Stephan Haggard and Marcus Noland, *Famine in North Korea* (New York, 2007), 42-44. The degree of the DPRK's dependence on aid remained twice that of sub-Saharan Africa. Nicholas Eberstadt, "Western Aid," 133.
21. Edward P. Reed, "Unlikely Partners in the Quest for Juche," Nautilus.org, 2004.
22. O Il-hwan, op. cit., 98.
23. There was also reference to Kim Jong Il's "military-centric thought." The relevant terms, respectively: *sŏn'gun hyŏngmyŏng sasang* and *kunsa chungsi sasang*. Here as in *chuch'e sasang* the second word is used in senses too broad to justify translating it as "idea" instead. To be sure, the KCNA translates *sŏn'gun sasang* (which soon became the standard term) as "military-first idea" in its English-language releases, but it has so little interest in generating clarity on meta-ideological issues that we should beware of following its translation practices. In one recent English-language article, for example, it referred to Kimilsungism-Kimjongilism as a) "the guiding idea" b) "ideas" and c) "the integrated Juche system of idea, theory and method." KCNA, "Kimilsungism-Kimjongilism, WP's Guiding Idea," 8 January 2013.
24. O Hyŏn-ch'ŏl, *Sŏn'gun kwa minjok ŭi unmyŏng* (Pyongyang, 2007), 40.
25. In South Korea's presidential election campaign in 2012, the left-wing presidential candidate Mun Jae-in issued the anodyne slogan "People first" only to find himself accused of preaching Juche. One conservative who made this aspersion in print was later fined for violating election laws. "Mun Chae-in 'saram i mŏnjŏda' sŭllogŏn e 'chuch'e sasang' pibang kwanggo Chi Man-wŏn pŏlgŭmhyŏng hwakchŏng," *Sŏul Sinmun*, 24 December 2013.
26. A fascinating example of that propaganda is Kim Nam-ho's novel *Mannam* [Encounter] (Pyongyang, 2001).
27. A typical account is Mike Chinoy's *Meltdown* (New York, 2009).
28. *Chosŏn taebaekkwa sajŏn* (Pyongyang, 2001), 19: 342-343. My translation can be found in Appendix 2 of this book.
29. *Widaehan suryŏng Kim Il-sŏng taewŏnsunim hyŏngmyŏng ryŏksa: chung 4* [The Revolutionary History of the Great Leader Marshal Kim Il Sung: Middle 4] (Pyongyang, 2003), 20-22.

30. Jiyeong Song, "The Right to Survival in the Democratic People's Republic of Korea," *European Journal of East Asian Studies*, March 2010, Vol. 9, Issue 1, 94.
31. "Sŏn'gun chŏngch'i nŭn p'ilsŭng ŭi pogŏm," KCNA, 30 April 2003. See also the title of the article cited in the footnote below.
32. "Rodong Sinmun p'yŏnjipkuk nonsŏl sŏn'gun chŏngch'i nŭn minjok ŭi chajusŏng ŭl wihan p'ilsŭng ŭi pogŏm," KCNA, 3 April 2003. I would have missed this article had Rüdiger Frank not referred to it in "The End of Socialism and a Wedding Gift for the Groom?" Nautilus.org, 11 December 2003.
33. Jiyeong Song, "The Right to Survival," 94.
34. See for example Park Young Soo, "Policies and Ideologies [sic] of the Kim Jong-un Regime in North Korea: Theoretical Implications," *Asian Studies Review*, Vol. 38 (2014), 9.
35. Tabassum Zakaria, "Clinton likens North Korea to unruly children," *Reuters*, 20 July 2009.
36. "Western aid," 142.
37. Bernard Brodie: "If there is one practically unvarying principle about the use within the government of outside experts as consultants, it is that they must be known to be friendly to the policy on which they are being consulted. They may be critical of details . . . but not of the fundamentals." *War and Politics*, 214.
38. The Juche myth's obfuscatory effect helps with the criminalization of pro-North expression and activity in the ROK. The court ruling issued on February 17, 2014 against the pro-Pyongyang legislator Yi Sŏk-ki and some of his comrades stressed North Korea's alleged commitment to a communizing unification (*chŏkhwa t'ongil*). The court took *chuch'e sasang* at face value as the North's guiding ideology while defining it in the terms that so angered Kim Jong Il in 1996, i.e., as "a variation of Marxism-Leninism." (See *Suwŏn chibang pŏbwŏn, che 12 hyŏngsabu*, 17 February 2014.) I suspect the South Korean state knows how much harder it would be to prosecute citizens for radical nationalist tendencies than for communist ones.
39. *Only Beautiful Please*, 140.

40. In fairness to the former US diplomats who grasp North Korean propaganda in this fashion, I concede that it is quite common for governments to assert the disingenuousness of their own propaganda in behind-the-scenes communication, and one can well argue, in regard to less intensely nationalist states, that such assertions are as often sincere as insincere. Taiwan, for example, told the Nixon administration not to take too seriously its formal public opposition to two-China representation at the UN, a line it claimed was for domestic consumption. (Monique Chu, "Taiwan and the United Nations," *Taipei Times*, 12 September 2001.) President Obama's so-called microphone gaffe of March 2012, in which he promised his Russian counterpart "more flexibility" after US elections, can be interpreted as an attempt to disavow his own public stance on Russia. I would be surprised, however, if Medvedev took it at face value. Even when the private disclaimer is not just a cynical effort to have things both ways, domestic propaganda puts the two-tongued government under some pressure to carry through on it. In any case, those Chinese and Eastern European diplomats who had far more extensive contact with the North Koreans than American diplomats did evidently agreed (as we have seen) that inner-track domestic propaganda was the better guide to regime intentions.
41. Hazel Smith, "Reconstituting Korean security dilemmas," *Reconstituting Korean Security* (Tokyo, 2007). 9.
42. The field suffers from its failure to enforce a friendly but principled distinction of the kind made between the Sinologist and the China hand. The growing influence of self-styled experts who cannot read Korean texts is worsening the tendency to cliquish mutual quotation – a journal recently got in trouble for this – and stifling the discussion of ideology in particular. Ian Robinson writes that "the understanding of their language is a precondition of seeing what sense the Athenians made themselves." *Holding the Centre* (Herefordshire, 2008), 8. Sometimes I feel tempted to put the sentence in the present tense, and "North Koreans" in the place of "Athenians." But close and critical reading even of translated texts can make up for a lot; Pfabigan understood Juche far better than Korean-speaking Pyongyang watchers have done.

43. Richard Saccone, *Negotiating with the North Koreans* (Seoul, 2003), 30-31.
44. "Juche has been the most extreme and uncompromising expression of national political and economic sovereignty in the world." Armstrong, *Tyranny of the Weak*, 53. This is almost as wrong if one applies the name Juche to the *de facto* ideology, which the regime felt compelled to restrict to inner-track propaganda for almost half a century, even distancing itself from it when called to account by patron states. A regime truly uncompromising in its expression of sovereignty (or "frank," "unrestrained," "freewheeling," etc, to recall other scholars' statements) would not have needed a Potemkin doctrine in the first place.
45. Suk-Young Kim, *Illusive Utopia* (Ann Arbor, 2010), 3-4; Armstrong, *The North Korean Revolution*, 3-4, 6. A partnered model argues that theatrical propaganda has succeeded in preserving Kim Il Sung's charisma; see for example Kwon and Cho's *Beyond Charismatic Politics* (2012). In North Korean studies one is used to seeing Kim's cult treated as a half-grassroots phenomenon that practically dictated a dynasty, when in fact it is the dynasty that has kept it going for so long. (Migrants' refusal to abandon the legend dinned into them as children is not in itself remarkable, especially considering the kid-gloves with which the outside world still handles it.) If the term *charismatic politics* is to be more than just an apologetic way of saying *hereditary personality cult*, someone must explain what charisma Kim ever manifested — in the Weberian sense of an ability to gain followers through sheer force of personal leadership — that the state could have then preserved over decades. His first audience rejected his heroic backstory precisely because he lacked the charisma needed to make it credible. (Illustrative is the less-famous photograph taken that day, which shows him simpering boyishly between two Red Army officers as his medal is fingered; to believe he had scared the Japanese eight years earlier requires no small leap of faith.) The Soviet authorities' installation of Kim after that lackluster debut was the textbook opposite of a charismatic rise to power. He then faced mounting contempt and disloyalty from inside the elite until (reluctantly, I believe) he started killing his critics. If his ghostwritten speeches tell us anything, it is that he had no great interest in being interesting. The hysteria he started

inducing in crowds after years of media worship had as little to do with innate magnetism as the reaction his grandson now elicits.

46. Andrei Lankov, "North Korea Dragged Back to the Past," *Asia Times*, 24 January 2008, and "Pyongyang Strikes Back," Asia Forum, 15 July 2009; and Victor Cha, *The Impossible State*, 59.
47. Asia Society Center on US-China Relations and University of Southern California Institute on Global Conflict and Cooperation, "North Korea Inside Out: The Case for Economic Engagement," October 2009, 22.
48. For a tautological chewing over of this platitude, see *Pulmyŏl ŭi chuch'e sasang*, 379-387. The few pages that deal with economy in the same handbook call only in vague terms for an independent economy; how it should be planned or organized is not defined (344-357). A later book on "Juche Economic Management Theory" quoted Kim Il Sung as having called for the state's leadership of the economy to fit "correctly" with the spontaneity of individual production units. *Chuch'e ŭi kyŏngje kwalli riron* (Pyongyang, 1992), 39. Such espousals of a vague golden mean abound, making it easy to reconcile even fundamental reforms with the leaders' writing.
49. A. James Gregor has pointed out that rule by pure coercion is a very expensive business. *Italian Fascism and Developmental Dictatorship* (Princeton, 1979), 38.
50. "Puk, singnyangnan sok P'yŏngyang kotkot sijang hwalbal," KBS News Nine broadcast, 10 August 2011.
51. That the public needed to be prepared for the succession is proof in itself, if I may take a swipe at another fallacy, that the personality cult is no religion. The Vatican picks a hitherto obscure man to be pope, and he is venerated that very day by the faithful.
52. I have long suspected that people in the northeast of the country, being more likely to run away, are not trusted with all the propaganda that their countrymen are. Migrants from that area are certainly less knowledgeable about the official culture than migrants from other areas (whom they greatly outnumber), but this may simply have to do with their lower social class.
53. To their credit most commentators, including Cumings, regarded the disingenuous conspiracy theories as beneath discussion. Had the South Korean

left really believed the ROK government or a US submarine was responsible for the deaths of those young men, there would have been months of candlelight demonstrations.

54. John Feffer, "Retaliate with Diplomacy," *Foreign Policy in Focus*, 21 May 2010. In fairness to Feffer, I admit that the title may have been imposed on him. I speak as someone who once had a *New York Times* op-ed published under the headline "To Beat a Dictator, Ignore Him."
55. Jimmy Carter, "North Korea's Consistent Message to the US," *Washington Post*, 24 November 2010.
56. Pak Min-hyŏk, "Mi, 'Puk konggyŏk hae ol kanŭngsŏng k'ŭda," *Donga Ilbo*, 20 December 2010.

10

The Myth Under Kim Jong Un

Let us turn at last from history to the state of affairs today. Most of the factors that encouraged the creation and maintenance of the Juche myth no longer play a big role. It has been almost half a century since a North Korean leader underwent a serious challenge to his rule. Marxism-Leninism ceased to matter so long ago that the idea of governance by theory would puzzle the country's pragmatic citizenry if anyone were to profess it in earnest. As for the personality cult, it no longer needs to explain itself. Unlike the first succession, the second did not need to be dressed up as a passing of the baton from the world's greatest philosopher to the next-greatest; the quasi-monarchist logic of a "Paektu bloodline" did most of the work.

Long gone too are the days in which the DPRK could destabilize the rival state by posing as the more progressive half of the peninsula. As can be confirmed by reading the *Hankyoreh* newspaper (or the *New York Times*' Choe Sang-hun, who writes in the same spirit), the ROK's nationalist left is now more anti-anti-Pyongyang than sympathetic. The few South Koreans who still admire the North do so for its right-wing credentials: its military might, its defiance of the West, its commitment to racial integrity.

"We do not speak empty words," an especially common slogan north of the DMZ, is as appealing to Koreans tired of liberal democracy as it is to those with no memory of it.

Things have changed even more dramatically on the foreign-policy front. The need for a decoy doctrine is greatly diminished. The regime is strong enough both to vaunt its race-thinking and to demand to be seen as dangerous. (Its popularity among Western neo-Nazis has grown accordingly.)[1] With the information cordon in tatters, the state could not maintain the two-track discourse even if it wanted to, at least not in its old Janus-like form. To go on pretending to an obsession with peace treaties and the like would be to undermine the domestic masses' pride in its iron resolve.

Small wonder, then, that despite slogans describing the young successor as the Kim Jong Il and Kim Il Sung of today, the personality cult has made no serious effort to present him as a theoretician in his own

right. A treatise he was alleged to have written in honor of his grandfather's hundredth birthday appeared in 2012, but it was just a panegyric run-through of both predecessors' achievements. The requisite tautologous excursion into *chuch'e sasang*, that "integrated system of a man-centered philosophical idea, revolutionary theory and leadership method," took up only 10% of the text.[2] Clearly the ghostwriter's main goal was to underscore a loyalty to everything subsumable under the term Kimilsungism-Kimjongilism, which had been formally proclaimed in April 2012 (after years of use in texts for South Korean consumption).[3] All the same, propaganda makes a show of treating Kim Jong Un's speeches as guiding texts, with posters showing young men holding up this or that bound edition.[4]

To judge from official documents secured by a South Korean broadcast company in late 2014, children in the DPRK continue to learn much more about their leaders than from them. In three years of high school each student is to spend a total of 389 hours studying, in separate courses, the lives of the three leaders. Another 42 hours are to be spent on the life of Kim Jong Suk, the Great Leader's wife. There is also an 88-hour course called Current Party Policies, but the name suggests something very different from *chuch'e sasang* instruction.[5]

So far Kim Jong Un has rather unwisely tried to present his regime as the embodiment of both Military-First resolve and the spirit of a "belt-loosening" age. There is little room for doctrinal aridities on either side of this dispensation. Lip service to *chuch'e sasang* is paid in briefer and less frequent doses than ever. Only every other month, for example, does the magazine *Ch'ŏllima* publish its "Subject Thought Study Room." It takes up but half a page. This is the first part of an instalment published under the title, "What does it mean to do things in accordance with actual conditions?"

> The Great Ruler Kim Jong Il spoke as follows.
> "The revolutionary movement demands that all problems be solved in accordance with both the changing and developing reality and a country's concrete conditions."
> Doing things in accordance with actual conditions means unceasingly solving problems in accordance with the changing and developing reality, and with the concrete conditions prevailing in a country.
> Revolution and construction do not stay in one place but are constantly changing and developing. Therefore the masses in every country must take into account the changing and developing reality and their country's concrete conditions, and solve all problems in accordance with them, if they are to carry out revolution and construction well.[6]

One can well imagine how little attention is paid to this sort of thing now that official media must compete with Seoul and Hollywood for citizens' leisure time. Granted, the doctrinal discourse was never intended to be read closely, but the brevity of these new articles precludes even the effect of intimidation. Whether intentionally or not, the regime has further lessened the doctrine's stature by churning out ever more competing slogans for model mindsets. Kim Jong Il Patriotism is but one of the new –isms. Our-Army-Number-One-ism jostles for space with Our-Leader-Number-One-ism, Light-Industry-Number-One-ism, Trade-Number-One-ism, and Our-Ideology-Number-One-ism.[7]

Kim Jong Un's New Year's greeting of 2013 was the first such greeting in decades to omit mention of *chuch'e sasang* altogether, though the first word did service in stock formulae like "the Great Subject Revolution."[8] The leader did not mention the doctrine on the next New Year's Day either, when the number of glittering-generality compounds dwindled to a mere three, nor did he speak of it on January 1, 2015. We should not make too much of these or any other outer-track texts. Besides, one occasionally sees the word *subject* used even in isolation to mean Subject Thought, or at least to make the discussion even more amorphous. (See for example the final sentence in Appendix 2.) All the same, there can be no mistaking the regime's readiness to convey a lack of interest in the Juche myth to the world at large. This although it could still perform useful smoke-and-mirrors service overseas without complicating the regime's posturing on the home front.

The change accords with other recent developments that bespeak either a growing contempt for foreign opinion or a decline in the ability to manipulate it. A prime example is the aid-for-good-behavior agreement signed between the US and the DPRK in February 2012, two months into Kim Jong Un's rule. Predictably enough, experts claimed a "new page" had been turned, a sign that North Korea's doves had gained the upper hand at last. (There was also doubt as to whether the Americans would keep their word.)[9] Mere weeks later the regime announced it would launch another long-range missile. The deal had obviously been signed only to put slack back in the rope, and sure enough, American punishment consisted only of cancellation of the promised aid, leaving the DPRK no worse off than before. This much was in the Kim Jong Il tradition. What was new was the almost comical rapidity with which the North Koreans had broken their word. To be sure, Kim Jong Un needed only to complain about the weeds at an amusement park for the slate to be wiped clean again, and have comparisons to Deng Xiaoping chalked on it.[10] But his father would not have pushed his luck so far, so quickly.

The regime went on to spend early 2013 rattling its nuclear saber. At one point it announced that if the republic's dignity were infringed upon, no one across the DMZ would be left alive to sign a surrender. This implied, probably unintentionally, a falling away of the old distinction between good and bad South Koreans. The propaganda apparatus went on to lampoon President Park Geun-hye in such crudely sexist terms that even the South Korean left felt compelled to object, as it had not done in regard to Pyongyang's death-threats against her predecessor.

More shocking to Western observers was the KCNA's decision in 2014 to print the following, purportedly the representative opinion of a laborer at the Ch'ŏllima Iron and Steel Works.

Hideous Monkey Man:
> Just looking at Obama's ugly mug turns my stomach almost to the point of vomiting. That blackish mug, the vacant, ash-colored eyes, the gaping nostrils: the more I study all this, the more he appears the spitting image of a monkey in an African jungle. . . . When I watch his squalid form jumping around anytime, anywhere, it's enough to doubt he's human, to think he's a monkey for sure; so closely does he resemble a monkey who can't sit still for a moment, who swings his scarlet buttocks as he clambers up this tree and that, stuffing himself with the fruit he picks, or eating whatever he finds on the ground. Not content with gorging himself on the south Korean territory he has crawled into, he is now ogling even the territory to the north. . . . [He] is a mongrel of indeterminate bloodline.[11]

That's only half of it. The racist rhetoric recalls Han Sŏrya's canonical anti-American novella *Jackals* (*Sŭngnyangi*, 1951).[12] But the above, in contrast, was online and therefore export propaganda, even if the KCNA had just enough residual discretion to refrain from providing an English version. The text was promptly translated by a blogger, forcing the North Korea commentariat to try to square it with the cherished failed-communist model.[13] The effort was nothing if not imaginative; it was claimed, for example, that the North had acquired its contempt for black people from the USSR.[14]

The KCNA outdid itself the following year by praising the "knife slashes of justice" inflicted on the US ambassador to the ROK on March 5, 2015. This rash expression of support for terrorism will only strengthen the South Korean president's case for tough action against the North's already spindly fifth column. But we should beware of seeing conscious policy shifts behind changes in propaganda policy that may well be just the result of a decline in professionalism; "somebody always does have the incapable people," as Margaret Oliphant pointed out. There are reports that Kim Jong Un has entrusted the propaganda apparatus to his younger sister, which if true would explain a lot, considering the inattentiveness she has been filmed displaying at official functions. It is unlikely that the regime will ever tell foreigners exactly what it tells its own citizens — no government does that — but the sophisticated dissimulation that gave rise to the Juche myth is already a thing of the past.

1. Nate Thayer, "White Power and Apocalyptic Cults: Pro-North Korean Americans Revealed," NK News, 6 May 2013.
2. Kim Jong Un, "The Great Kim Il Sung is the Eternal Leader of Our Party and Our People: Treatise to Mark the Centenary of the Birth of President Kim Il Sung," 2012, 6-7.
3. The term featured in the new preamble to the WP's statutes, which the KCNA made public in April 2012. (The statutes themselves, which may or may not have been changed, were not published, perhaps so that outsiders could no longer comment on the regime's flouting of them.) The new preamble defines the WP's goal as the permeation of (North *and* South) Korean society in Kimilsungism-Kimjongilism. The former version had talked of *chuch'e-sasang-hwa* instead. Yet a sentence near the end of the preamble declares not only a commitment to the strengthening of education in *chuch'e sasang*, but also the party's adherence to the "revolutionary principles of Marxism-Leninism." This last may well have been included to preserve the special party-to-party relationship with Beijing. (Nevertheless, the giant portraits of Marx and Lenin that had hung for so long in Kim Il Sung Square were quietly removed a few months later.) "Puk, Chosŏn rodongdang kyuyak chŏnmun," newfocus.co.kr, 12 April 2012. Whether the inner-track version of the preamble is the same is anyone's guess.
4. See for example the poster on the inside back page of the woman's magazine *Chosŏn Nyŏsŏng*, June 2014.
5. Yu Kwang-sŏk, "Puk, Kim Chŏng-ŭn hyŏngmyŏng yŏksa to kogyo chŏnggyu kwamok ch'aetaek," KBS News, 24 November 2014.
6. "Siljŏng e matke handanŭn kŏs ŭn muot ŭl ŭimi hanŭnga?", *Ch'ŏllima*, December 2012, 38.
7. The last term: *uri sasang cheiljuŭi*. Kim Sun-gil, "Pukhansik cheiljuŭi ŭi hŏsang kwa chinsil," Radio Free Asia, 7 February 2014.
8. Mok Yong-jae, "Kim Chŏng-ŭn sinnyŏn insa 'chuch'e sasang' ŏn'gŭp an toen iyu nŭn?" *Daily NK*, 1 January 2013.
9. See for example Chris McGreal, "North Korea pledges to halt nuclear program in exchange for US aid," *The Guardian*, 29 February 2012.

10. John Delury, "Reform sprouts in North Korea?" YaleGlobal, 26 July 2012.
11. "Sesang e hana pakk e ŏmnŭn pullyanga Obama ege ch'ŏnbŏl ŭl," KCNA, 5 May 2014.
12. For my translation of the novella, see *Han Sŏrya and North Korean Literature*, 157-188. A while back I read with amusement that I shouldn't have translated the anti-Yankee epithet *sŭngnyangi* as "jackals," because jackals are not indigenous to the peninsula. And just the other day someone felt it necessary to tell me that the Korean word literally means "dhole." Evidently I was wrong in thinking the title *Dholes* so obviously inappropriate, because obscure and affectless, that it could be rejected without explanation. I settled on *Jackals* because that word (unlike *Wild Dogs* or *Wolves*) carries *Sŭngnyangi*'s connotations of cowardly rapacity and low cunning. Only much later did I learn that jackals and dholes are closely related, and look very similar. See Claudio Sillero-Zibiri, *Canids* (2004), 210.
13. The story was broken on May 7, 2014 by Joshua Stanton on his blog One Free Korea.
14. See the experts' remarks recorded by Chad O'Carroll in "President Obama a 'Wicked Black Monkey,'" *NK News,* 9 May 2014. 87

Conclusion

THE NEAR-UNANIMOUS CONSENSUS in regard to Juche's centrality to North Korean ideology has always accommodated varying assessments of its practical importance. These have generally become more dismissive in recent years, in accordance with the ongoing economization of the experts' own thinking; the current assumption seems to be that Juche is the ruling ideology *and* no big deal. My main purpose has been to establish the true function of Juche, not the degree of its importance. Still, I hope to have shown that as a textual prop in the personality cult, it has been a very big deal indeed. By crediting Kim Il Sung with an original, world-renowned doctrine the propaganda apparatus enhanced his prestige, undermined internal challenges to his rule, strengthened pride in the DPRK, and helped save the regime's face when its patron-states collapsed. Although the Juche torch never dazzled the outside world quite as intended, it continues to cast a respectable red glow over the olive-brown reality, thereby aiding the country's effort to maximize aid revenues while arming itself to the hilt. The function that Juche doctrine has never performed, except perhaps briefly in South Korea's student movement, is that of an ideology.

There should be no more talk of multiple official ideologies operating inside the DPRK at fluctuating degrees of intensity. As I have already pointed out, a political ideology is a worldview. No regime can want to follow two at once, nor can it have an interest in simultaneously propagating two in earnest to the same domestic public. (Kim Il Sung did not purge the Soviet Koreans for nothing.) If militarist ultra-nationalism and the humanist universalism of Juche are irreconcilable worldviews, as I believe, one must decide which of the two has been calling the shots.

I will risk assuming that when ethnic Korean Pyongyang watchers talk of the DPRK's ideologies in English (and they seem to do it most often) they are thinking of multiple *sasang* instead, as elements of one big worldview. And a line of retreat for our traditionalists may well be to argue that while *chuch'e sasang* is no ideology in its own right, it at least functions — as the DPRK itself claims — as an integral part of the overarching ideology, which now goes by the name of Kimilsungism-Kimjongilism. They might even think of a plausible way to reconcile universal, peace-minded humanism with the militarist, paranoid-nationalist personality cult. European fascist thinkers did something comparable in their own writings in the 1920s and 1930s. The task is made more difficult here, however, by the fact that Kim Il Sung explicitly disparaged nationalism in his *chuch'e sasang* talks. Would-be salvagers of the Juche myth must also answer questions begged by the lateness of the doctrine's emergence. Just how did its content alter the ideology that had been preached in the inner track from the start? And more importantly: How did policy-making change as a result? The Juche of the 1970s, which consisted of such innocuous commonplaces that prominent people across the global political spectrum felt safe in praising it, was as water in comparison to the hard liquor of the inner track. The only effect an ideologically-functioning Juche could possibly have brought about in those years was a dilution or moderation of the official culture, something that clearly did not take place.

In any case, there is no justifying the attribution to the DPRK of a distinguishing commitment to self-reliance. In neither the *pro forma* canon (the leaders' writings) nor the *de facto* one (the mytho-biographies) has self-reliance played a more important role, or been defined in more radical terms, than one would expect from any nationalist state. As for real-world policy-making, the regime has always been more interested

CONCLUSION

in racial isolation than self-reliance. Indeed, the former has long been bought at the cost of the latter.[1]

As we saw in an earlier chapter, the West took a remarkably subjective (*chuch'ejŏk*) role in its own befuddlement. Pyongyang watchers began talking of Kim Il Sung's Juche even before the North Koreans did. It is unlikely that tendentiousness was to blame. Most observers in those days were researchers of the peninsula in general. With one or two exceptions, none had special knowledge of communism. The general shakiness of their Korean skills contributed to a neglect of ideological matters. We mustn't be too hard on them for thinking that the creative application of Marxism-Leninism to local conditions was a bravely original thing to call for. What country specialist does not want to make his country special?

It was only in 1965, with Joan Robinson's encouragement, that observers united in describing Juche as a nationalist-communist ideology of self-reliance. This error too was made without much official encouragement from the DPRK, which preferred to be seen overseas as a bastion of internationalist non-alignment instead. Kim Il Sung explicitly rejected nationalism and — with far more sincerity — disclaimed any intention of rejecting aid or "fraternal" trade.

In the late 1960s and the 1970s the North tried to promote and steer the Juche myth by sending out foreign-language versions of Kim's ghostwritten works. This time Pyongyang watchers made the error of thinking that if Juche comprised the bulk of export propaganda, it had to be central to the domestic kind too. A few hours with the *Rodong Sinmun* would have set them straight. To be sure, the showcase ideology did not blind Westerners entirely to the real one, not least because it failed to hold their attention for long. All that sank in was the impression of a leader focused on a North-internal vision of some sort, but that was cosmetic service enough.

We can all agree, I hope, that the ruling ideology does indeed call for "putting Korea first in everything." Let us leave aside the question of whether this is a Japanese-influenced blood-nationalism, as I contend, or that more respectable, communist nationalism which most observers prefer to imagine. It should go without saying that putting Korea first means putting unification first. It is hardly surprising that the memory of American carpet-bombing did not stop Kim Il Sung from trying to win his allies' approval for another invasion of the South, as we now know from communist-camp archives. A radical nationalism that resigned itself to a foreign-drawn demarcation line would be a contradiction in terms.[2]

The most dangerous effect of the Juche myth has been to make the world believe that North Korea's main interest lies in becoming self-contained, or at least whole unto itself. Its nationalism has thus been denatured into something that hardly sounds like nationalism at all, enabling apologists to play up the perceived righteousness of it without acknowledging the obvious ideo-*logical* implications. Western college students have been taught to respect the "guerrilla state" on nationalist grounds if on no others — and at the same time to regard Syngman Rhee and Park Chung Hee as fabricators of northern-peril scares.

For decades now, the North has pursued a mass-impoverishing armament program, steadily increased the militarization of its society, and undertaken occasional attacks on the ROK. The last of these, at time of writing, consisted of the surreptitious planting of new land mines on the South Korean side of the DMZ, which maimed two ROK soldiers on August 4, 2015. The Juche myth has encouraged the Western commentariat to pass off this consistent pattern of behavior as a matter of "reactive" and "self-defeating" bids for, of all things, a more stable status quo. (As if any militarism, let alone that of a radical-nationalist state, would be content to play defense forever.) A truly disinterested community of scholars would have seen things differently even if it had made the same honest errors at the beginning. Ho Chi Minh stressed the need for national self-reliance before and during the Vietnam War, and one of Syngman Rhee's reasons for wanting a "march to the north" was his belief that the ROK would never stand on its own feet without the rich resources there.[3] There was no reason to believe that an obsession with self-reliance would weaken the North Korean regime's commitment to its original goal.

Our Juche-mythmakers appear to have recognized this problem on some level or another. They must certainly have known that the degree of the DPRK's dependence on aid has always been excessive even by sub-Saharan standards, let alone by the standards they have attributed to it. Hence their compensatory assertions that Juche is beyond Western understanding, knowable only to the solipsistic North Koreans themselves; we may translate the term as self-reliance at a pinch, but there is *so* much more to it than that. This bluster should have aroused suspicion when it was first trotted out in the 1980s. Instead the nuclear crisis enhanced the popularity of the Juche myth in the wishfully-thinking West even as the word receded from the *Rodong Sinmun*'s headlines.

As I mentioned in my introduction, the decoy now works in a way that neither Kim Il Sung nor Kim Jong Il could have foreseen. Faced with the North Koreans' obvious indifference to communism and self-reliance, and misperceiving it as a new phenomenon, more and more observers are claiming that ideology no longer matters there.[4] It's as if Iran watchers visited Tehran expecting to find a bastion of Catholicism, and then concluded that the locals had given up on religion altogether.

The end-of-ideology fallacy encourages those North Korea hands who set great store by such things as academic and professional exchanges, including the training of WP propagandists in Western media techniques.[5] There is no disabusing some people of the belief that mutual mistrust is undermined by contact between nations.[6] (As Spengler said, the big problems are always falsified down, with "almost criminal optimism," into little ones.)[7] It is odd to hear the strategy of "subversive engagement" called for in public, as if the North Koreans would never think to listen in.[8] This underestimation of the country has more to do with mirror-imaging than racism; the West now projects its own unseriousness onto the rest of the world. Even our political scientists believe that the DPRK wants Washington's help in preserving its distinctiveness from South Korean encroachment.[9] In fact that distinctiveness lies primarily — and to a growing degree as the economy liberalizes — in hostility to America. Normal relations would be the end of it. Carl Schmitt's assertion that the definition of the enemy is the definition of the political is especially true in this context.[10]

Retiring the Juche myth does not mean exchanging the old reductionism for a new kind, and seeing a religion of ROK-conquest behind the regime's every move. Nor does it mean rejecting the possibility that Kim Jong Un might someday be induced to take the allegedly pragmatic road the West wants him to. It means acknowledging that for now, at least, militarist nationalism continues to guide and unify the DPRK. Capitalism is so reconcilable with it that North Koreans can violate mere economic regulations and still consider themselves loyal citizens, loyal ideologues even. One is reminded of wartime Japan, another militarist state supported by a nation of black marketeers.

By making clear and world-defying progress on the nuclear front, the regime in Pyongyang has earned the right to the slogan, "We don't speak empty words!" Therein lies much of the appeal this far-right dictatorship exerts on its citizens, who, however docile they may appear to be, keep a certain pressure on it in return. What is a dominant ideology, if not the values by which ruler and people agree that his performance is to be judged? Whether either side believes in them with any great fervor is a matter of secondary importance. Kim Jong Un knows, then, that he must continue taking visible steps toward the main ideological goal. We should at least recognize what it is.

CONCLUSION

1. The DPRK is thus more properly likened to a *hikikomori* than a hermit. *The Cleanest Race*, 49-50.
2. South Korea's ruling ideology therefore ceased to merit being called radical-nationalist when (circa 1960-1961) it stopped prioritizing unification above all else.
3. Laura M. Calkins, *China and the First Vietnam War, 1947-54* (New York, 2013), 26. Imperial Japan and Nazi Germany invaded foreign countries with an explicit design to make the motherland self-sufficient, as appalling as the word may seem in this context. Jerome B. Cohen, *Japan's Economy in War and Construction* (Minneapolis, 1949), 33.
4. Also at work is the educated Westerner's tendency to think of ideology as something (like propaganda) that only other people believe in. The perceived triumph of Western-style consumerism over communism in the DPRK is thus regarded not as the replacement of one ideology with another, but as the rout of ideology by good sense and progress.
5. Claire Carter, "British taxpayers fund UK-based media course for Kim Jong Un's spin doctors," *Daily Mirror*, 14 December 2014.
6. Walker Connor laments this conviction in *Ethnonationalism*, 47-48. He writes that "increasing awareness of a second group . . . is at least as likely to produce, on balance, a negative response." Ibid., 48. The point is amply illustrated by how animosity between South Korea and Japan has risen since the 1990s.
7. *Jahre der Entscheidung* (1933, repr. Munich, 2007), 140, 145.
8. The leading advocate of this approach is Andrei Lankov. (See for example, "The North Korean Paradox and the Subversive Truth," American Enterprise Institute, 3 March 2009.) He is no less publicly agreed with. The apparent assumption is that Pyongyang can neither do without things like academic exchanges nor take effective counter-measures, even if it does know our motives.
9. Bruce Cumings, *North Korea* (New York, 2004), x.
10. *Der Begriff des Politischen* (Berlin, 1963), 26ff.

Appendix 1

On Eliminating Dogmatism and Formalism and Establishing the Subject in Ideological Work: Speech to Workers in Party Propaganda and Agitation, December 28, 1955

[The following is my translation of the earliest extant version of the speech, i.e. the one published in Kim's Selected Works *in 1960. The paragraphing of that version has been retained. I have underlined and appended footnotes to words and phrases omitted or changed in later editions. Other footnotes supply additional information not already discussed in the relevant chapter. — BRM]*

Today I would like to express a few opinions to you comrades on the shortcomings in our party's ideological work and on how to eliminate them in the future. As you learned at yesterday's session, big ideological errors have been made on the literary front.

Obviously, then, our propaganda work cannot have gone well either. Unfortunately it has lapsed into dogmatism and formalism in many respects.

The most fundamental shortcoming of ideological work is the failure to delve deeply into all matters and the absence of a subject. It may not be correct to say that there is no subject, but the truth is that it has not yet been firmly established. This is a serious matter. We must thoroughly rectify this shortcoming. Unless this problem is solved, we cannot hope for good results in ideological work. Why does our ideological work suffer from dogmatism and formalism? There is a need for serious reflection on the questions of why our propaganda and agitation workers only concern themselves with appearances, failing to go deeply into matters, and why they merely copy and memorize foreign things instead of working creatively.

What is the subject in our party's ideological work? What are we doing? We are engaged in Korea's revolution and not some other country's. Precisely this Korean revolution is the subject of our party's ideological work, all of which must therefore be made to serve its interests. Whether we research the history of the Communist Party of the Soviet Union, the history of the Chinese revolution, or the general principles of Marxism-Leninism, it is all in order to carry out our own revolution correctly.

By saying that the subject is missing from our party's ideological work, I do not mean, of course, that we did not carry out a revolution, or that our revolutionary work was undertaken by some passer-by. But the subject has not been firmly established in ideological work, for which reason dogmatist and formalist errors have been made, doing much harm to our revolutionary cause.

To carry out a revolution in Korea, we must know Korean history and geography as well as the customs of the Korean people. Only then is it possible to educate our people in a way that suits them, and to inspire in them an ardent love for their native region and their homeland. Before anything else, the most important thing is to research the history of our country and of our people's struggle, and to make it widely known among the working people.

This is not the first time we have raised this question. As far back as the autumn of 1945, immediately after liberation, we emphasized the need to study the history of the nation's struggle[1] and to inherit its fine tradition. Only when we educate our people in the history and tradition of their own struggle, can we stimulate their national pride and rouse the broad mass of people to revolutionary struggle. Yet many of our cadres are ignorant of the country's history and do not strive to discover, inherit and carry forward its fine tradition. Unless this is corrected, it will lapse, in the long run, into the negation of Korean history.

---

[1] Throughout this text the words *nation*, *national* (*minjok*, *minjokchŏk*) are to be understood in the sense of the pan-Korean ethnic community, not just citizens of the DPRK.

APPENDIX 1

Those mistakes too which have recently been made by Pak Ch'ang-ok and others are due to their negation of the history of the Korean literary movement. The struggle waged by the fine writers of the KAPF, namely the Korean Proletarian Literature League,[2] and the fine works of progressive scholars and writers like Pak Yŏn-am and Chŏng Ta-san[3] are not in their field of vision. We told them to study such things deeply and make them widely known, but they did not do so.

Today, ten years after liberation, we possess all the conditions for collecting material on our literary legacy and putting it to sufficient use, yet our propaganda cadres do not show the slightest interest.

At the fifth plenum of the party's Central Committee[4] it was decided to actively publicize the history of our people's struggle and our precious cultural legacy, but cadres in the field of propaganda failed to do so. They even went so far as to forbid newspapers to carry articles on the anti-Japanese struggle of the Korean people.

The Kwangju Student Incident, for example, was a mass struggle in which tens of thousands of Korean students and other young people rose up against Japanese imperialism; it played a huge part in instilling anti-Japanese spirit in broad sections of Korean youth.[5] Accordingly, we should publicize this movement widely, and educate our students and other young people in the brave fighting spirit displayed by their forerunners. While our propaganda cadres fail to do this, Syngman Rhee has been making use of this movement in his propaganda.[6] In this way communists have ended up looking like disregarders of national traditions. How dangerous

---

[2] The acronym reflects the group's Esperanto name, which is rendered in various spellings. The most common of these is Korea Artista Proletaria Federatio.

[3] Omitted from later editions.

[4] 15-18 December 1952.

[5] Reference is to the Kwangju Student Movement, an umbrella term for student demonstrations and civil disobedience set off by Japanese students' alleged harassment of Korean schoolgirls near Kwangju. The unrest began on November 3, 1929 and continued until May the following year.

[6] In October 1953 Rhee had designated November 3 as "Students' Day," in honor of the Kwangju movement initiated on that day.

a thing this is! We will never win over the south Korean youth in this manner.

Up to now, such publicity and education work has been dropped and laid aside, without anyone's having issued an instruction to that effect. Newspapers do not write about [the student movement], nor are meetings held to commemorate it. <u>In China the May Fourth movement is commemorated as a great event in the youth movement.</u>[7] Our country's[8] Kwangju Student Incident is a magnificent model for our young students' struggle against imperialism.

The same must be said of the June Tenth *Manse* Incident.[9] This was another mass struggle in which the Korean people rose up against Japanese imperialism. It is true that the struggle was greatly damaged by the factionalists who had wormed their way into it. Considering that even after liberation, the spy clique led by Pak Hŏn-yŏng and Yi Sŭng-yŏp[10] crept into our ranks and wrought mischief, it goes without saying that in those days it was easier for factionalists to carry out subversive activity. But does saying so make the struggle itself bad? That cannot be. It ended in failure because of a few scoundrels mixed in with the organization's leadership, but we cannot deny its revolutionary character, and should look for lessons in its failure.

---

[7] Reference is to student demonstrations against the Versailles Treaty which took place in Beijing on May 4, 1919. In later editions of Kim's work this sentence was replaced with one reading: "Events like the Kwangju Student Incident ought to be taken up by the Democratic Youth League."

[8] Omitted from later editions, because the preceding reference to China had been omitted too.

[9] *Manse* is the Korean equivalent of the Japanese *banzai* and our own *viva* or *long live* (so-and-so or something). The June Tenth Movement is the more common term in South Korea for these student demonstrations in 1926, which were inspired by the burial of Sunjong, who had been emperor at the time of Korea's annexation. Naturally Kim wants the demonstrations' monarchist aspect dismissed as the result of "factionalist" infiltration.

[10] Pak, the former foreign minister of the DPRK, had been sentenced to death on trumped-up spy charges mere weeks before Kim's speech. He was evidently not executed until well into 1956. Yi had been the DPRK's first Minister of Justice. Purged in 1953 on similar grounds, he was apparently executed earlier than Pak.

APPENDIX 1

Even worse, no publicity has been given to the March First Movement either.[11] Progressive people with a national conscience cannot be led along the right path in this way, to say nothing of communists. The lack of Communist Party leadership was the principal cause of the failure of the March First Movement. But who would deny that it was a nationwide resistance movement against Japanese imperialism? Accordingly we ought to make the people aware of the historic significance of this movement and use its lessons to educate them.

In the past many of our country's revolutionary movements failed due to scoundrels who infiltrated into their leadership, but there is no denying that they were mass struggles. The mass of the people has always fought courageously. Pak Ch'ang-ok may have arbitrarily denied this. But no true Marxist-Leninist would dare deny the achievements of the people's struggle.

When I asked Pak Ch'ang-ok and the people following him why they rejected KAPF, they answered that they did so because some renegades were involved in it.[12] So does this mean that the KAPF, in which Comrades Han Sŏrya and Yi Ki-yŏng[13] were active as the main core, was something of no importance? We must highly value the fighting achievements of these people, and put them in the center of our literature's development.[14]

On what principal will the revolution be carried out if our people's struggle is denied? Casting all these things aside makes them seem to

---

[11] A declaration of Korean independence was read out on March 1, 1919 at a park in downtown Seoul, setting off nationwide demonstrations which were brutally suppressed. Kim's mentioning of this the most important colonial-era incident in third place is another indication that he was either speaking impromptu or referring to very rudimentary notes.

[12] Reference is to those who betrayed the movement by formally renouncing it in written statements to the colonial authorities. In fact every member of KAPF signed a declaration of *chŏnhyang* or apostasy and went on to conform to the status quo. (Myers, *Han Sŏrya*, 29.) The Soviet Koreans' lack of enthusiasm for KAPF is therefore understandable.

[13] Although only Han was later purged — evidently at Kim Ch'ang-man's urging — both Han and Yi's names were substituted in later editions with the words "prominent proletarian writers."

[14] Changed in later editions to read only: "We must highly value the fighting attainments of the KAPF."

have done nothing. As Comrade Han Sŏrya told you yesterday,[15] there is much to be proud of in our country's peasant movement. In recent years, however, one cannot find any articles dealing with it in our newspapers.

In schools, too, there is a tendency to neglect courses on Korean history. During the war, the Central Party School's curriculum allotted 160 hours a year to the study of world history, but very few hours to Korean history. The party's own school being managed in this way, our cadres cannot help but be ignorant of their country's history.

In our propaganda and agitation work, numerous examples can be found of extolling only foreign things while slighting our own.

Once I visited a People's Army rest home, where there was a picture of the Siberian steppe on the wall. That landscape probably appeals to Russians. But the beautiful birds and beasts, mountains and rivers of our own country appeal to Korean people more. There are beautiful mountains in our country, such as the Kŭmgang and Myohyang ranges. There are clear streams, the blue sea with its rolling waves and fields with their ripening grain. If we are to inspire in our People's Army soldiers a love for their native place and their country, we must display many pictures of our landscapes.

One day this summer when I dropped in at a provincial room for democratic propaganda, I saw diagrams of the Soviet Union's Five-Year Plan, but not a single one illustrating our own Three-Year Plan. Moreover, there were grand pictures of factories in foreign countries, but not a single photograph of the factories we are reconstructing or building. They do not even put up any diagrams and pictures showing our economic construction, much less research our country's history.

Visiting a primary school I saw that all the portraits on the walls were of foreigners, such as Mayakovsky and Pushkin, with not one of a Korean. With this sort of education, how can children be expected to have national pride?

To give a ridiculous example, foreign ways are aped even when it comes to putting tables of contents in books, so that they are put in the

---

[15] Omitted from editions published after Han's fall from grace in 1962.

APPENDIX 1

back. We should of course learn from the good experiences of [other countries'] socialist construction, but where on earth is the need to put tables of contents at the back, foreign-style? This does not suit Korean taste. Accordingly, shouldn't we put a book's table of contents in the front?

In compiling schoolbooks, too, material is not taken from our country's literary works but from other countries'. All this is because the subject is lacking.

The result of this forgetting of the subject in propaganda work is that much harm has been done to party work.

For the same reason, many comrades do not respect our revolutionaries. At present more than 100 comrades who took part in revolutionary struggle in the past are attending the Central Party School, but until recently they were buried in obscurity.

We sent many revolutionaries to the Ministry of the Interior, but many of them were driven out on the ground that they lacked skills. At the Central Party School, I once met a comrade who had taken part in revolutionary activities in the past. He had been left in his post as chief of a county's internal affairs for eight years. This is a very wrong attitude to take towards revolutionaries.

Today our cadres have become rude people who do not acknowledge their seniors. They have been allowed to fall into such a habit, in spite of the fact that Communists are supposed to have a higher moral sense than others and hold their revolutionary seniors in high esteem.

As the result of a vigorous struggle waged in our People's Army to establish[16] revolutionary traditions, most veterans of revolutionary activities have become either regimental or divisional commanders.

If we had not organized the People's Army with old revolutionary cadres at its core, what would have been the outcome of the last war? We would not have been able to defeat the enemy and win a great victory under such difficult conditions.

During our retreat, certain foreigners predicted that most of our army units, trapped by enemy encirclement, would not be able to return [from

---

[16] Changed in later editions to read "inherit" or "carry on."

the south]. But we were firmly convinced that all of them would, whatever it took. In fact, all of them returned except those who were killed. The foreigners looked with much fond approval on our boys[17] and said there were few armies like ours in the world. How did this come about? The explanation is that our army cadres were comrades who had taken part in guerrilla warfare or in local revolutionary movements in the past. That is precisely why our army is strong.

Ten years have passed since our party was founded. Therefore, party members should naturally be taught the history of our party. If our cadres are not taught the revolutionary history of our country, they will be unable to carry our fine revolutionary traditions forward, nor will they be able to know which direction to take in the struggle, or show enthusiasm and initiative in their revolutionary activities.

We should research our own things in earnest and get to know them well. Otherwise we shall be unable to solve creatively, in keeping with our actual conditions, the new problems that will crop up one after another in practical administration.

It is true that the form of our government should also be suited to our country's specific conditions. Does our people's power take exactly the same form as that in other socialist countries? No. They are alike in proceeding from Marxist-Leninist principles, but their forms differ from each other. There is no doubt, too, that our platform is one in keeping with the realities of our country. Our 20-item program was developed from the program of the Association for the Restoration of the Homeland.[18] As you all know, this association existed before liberation.

---

[17] The very un-nationalist choice of words in the original (*maeu kit'ŭk hage yŏgimyŏnsŏ*) implies that the foreigners were somehow superior. It was changed in later editions to read "greatly admired this."

[18] Reference is to the program Kim had announced on March 31, 1946, when he was still chairman of the North Korean Provincial People's Committee. No doubt formulated under Soviet guidance, it included a commitment to the purge of former pro-Japanese elements and to land reform. Kim is here claiming that the program originated with the colonial-era *Choguk kwangbokhoe*, a resistance organization founded in Kapsan county in Hamgyŏng Province.

APPENDIX 1

Because our cadres do not understand these matters well, they keep making errors.

Some people even think it strange that our agricultural collectivization movement is progressing rapidly. There is nothing strange about this. In the past, the Korean peasantry's economic base was very weak <u>and the soil bad</u>.[19] Under Japanese imperialist rule, the peasant movement grew and the peasants' revolutionary spirit was very strong. After liberation they were tempered politically all the more by the building of democracy and the bitter years of war, so it is natural that the agricultural collectivization movement should be making rapid progress in our country today.

<u>Comrade</u>[20] Pak Yong-bin, on returning from a visit to the Soviet Union, said that since it was following the line of easing international tension, we too should drop our slogan of resisting US imperialism. Such an assertion has nothing to do with revolutionary initiative, and would nullify our people's revolutionary vigilance. Are they not our arch-enemies, these US imperialists who set fire to our territory, massacred innocent people, and continue to occupy the southern half of our country by force?

It is utterly ridiculous to think that our people's struggle against the US imperialists conflicts with the efforts of the Soviet people to ease international tension. Our people's condemnation of and struggle against the US imperialists' policy of aggression against Korea do not undermine but rather conduce to the struggle of the peoples of the world to lessen international tension and defend peace. At the same time, the struggle to ease tension on the part of the peace-loving people the world over, including the Soviet people, creates more favorable conditions for our people's anti-imperialist struggle.

Because Pak Ch'ang-ok did not study our country's history and current reality, he became ideologically linked to the reactionary bourgeois writer Yi Tae-jun.[21] Of course Pak too had remnants of bourgeois ideology in his mind, but he was conceited enough to think he knew everything,

---

[19] Omitted from later editions for obvious reasons.
[20] Omitted from later editions for obvious reasons.
[21] A fiction writer who came north in 1947, Yi T'ae-jun enjoyed the Soviet Koreans' patronage until his fall from grace in 1954.

without even studying the realities of our country. Consequently, things went wrong. The harm he did to our ideological work is very serious.

After liberation, these people said that since Yi Kwang-su was a talented man, it would be better to give him prominence, but I pointed out that it would be wrong to do so.[22] He had written a novel, *A Revolutionary's Wife*, in which he insulted revolutionaries released from prison.[23] In addition he was a scoundrel who used to rave that Koreans came from "one and the same ancestry and the same roots" as the Japanese imperialists. Therefore, I blocked the plan, saying it was unthinkable to give prominence to such a man and that they could not do so. <u>At that time Comrade Han Sŏrya also criticized Yi Kwang-su strongly.</u>[24]

Some comrades working in the party's Department of Propaganda and Agitation to copy mechanically from the Soviet Union in all their work, because they had no intention of studying our realities and lacked the true Marxist-Leninist approach to educating the people in our own good things and revolutionary traditions. Many comrades swallow Marxism-Leninism whole, without digesting and assimilating it. It is self-evident, therefore, that they are unable to display revolutionary initiative.

<u>We have</u>[25] so far failed to organize the business of researching our history and our national culture systematically. Ten years have passed since liberation, yet we have failed to tackle the matter actively, treating it as an optional one. We lacked cadres before, but now we have scholars, funds and material, and sufficient resources for doing it. It is quite possible if only you comrades research well and organize the work. Every effort

---

[22] The novelist Yi Kwang-su was the most notorious of all Japan's intellectual collaborators on the peninsula. There were attempts in the late 1940s to induce him to come North, and during the war he was simply forced to. He is thought to have died on the road. The common assumption that Pyongyang wanted not to recruit but to punish him is belied (as are Kim's disparaging remarks above) by the stately, respectfully-inscribed tombstone on his North Korean grave.

[23] Reference is to *Hyŏngmyŏng ŭi anae* (1930), which the KAPF writer Yi Ki-yŏng had reviewed very critically at the time.

[24] Omitted from editions published after Han's fall from grace in 1962.

[25] Changed in later editions, to preserve Kim's reputation for infallibility, to read "The sector of propaganda work has . . ."

APPENDIX 1

should be made to ascertain, uphold and promote our national heritage. We must absorb internationally progressive things <u>to the utmost</u>,[26] but we should develop the fine things of our own as we take in advanced culture. Otherwise, our people will lose faith in their own ability and become an effete people who only try to copy from others.

Hearing us say that it is necessary to establish the subject, some comrades might take it in a simple way, and get the wrong the idea that we need not learn from foreign countries, but it's not that way at all. <u>We must learn from all socialist countries, especially from the Soviet Union.</u>[27]

The important thing is to know what the goal of our learning is. It is to put the advanced experience of the Soviet Union and other socialist countries to good use in our Korean revolution.

During the war, Hŏ Ka-i, Kim Chae-uk and Pak Il-u once quarreled pointlessly among themselves over how to do political work in the army.[28] [Korean] people from the Soviet Union insisted upon doing things Soviet style, those who had come from China wanted to do things Chinese style. So they quarreled, saying Soviet style is good, Chinese style is good. This is foolishness.

When you're eating, it does not matter whether you use the right hand or the left, whether you use a spoon or chopsticks. No matter how you eat, it is the same so long as food is put into your mouth, isn't it? Why does one have to fuss over "style" in wartime? We do political work to strengthen our People's Army and win battles, and any way will do so long as our aim is achieved. Yet Hŏ Ka-i and Pak Il-u picked fights about such trifles. This does nothing but weaken discipline within the party. At that time, the party center maintained that we should learn <u>Soviet things and Chinese</u>

---

[26] "To the utmost" was replaced in later editions with "actively."

[27] The sentence was changed in later editions to read simply, "We must learn from the good experiences of socialist countries."

[28] Hŏ (a.k.a. A.I. Hegai) led the Soviet Korean faction inside the ruling elite until his purge in 1953. Kim Chae-uk, another Soviet Korean, had been vice-minister of agriculture. Pak Il-u, the former Minister of the Interior, had been a prominent member of the so-called Yan'an faction; he was purged in 1954.

things²⁹ and, on this basis, create a method of political work suitable to our actual conditions.

It is important in our work to grasp revolutionary truth, Marxist-Leninist truth, and apply it correctly to our actual conditions. There can be no principle that we must do things Soviet style. Some advocate the Soviet style and others the Chinese, but is it not high time we made our own style?

The point is that we should not mechanically follow the Soviet Union's forms and methods, but should learn from its experience in struggle and from the truth of Marxism-Leninism. So, while continuing to learn consistently from the Soviet Union,³⁰ we must put stress not on the form but on the essence of its experience.

In learning from the Soviet Union³¹ there is a marked tendency merely to model ourselves on the external form. If *Pravda* puts out a headline "A Day in Our Country," our *Rodong Sinmun* carries the same title, "A Day in Our Country." Where is the need to follow it so closely? The same holds for clothing. When there is very magnificent Korean clothing for our women, do they have to discard it and put on clothes that don't suit them? There is no need to do this. I suggested to Comrade Pak Chŏng-ae³² that our women dress in Korean clothes as far as possible.

Merely copying the forms used by others instead of learning the truth of Marxism-Leninism does no good, only harm.

Whether in revolutionary struggle or construction, we should thoroughly adhere to Marxist-Leninist principles, applying them in a creative way to suit the specific conditions and national characteristics of our country.

---

[29] Changed in later editions to read "the good things from the Soviet Union and China."
[30] Changed in later editions to read "while learning from the experience of the Soviet Union."
[31] Changed in later editions to read "from the experience of the Soviet Union."
[32] A Central Committee member and the DPRK's most prominent female official, Pak was one of very few Soviet Koreans to stay in the dictator's good graces. Yet later editions dropped the "Comrade," then replaced Pak's name with "Women's League functionaries."

APPENDIX 1

If we ignore our country's history and our people's tradition and mechanically apply foreign experience, paying no heed to our own reality or the degree of our people's [political] awareness, we will commit dogmatic errors and do great harm to the revolutionary cause. Doing this is not being loyal to Marxism-Leninism, nor is being loyal to internationalism; it runs counter to both.

Marxism-Leninism is not a dogma, it is a guide to action and a creative theory.[33] So only when it is applied creatively to suit the specific conditions of each country can it display its indestructible vitality. It's the same with the experience of fraternal parties. It will prove valuable to us only when we study it, grasp its essence and properly apply it to our realities. If we don't do that, and just gulp it down, spoiling our work, it will not only harm our endeavor, but also lead to discrediting that valuable experience of the fraternal parties.

Regarding the problem of establishing the subject, I think it necessary to speak about internationalism and patriotism.

Internationalism and patriotism are inseparably linked with each other. You must realize that Korean communists' love for their country does not conflict with proletarian internationalism, but fully conforms with it. Loving Korea is the same as loving the Soviet Union and the socialist camp and, likewise, loving the Soviet Union and the socialist camp means loving Korea.[34] It's a complete whole. This is because there are no borders in the great cause of the working class, and our revolutionary cause is one part of the international revolutionary cause of the world's working class. The only paramount goal of the working class of all countries is to build a communist society. If there is a difference between them it is only the fact that some countries will do this earlier and others later.

---

[33] Lenin: "'Our theory is not a dogma, but a guide to action,' Marx and Engels always said, rightly ridiculing the mere memorizing and repetition of 'formulae,' that at best are capable only of marking out general tasks, which are necessarily modifiable by the concrete economic and political conditions of each particular period of the historical process." "Letters on Tactics," 8-13 April 1917, MIA.

[34] Softened in English translation to read "Loving Korea is as good as loving the Soviet Union and the socialist camp, and likewise, loving the Soviet Union and the socialist camp is as good as loving Korea." The Korean version was not changed.

It would be wrong to shout "patriotism!" while neglecting internationalist solidarity. For the victory of the Korean revolution, for the great cause of the international working class, we must strengthen our solidarity with the people of the Soviet Union, <u>our liberator and benefactor</u>,[35] and with the peoples of all socialist countries. This is our sacred internationalist duty. The Soviet people, too, are doing all they can to strengthen unity not only with the countries of the socialist camp but also with the working class of the whole world, both for the building of communism in their own country and for the victory of the world revolution.

Patriotism and internationalism are thus inseparable. Someone who does not love his own country cannot be loyal to internationalism, and someone disloyal to internationalism cannot be loyal to his own country and people. A true patriot is an internationalist, and vice versa.

If we cast aside everything good in our country and only copy and memorize things foreign in ideological work, we will certainly bring damage to our revolution, and thereby fail to fulfill our obligations to the international revolutionary cause properly.

In the report to the Second Party Congress, I quoted the following passage from the statement of the commander of the Soviet army, published on the day the army entered our country: "Korean people! ... Happiness is in your hands. ... The Korean people must become creators of their own happiness."[36] This statement is perfectly correct, and if we fail to act accordingly, we may lose the broader public.

Our propaganda workers' formalism also finds expression in exaggeration in propaganda work. For example, such bombastic expressions as "all have risen up," "all have been mobilized," etc, have long been in fashion in speeches and articles.

We advised Pak Ch'ang-ok more than once on this point. He made mistakes because he could not break away from this "all" type of bombast he had created. Later he took a fancy to the superlative of "big," and

---

[35] Omitted from later editions for obvious reasons.
[36] The second party congress was held in March 1948. The Russian quoted: I. M. Chistiakov, commander of the 25th Army of the First Far Eastern Front, which liberated Korea. Lankov, *From Stalin to Kim Il Sung*, 1-2.

APPENDIX 1

carelessly applied the adjective "great" to everything. There's no knowing whether this was due to his ignorance of Chinese characters or to errors in his ideological perspective.

If propaganda work is done not with substance but with such empty exaggeration, it will lead people to be carried away by victory and become complacent. The spurious reports handed in by lower-level cadres also have their origin in this bad practice.

The use of an adjective may seem a simple matter, but its misuse may be the cause of failure in our work. From now on, this should be thoroughly corrected.

Next, I would like to talk about a few other problems which have arisen in ideological work.

To help in the study of the documents of the April [1955] plenum the party's Central Committee has handed down written material on the nature and tasks of our revolution. So I will not make any additional comment on this.

I would just like to emphasize, once again, the road ahead for our revolution. There are two kinds of road ahead. One is the peaceful reunification of our country, and the other is the realization of reunification under the condition that the forces of imperialism are drastically weakened by a big war.

Of course we have been striving with all our might to realize the first prospect.

Our struggle for peaceful reunification comes down to two problems – carrying out construction successfully in the northern half of the country, while directing effective political work towards the southern half. If we strengthen the democratic base by promoting socialist construction in the north and, through effective political work, rouse the masses in the south to rise up in a struggle for liberation, peaceful reunification can be realized.

Political work directed towards the south means strengthening the north's influence on the masses in the south and getting the broader public there to support us. To this end, socialist construction in the north should be carried out successfully. By developing the economy well, the economic base must be strengthened and the people's living standards should be raised, and the entire people united around our party. Then, no matter how desperately Syngman Rhee may try, he will never be able to keep the southern people's fighting spirit from being encouraged by the north's socialist development.

A while ago a man who came over from the south said, "Syngman Rhee's propaganda says that the north has a population of only 3 million, and that nothing's left of Pyongyang but a heap of ashes. But now that I've come here I see that the bridge over the Taedong River has been restored, and Pyongyang is being built into a much more magnificent city than before. Syngman Rhee has been talking nonsense." This is what happens when we carry out construction successfully.

In 1948, when a joint conference of political parties and social organizations from north and south Korea was held,[37] we in the north did not have much to our credit in construction. But apart from Syngman Rhee and Kim Sŏng-su,[38] even the right-wing personalities of south Korea came. The joint conference is of very great significance. Many who came to the north at that time remained here.

This is what Kim Ku[39] said: "I have found north Korea to my liking. I have seen many communists both in Shanghai and in south Korea (if he met any, they must have been those of the Tuesday group or the M-L group),[40] but north Korean communists are different. I thought before that communists were narrow-minded and evil, but coming here and looking around, I have found you are broad-minded and generous people with whom all manner of cooperation is possible. Being old I have no desire for

---

[37] This conference took place in Pyongyang from April 19-23, 1948.

[38] The founder of Korea University and the *Dong-a Ilbo* newspaper, Kim Sŏng-su later became the second vice-president of the ROK (1951-1952).

[39] Later that year Kim Ku, a popular hero of the anti-Japanese resistance, became a candidate for the ROK presidency. In 1949 a rightist assassinated him in Seoul.

[40] The "Tuesday group" or "Tuesday Association," purportedly named after the day Marx was born, was a communist organization founded in 1924, to which both Pak Hŏn-yŏng and the later South Korean presidential candidate Cho Pong-am belonged. The "ML group," a rival organization, formed in 1926. Kim's parenthetical reference to these groups is of course dismissive in tone.

APPENDIX 1

power. If I do not go back to south Korea, Syngman Rhee will certainly claim I have been detained. As for me, I must go and make known the fine things I have seen here, so I have to go back. Do not think I am going to collaborate with the Yankees. When I return again later, I hope you will give me an apple orchard or something, because I want to live out my life in peace in the countryside." Kim Kyu-sik spoke in the same vein.[41] Afterwards, Kim Ku fought against the Yankees.

As everyone knows, Kim Ku was a nationalist. From the beginning he was against both imperialism and communism, and he came to us saying he would try negotiating with the communists. If even Kim Ku, who once regarded communism as his eternal enemy, corrected his way of thinking about our struggle for homeland construction, one can imagine all the more easily what workers, peasants and public figures with a national conscience in south Korea will think if they come and see the northern half of our country.

Before liberation, merely to hear that in the Soviet Union the working class held power and was building socialism made us yearn greatly for that country we had never even visited. How then can the people in the south not admire the socialist construction in the north carried out by people who are of the same stock?

That is why successful construction in the north is more important than anything else.

Thus, when the north's successful socialist construction and its effective south-oriented political work rouses the people in the south to rise up against US imperialism and the Syngman Rhee regime, peaceful reunification can become reality in our country.

This is the internal factor which makes peaceful reunification possible.

External factors conducive to peaceful reunification should also be taken into consideration. If we succeed in maintaining peace for a five to ten year period, China, with her population of more than 600 million, to

---

[41] A former leading member of the colonial-era provisional government based in Shanghai, Kim Kyu-sik was considered a moderate conservative. He is unlikely to have been as impressed by the Soviet zone as Kim Il Sung implies. During the Korean War he was forcibly taken to the north, where he evidently died in late 1950.

say nothing of the Soviet Union, will grow incomparably stronger and the capabilities of the whole socialist camp will be further strengthened.

As the might of the socialist camp grows, the national liberation movement of the people in colonial and dependent countries has been further strengthened, and many countries have won national independence. The peoples of India, Indonesia, Burma and other independent states in Asia and the peoples of the Arab countries are opposing imperialist invasion and struggling for peace.

All this constitutes a severe blow to imperialism, especially US imperialism. As the forces of peace, democracy and socialism grow stronger, the US imperialists will finally be compelled to withdraw from Korea.

Of course, the struggle for the peaceful reunification of our country is an arduous and protracted one. But when we grow stronger and the international forces of peace, democracy and socialism become more powerful, we will be able to achieve peaceful reunification. This is one prospect for the development of the revolution in Korea and for reunification.

The problem of reunification might also be solved by war, not by peaceful means. If the imperialists unleash war on a worldwide scale, we will have no alternative but to fight, and then it would be quite possible for us to defeat the US imperialists in Korea by our own strength. Although it would be rather hard for us to fight against US imperialism single-handed, we should be able to defeat it relatively easily if it is compelled to disperse its forces all over the world. In that case we shall sweep the forces of US imperialism from Korea and achieve the reunification of our country. This is the other prospect for the development of the Korean revolution and for the country's reunification.

But we do not want this prospect. We desire the first prospect, that is, reunification by peaceful means, and we are struggling to achieve it.

No matter which prospect for the country's reunification comes about, the most important thing of all is to strengthen our party and temper the members' party spirit.

In case negotiations start between the north and the south, then the barriers between them are torn down and we go to work among south

APPENDIX 1

Koreans, can our party get away with not being strong? Only if strong can it take advantage of such a favorable state of affairs.

The proportion of our party membership to the population is now one to ten, as we have a million members out of a population of 10 million. This is indeed not a small proportion. But when compared with Korea's entire population of 30 million, one million is by no means a big number.

In south Korea the growth of the party cannot help but be seriously limited by the extremely difficult circumstances in which the underground movement must operate.

After reunification, it will be difficult to carry on our work with a small number of party members, although the number will grow in south Korea too. What is wrong with our training a large number of party members in the northern half from now on and assigning them to work both in the north and south after reunification? Nothing at all. Yet at the time of the fourth plenum of the party's Central Committee, Hŏ Ka-i insisted that the party close its doors, despite its having no more than 600,000 members. The party criticized his view then, and has continued increasing its membership.

The problem now is to educate our one million party members well. Among our members there may be some who are not even at the level of the non-party masses. But even so, these people must not be expelled from the party. They must be kept in and educated; otherwise, if they are expelled, our party might be weakened. This is all the more so since ours is not the only party.

It is our consistent organizational line to constantly train the core of the cells while building up a mass-based party. By the core we mean those party members who know communist truth and can follow the road of revolution without vacillating. It is difficult to arm one million party members overnight with an equal degree of communist consciousness. We must follow the line of first training a core and then gradually raising the political level of all party members.

Our line is to use the core to educate party members. So, since the fourth plenum, the party has put special emphasis on the question of training the core members of the cells. It will be all the more gratifying if their number increases from five today to ten tomorrow so that all party members become part of the core. But it will be good even if only 50 percent of the party membership does so.

The merging of the Communist Party and the New Democratic Party was of great significance in turning our party into a mass political party.[42] As a result of our correct organizational line and energetic struggle to win over the broad mass of the working people, our party has now become a mass political party embracing one million members. This success was by no means easy, but was achieved through a very arduous struggle.

We fight for democratic rights and freedoms in south Korea – freedom of speech, the press, assembly and association – which are prerequisites for the peaceful reunification of the country. We aim at securing conditions for our own free activities in the southern half in return for allowing political parties of south Korea to conduct political activities freely in the northern half.

When free political competition in north and south is thereby brought about, victory or defeat will be decided in accordance with which side wins over more of the people. It is therefore of the greatest importance to strengthen our party and the party spirit of its members.

In order to strengthen the party spirit of our members, we should get all of them to make a constant and deep study of the documents of the Central Committee's fourth and fifth plenums.

Our comrades must not immerse themselves only in economic campaigns, but instead direct more effort to the party's organizational and propaganda work. Party cells must be built up well and party members educated by the cell core. It is particularly necessary to temper the party spirit of those members who hold leading posts – ministers, vice-ministers and bureau directors. Throughout the party, vigorous educational measures should be taken to temper party spirit.

---

[42] The merger in question took place in July 1946. The Workers' Party of North Korea held its founding congress in the following month.

APPENDIX 1

<u>Strong education measures must be implemented across the entire party. We too need to carry out a rectification, like the Chinese party. All rectification means is training in party spirit and education in ideology.</u>[43]

The composition of our party is very complex. All sorts of people have joined it: those who once belonged to the Tuesday group and the M-L group, those who joined the Workers' Party after liberation, and others. Many had in the past been under the factionalists' influence. These people are to be found both among responsible cadres in the central organs and among the members of the party's Central Committee.

Are all of these people worthless? No. Education will make them all useful. But their education must not be conducted in a short-term campaign. Prolonged, patient education and criticism are needed.

We must wage a determined struggle to arm every party member firmly with our party's ideology and eliminate the remnants of bourgeois ideology which persist in the minds of party members and the working people. Our members' party spirit should be thoroughly steeled until their shortcomings have been purged and their ideological illnesses completely remedied.

We were too late in criticizing Pak Ch'ang-ok and Ki Sŏk-pok.[44] If they had been criticized at the time of the party Central Committee's fifth plenum, things would not have come to this pass. Therefore it is especially important to reshape the thinking of those leading cadres who were influenced by Hŏ Ka-i or Pak Il-u and make them firmly establish the Party's ideological system. This kind of work must be done by the party's Department of Organizational Leadership and its Department of Propaganda and Agitation.

The important thing in educating party members is to get them, especially the officials, to establish a mass-oriented perspective. Because this is lacking, bureaucracy continues to manifest itself. This a big shortcoming of our party work.

---

[43] Omitted from later editions for obvious reasons.
[44] Ki, another Soviet Korean, was editor of the party organ *Rodong Sinmun*, thus the target of Kim's criticism (re *Pravda* headlines) earlier in the speech.

If we are to achieve our lofty goal of reuniting the country and building socialism and communism, we must win over the people. We must be clear on how much damage bureaucracy can cause to the revolution.

Keeping an ear on the people's voice and championing their interests is fundamentally different from basing one's work on incorrect opinions floating around in the street. The latter has nothing in common with a revolutionary mass-oriented perspective. By the people we mean the basic people we rely on – the workers and the peasants, and our allies who support and follow us. We have to listen to them accordingly and champion their interests.

Everyone, whether a Party cadre, an administrative worker or a functionary in a social organization, must work consistently in the interests of the revolution and the people.

How was it possible for the anti-Japanese partisans to hold out for such a long time? Why couldn't the Japanese destroy us despite their great military strength? Because the partisans had the correct mass-oriented viewpoint and the people's support. When partisans were wounded and entered a village, the peasants took care of us as though we were their own children, getting hold of the rice they could not afford to eat themselves and cooking it for us. Even the peasants living inside the earth walls of the concentration villages set up by the Japanese imperialists sent food [to us] outside the walls.

The people supported and protected us in this way because we had always defended their interests and fought for them at the risk of our lives. All party members must learn from the partisans' attitude toward the people.

In the days of Japanese imperialist rule everything was imposed upon us by force – compulsory military service, compulsory labor, compulsory delivery of farm produce, etc. We are resolutely opposed to such practices.

A party divorced from the people is like a fish that has left the water.[45] How can a party without a public carry out a revolution? A party divorced

---

[45] Compare to Mao's famous statement (*Aspects of China's Anti-Japanese Struggle*, 1948) that "the people are like water and the army is like fish."

from the people not only cannot bring the revolution to victory, but will eventually find its own existence endangered.

The party issues a program and takes political power also solely for the purpose of protecting the interests of the people. So wouldn't it go against the goals of the party and the revolution to harm the interests of the people?

There can be no disputing that our laws and decisions are good. But they will all come to nothing if our officials harm the interests of the people in the process of implementing them. You comrades must bear this in mind, and strengthen educational work among party members so that they can purge bureaucratist tendencies and acquire a correct mass-oriented viewpoint. If only 50% of all party members acquire this viewpoint, it will mean a complete change of our party.

At the moment quite a few party members are not firmly equipped with the correct viewpoint. It's worse among officials in particular. Whether a party member has the correct mass-oriented viewpoint or not also depends on his party spirit. So tempering party spirit is of decisive importance in this respect too.

Next, it is important to cultivate party members' faith and optimism regarding the road ahead for the revolution. If they lack firm faith in the final victory of our cause and optimism regarding the road ahead, whatever the surrounding circumstances may be, they will not be able to overcome the difficulties inevitably encountered in the course of revolutionary struggle.

To make our party members unyielding fighters who are always optimistic about the future of the revolution, the work of Marxist-Leninist education must be strengthened. Without a clear understanding of the laws of social development and the inevitability of the triumph of socialism and communism, one can neither have faith in victory nor have the lofty spirit and combativeness that remains firm in the most difficult situations.

Let me give you an example of wavering and defection in the revolutionary ranks caused by a lack of knowledge of the laws of social development and of a clear understanding of the trend of developments in a complex situation.

When the defeat of Japanese imperialism was in sight, some people in partisan detachments lost faith and deserted. This was partly because of certain formalistic shortcomings in our propaganda work at the time.

In those days propaganda about the Soviet Union had especially important significance, and <u>we propagandized</u>[46] that, "A big collision will occur between the USSR and the imperialist countries due to fundamental contradictions existing between them, at which time Japanese imperialism will be ruined and our country will be able to gain independence." That was wrong. It was right to propagandize about the contradictions between the socialist state and the imperialist countries, but the truth about these developments was not disseminated. As a result, when a treaty of neutrality was concluded between the Soviet Union and Japan in 1941, and a non-aggression pact between the Soviet Union and Hitler Germany signed, some elements in the partisan ranks lost hope in the future and wavered. Saying that after 10 years with the guerrillas they only saw a dark future, uncertain whether they would have to spend another 10 or 20 years fighting, they left our ranks and ran away, So we explained the revolutionary situation and the truth about the revolution fully to the partisans. After that, there were no more deserters.

There can be no doubt that soon we shall see the great revolutionary event come about. As I have already said, it may occur peacefully or non-peacefully. Whatever form it takes, we must always be prepared to meet it.

To do so the members' party spirit should be steeled. They should be educated to have a correct mass-oriented viewpoint, as well as faith in victory and optimism regarding the road ahead for the revolution.

Another important thing is to carry out the struggle correctly against all anti-party tendencies. Had we not had the experience of fighting the

---

[46] Later changed, with a view to preserving Kim's reputation for infallibility, to read "among partisans it was propagandized."

APPENDIX 1

Minsaengdan in Kando in the past,[47] we would not have been able correctly to lead the struggle against the counter-revolutionaries in Korea after liberation, especially during the war.

The Japs set up a counter-revolutionary espionage organization called Minsaengdan and infiltrated its agents into the revolutionary districts of Kando. In this way they schemed to drive a wedge between Koreans and Chinese and turn Koreans against each other. Ensnared for a time in the enemy's scheme, people in the revolutionary camp killed one another, with the result that many lives were sacrificed to no clear purpose.

This became an important experience when dealing with the case of the Pak Hŏn-yŏng clique. We strongly established the principle of drawing a sharp distinction between spies and non-spies.[48] We emphasized this many times in the Political Committee. Had we made a mistake, we would have played into the hands of the Yankees, and made many people unable to be used.

Of course the struggle must be relentless. Otherwise there may be some spies who slip away and escape. But the struggle must always be carried on as an ideological one.

Just because someone was influenced by Pak Hŏn-yŏng does not make him a member of the Pak Hŏn-yŏng clique, nor does it make him a spy. But in these people's minds his ideological influence still remains. This must be fought against.

The experience acquired in the struggle against the Pak Hŏn-yŏng clique and in the counter-espionage struggle should be made thoroughly known to party members, so that they know how to wage a relentless struggle against spies, and how to correctly distinguish spies. If this is not done, and instead everybody is suspected, in the end one ends up not trusting one's own shadow.

---

[47] The Minsaengdan was a pro-Japanese, anti-communist organization founded by Korean settlers in the Kando region of Manchuria in 1932. The Chinese communist party went on to purge many of the Koreans in its own ranks under suspicion that they were secret Minsaengdan members. Kim Il Sung was detained but soon exonerated.

[48] Needless to say, this is untrue, as none of the arrested and executed members of the "clique," least of all the poet Yim Hwa, was really conducting espionage for the enemy.

To corrode our ranks from within, the enemies always scheme to make people distrust one another and set them at odds. You must learn to discern sharply such plots and slanders concocted by the counter-revolutionaries, and know how to fight against them. Party members should be trained to be able to spot spies, as well as to be able to spot waverers, nepotists, parochialists and factionalists.

Such a struggle can be conducted properly only when party officials and all party members have a high political level. Without attaining a high level of Marxist-Leninist knowledge, party members cannot properly carry out such a difficult task. To enable them to fight skillfully against the counter-revolutionaries, it is necessary to strengthen their Marxist-Leninist education and, at the same time, acquaint them with our experience in the struggle against counter-revolution.

Next, propaganda and agitation must be stepped up among the broad masses. Education of the people in socialist ideology should be the main content of our agitprop work. The most important thing here is to make the workers and peasants, especially the workers, clearly aware that they are masters of political power. When they are highly conscious of this fact, the workers will act as masters in everything – loving their places of work, machinery and equipment, working hard, maintaining discipline well and effectively fighting against counter-revolutionary elements.

The same is true of the peasants. If they realize that the working class is not only their ally but also their leader, and that they too are masters of political power, they will work their land well, take good care of their implements and willingly pay the tax in kind.

Everyone shows enthusiasm when he realizes that he is the master. When we were engaged in revolutionary activities in the past, who would have done it only on the condition that he were paid? We fought without sleep and forgot our hunger because we were aware that by making revolution we could not only forge our own destiny but save our homeland. The workers will likewise put all their strength and passion into their work when they are clearly aware that their labor is for their own happiness and for the prosperity of society.

APPENDIX 1

Prolonged, persistent education is needed to get all the working people to attain to this kind of awareness. We must patiently educate the people and unite them more closely around the party.

Finally, I want to express a few opinions about our newspapers. They still do not thoroughly discharge their duties.

The central task of the *Rodong Sinmun*, our party organ, is to educate party members through day-to-day explanation of the party's lines and policies and their fighting tasks, while the central task of the *Minju Chosŏn*[49] is to mobilize the people to put state policies into effect by fully explaining the laws and regulations of the people's government and the policies of the state. The papers of the General Federation of Trade Unions, the Democratic Youth League, and other organizations should likewise be edited in accordance with their respective nature and tasks.

Whether it's because our newspapers all receive material from the Korean Central News Agency or because some of them have few pages, they have no specific character, which is a big failing.

Here, too, a lot of formalism and dogmatism finds expression. I think there must be a serious investigation of this.

Today I have spoken about some problems in our party's ideological work. I hope you comrades will take them into consideration, eliminate the shortcomings that have become apparent so far, and strive to raise our party's ideological work to a higher level.

---

[49] Ostensibly the state counterpart to the party newspaper *Rodong Sinmun*, *Minju Chosŏn* is the organ of the DPRK's cabinet.

APPENDIX 2

"SUBJECT THOUGHT" (ENCYCLOPEDIA ENTRY, "*CHUCH'E SASANG*," 2001)

[*This is my translation of the entry for* chuch'e sasang *in 19:342-343 of the encyclopedia* Chosŏn taebaekkwa sajŏn, *published in Pyongyang in 2001. The almost complete lack of paragraphing has been preserved, as has the use of bold print. — BRM*]

A MAIN CONSTITUENT ELEMENT that comprises the essence of the Great Leader Comrade Kim Il Sung's revolutionary ideology. It forms the theoretical and methodological foundation of the Great Leader Comrade Kim Il Sung's revolutionary ideology. Subject Thought, which was conceived by the Great Leader Comrade Kim Il Sung and has been constantly deepened and developed by the Great Ruler Comrade Kim Jong Il, is the working class's most scientific and revolutionary body of thought.
The Great Ruler Comrade Kim Jong Il spoke as follows:
"Subject Thought is an original body of thought that not only reveals new philosophical and socio-historical principles but also reveals the leading principles of revolution and construction."
Subject Thought is a constituent element of the philosophical principles and socio-historical principles of the subject as well as of the leading principles of revolution and construction. Subject Thought is an important constituent element of the philosophical principles. Of the philosophical principles inside Subject Thought, the representative one is the principle that reveals the fundamental nature of man's position and role in the world. Of Subject Thought's philosophical principles, the one occupying the most important place is the principle revealing man's position and role in the world, namely, the principle that man is the master of all things and

decides all things. This philosophical principle is a basic principle that provides the answer to Subject Philosophy's fundamental question regarding man's position and role in the world, and therefore forms the basis of all other philosophical principles while representing the whole of Juche's philosophical foundation. The statement that man is the master of all things means that man is master of the world and his fate. In other words, man is not subordinate to the external world that surrounds him, but is instead the only being who subordinates and dominates nature and society according to his own intentions and demands. Thus is revealed the position man occupies in the world. The statement that man occupies the position of master in the world does not mean that he actually dominates everything in the infinite world. Its true meaning is the principle that the external world does not dominate man, but rather, man is the master of all things, a being who dominates all of nature and society, The statement that man decides all things means that man plays a decisive role in reshaping the world and developing his own fate. In other words, it means that man is the only being who reshapes and develops the world. This revealed the role that man plays in reshaping and developing the world. By no means does the statement that man decides everything mean that all changes and developments in the world are effected by man. The true meaning is the principle that the decisive role played in the reshaping and reforming of the world are not the objective conditions but rather the activity of man, who thus decides all things. Another thing that occupies an important place in Subject Thought's philosophical principles is the principle that exposes man's fundamental characteristics. The philosophical principles of Subject Thought not only expose the fundamental principles of a man-centered philosophical worldview, but also offer an original elucidation of man's fundamental characteristics, establishing a perfect philosophical understanding of man as a social being in possession of autonomy, creativity and consciousness. Autonomy is social man's attribute of seeking to live and develop autonomously as the master of world and his fate; creativity is social man's attribute of reshaping the world and exploiting his destiny with a sense of purpose; and consciousness is social

APPENDIX 2

man's attribute of regulating all activity aimed at grasping and changing himself and the world. By possessing the fundamental characteristics of autonomy, creativity and consciousness, man becomes the world's strongest and most precious being, and the world's only lord and remodeler. Through the philosophical principles of Subject Thought, man's nature was explained perfectly in a scientific fashion, man's position and role as the world's only lord and remodeler was established, and man's dignity and value ascended to the highest stage. Joining into one monolithic system, the philosophical principles of Subject Thought illuminate views, aspects and standpoints in regard to the world and tie them closely together, thereby placing man in the center of all philosophical inquiry about the world, and forming a man-centered philosophical system: the philosophical worldview of the subject. From the philosophical principles of Subject Thought derive all other constituent elements of Subject Thought, as well as the methodological foundation by which they are to be understood. Socio-historical principles are an important part of Subject Thought. Of the socio-historical principles of Subject Thought, the principle with the most basic significance is the principle that the masses are the subject of social history; but there are many other principles illuminating society's nature, characteristics and structure, as well as the legitimacy of social development, such as the principle that the social movement is an autonomous, creative and conscious movement of the masses; and the principle that the masses' autonomous ideological consciousness plays a decisive role in revolutionary struggle. The principle that the masses are the subject of history, which forms the basis of Subject Thought's socio-historical principles, enables a perfect understanding of the subject and dynamic of history. Unlike the dynamic of nature, the socio-historical dynamic has a subject; it is generated and develops in accordance with the leading role and effects of that subject. That which propels the social dynamic forward are the masses, and it is by the masses that all of society is created, and history developed; the masses' creative power is the prime force in all social development. In its essence the social dynamic is an autonomous dynamic by which its subject, the masses, seek to fulfill their autonomy in accordance with socio-historical principles, such as the principle that the social dynamic is the masses' autonomous, creative and conscious dynamic; and the social dynamic proceeds through the struggle to reshape man, nature and society, in accordance with the autonomous, ideological-conscious and creative capabilities of people; it is a rational process by which social resources increase and social relationships are reformed, a process that elevates the position and role of the masses. Overcoming the limitations of the materialist view, which looks at the process of social development as a natural-historical process, the legitimacy of social development is perfectly illuminated: social development takes place in accordance with the leading role and effects of its subject, and thus in accordance with the autonomous ideological consciousness and creative capabilities of the masses that comprise that subject; and through the three main reforming tasks that constitute its main domain. Due to the comprehensive exposure, in accordance with Subject Thought's socio-historical principles, of society, the socio-historical dynamic, the rationality of socio-historical development, and views and standpoints in regard to historical development and social revolution, the socio-historical view of the working class underwent a fundamental shift from a material and economic-centered socio-historical view to a socio-historical view centered on man and the masses, thus bringing its development to its highest stage. Together with the philosophical principles and socio-historical principles of the subject, Subject Thought is an important constituent element of the leading principles that must be adhered to in revolution and construction. Among the leading principles of Subject Thought are principles pertaining to the adherence to an autonomous standpoint, the implementation of creative methods, and the use of ideology as a foundation. The principle of adherence to an autonomous standpoint, being a principle for the fulfillment of man's autonomy in all areas of party and national activity, of revolution and construction, is a fundamental guiding principle according to which the masses guard the standpoint of a master of revolution and construction. This includes the principles of subjectivity in ideology, autonomy in politics, independence in economic affairs, and

APPENDIX 2

self-defense in national defense. Ideologically and politically, as well as materially and militarily, the principles of subjectivity, autonomy, independence and self-defense firmly safeguard the masses' position, enabling the realization of the masses' autonomy in all areas of social life, and enabling social struggle and the work of construction to proceed down the straight and right path toward victory, and therefore comprise the most scientific and revolutionary leading guideline. The principle of implementing a creative method calls primarily for methods that depend on the masses, and methods that adjust to the actual circumstances. Methods that depend on the masses and methods that adjust to the actual circumstances are the most scientific and revolutionary methods, for they highly cultivate the masses' revolutionary fervor and creative positivity, endlessly elevate their role as master, and spur them on to acquit the revolutionary struggle and work of construction with exceptional speed. The principle of using ideology as a foundation is a principle aimed at realizing consciousness in all areas of party and state activity, in revolution and construction. This principle is a principle that ascribes decisive importance to ideological elements of revolution and construction while solving all problems through elevating the role of people's ideological consciousness. The basic content of the principle of proceeding from an ideological foundation pertains to the placing of ideological re-shaping work and political re-shaping work at the start of all work. Subject Thought focused all worldview problems on man, thereby raising them anew while solving them perfectly, and thus brought about a fundamental change in the development of mankind's philosophical worldview. Subject Thought contains incomparably deep, abundant, new and original ideological and theoretical content, unfolded and systematized with man at its center, thereby becoming the most scientific and revolutionary worldview, equally representative of previous historical ages, our own time, and the communist future. Used in its broad sense, Subject Thought encompasses all of the Great Leader Kim Il Sung's revolutionary thought, the ideology, theory and methods of the subject.

REFERENCES

SOURCES IN KOREAN (DPRK)

"1952-nyŏn tang chung'ang wiwŏnhoe che 5 ch'a chŏnwonhoe ŭi ryŏksajŏk ŭiŭi"[The historical significance of the Party Central Committee's fifth joint plenum in 1952]. *Rodong Sinmun,* 19 December 1962.

"Chakka tongmaeng esŏ" [From the Writers' League]. *Chosŏn Munhak,* February 1956, 214-218.

Chang U-jong. "Tang haksŭp esŏ hyŏngsikchuŭi wa kyojojuŭi rŭl kŭnjŏl haja" [Let us eliminate formalism and dogmatism in Party instruction]. *Rodong Sinmun,* 29 January 1956.

"Chapchi <Ryŏksa kwahak> ŭi chil ŭl tŏuk nop'ija" [Let us raise the quality of the magazine *The Science of History*]. *Kŭlloja,* 15 February 1960, 57-64.

Ch'oe Ch'ŏl-ung. "Chuch'e sasang ŭn hyŏngmyŏng kwa kŏnsŏl ŭi chuin ŭn inmin taejung'imyŏ kŭ kŏs ŭl ch'udong hanŭn him to inmin taejung ege ittanŭn sasang" [Subject Thought is the body of thought that says the masters of revolution and construction are the masses, and that they are the driving force behind them as well]. *Ch'ŏllima,* June 1974, 13-15.

Ch'oe Yŏng-nim. "Uri sik ŭi tokt'ŭk han sahoejuŭi rŭl pit'naeyŏ naganŭn tang" [The great Party giving luster to our style of special socialism]. *Kŭlloja,* February 1991, 17-22.

Chŏngch'i sajŏn [Political dictionary]. Sahoe kwahak ch'ulp'ansa. Pyongyang, 1973.

"Chŏngdang ŭi chuch'esasanghwa nŭn hyŏngmyŏngjŏk tang kŏnsŏl ŭi kangnyŏngjŏk chich'im" [A party's permeation in Subject-Thought is the essential guide to the construction of a revolutionary party]. *Ch'ŏllima*, August 1994, 77-82.

Ch'ŏrhak sajŏn [Philosophical dictionary]. Sahoe kwahak ch'ulp'ansa. Pyongyang, 1957.

Ch'ŏrhak sajŏn [Philosophical dictionary]. Sahoe kwahak ch'ulp'ansa. Pyongyang, 1970.

"Chosŏn minjujuŭi inmin konghwaguk sahoejuŭi hŏnbŏp" [Socialist constitution of the Democratic People's Republic of Korea]. *Kŭlloja*, January 1973, 29-42.

Chosŏn munhakt'ongsa [History of Korean literature]. Kwahagwŏn ch'ulp'ansa. Pyongyang, 1959.

Chosŏn'ŏ sosajŏn [A small dictionary of the Korean language]. Chosŏn rodongdang ch'ulp'ansa. Pyongyang, 1956.

Chosŏn rodongdang che 4 ch'a taehoe chuyo munhŏnjip [Documents of the Fourth Party Congress of the Workers' Party of Korea]. Chosŏn rodongdang ch'ulp'ansa. Pyongyang, 1961.

"Chosŏn rodongdang chungang wiwŏnhoe saŏp ch'onggyŏl pogo e taehan Chosŏn rodongdang che-3 ch'a taehoe ŭi kyŏljŏngsŏ" [Resolution of the Korean Workers' Party's 3rd Congress in regard to the final report of the Korean Workers' Party's Central Committee]. In *Chosŏn chungang nyŏn'gam*. Chosŏn chungang t'ongsinsa. Pyongyang, 1957. 7-17.

"Chuch'e ch'ŏrhak ŭn hyŏngmyŏng kwa kŏnsŏl e kwanhan kwahakchŏgin haksŏl" [Subject Philosophy is a scientific doctrine regarding revolution and construction]. *Chosŏn Munhak*, December 1972, 5-7.

Chuch'e sasang ŭi widaehan sŭngni [The great victory of Subject Thought]. In 3 volumes. Chosŏn rodongdang ch'ulp'ansa. Pyongyang, 1981-1982.

"Chuch'e sasang ŭl ch'ŏljŏhi kuhyŏn hanŭn kŏs ŭn uri hyŏngmyŏng sŭngni ŭi hwakko han tambo" [Thoroughly embodying Subject Thought is the firm guarantor of the victory of our revolution]. *Rodong Sinmun*, 28 December 1967.

REFERENCES

"Chuch'e ŭi hyŏngmyŏnggwan ŭn suryŏnggwan, chojikkwan, kunjunggwan, todŏkkwan ŭro iruŏjin chŏn'iljŏgin hyŏngmyŏnggwan" [The subject's view of revolution is an integral one made of a view of the leader, of organization, of the masses and of morality]. *Kŭlloja*, November 1988, 23-28.

"Chuch'e wa ch'ŏllima sasang manse" [Long live Subject and Ch'ŏllima Thought]. *Rodong Sinmun*, 13 September 1968.

"Ch'ullo nŭn minjok ŭi chaju t'ong'il e itta" [The way out lies in the nation's autonomous unification]. *Kŭlloja*, 20 April 1963, 10-18.

Erŭman Elleiruarŭ. "Chuch'e, i nŭn hyŏngmyŏng ŭi kich'i" [Juche, this is the banner of revolution]. *Chosŏn Munhak*, April 1971, 58.

Han Sŏrya. "Yŏn-am Pak Chi-wŏn ŭi saengae wa hwaldong" [The career and activity of Pak Yŏn-am]. *Chosŏn Munhak*, January 1956, 137-156.

Han Yun-ho. "Kagarin sojwa ege" [To Major Gagarin]. *Munhak Sinmun*, 14 April 1961.

Hang'il ppaltchisan ch'amgajadŭl ŭi chŏnt'u hoesanggi 1 [Battle reminiscences of participants in the anti-Japanese partisan struggle]. Chosŏn inmin'gun ch'ulp'ansa. Tokyo, 1963.

Hong Sŏn-bong *et al. Uri tang ŭi chuch'e sasang kwa sahoejuŭijŏk aegukchuŭi* [Our party's subject(ive) thought and socialist patriotism]. Chosŏn rodongdang ch'ulp'ansa. Pyongyang, 1966.

Hyŏndae chosŏnmal sajŏn [Modern dictionary of the Korean language]. Sahoe kwahagwŏn ch'ulp'ansa. Pyongyang, 1968.

"Hyŏngmyŏng chŏnt'ong kyoyang ŭl tŏuk simhwa haja" [Let us further deepen education about the revolutionary tradition]. *Kŭlloja*, 20 January 1965, 2-14.

Kang Hyŏn-se. "Suryŏngnim ŭi hyongmyŏng sasang ŭl simjang e saegimyŏ" [Engraving the Leader's revolutionary thought in the heart]. *Chosŏn Munhak*, January 1970, 26-27.

Ki Sŏk-pok. "Renin, Ssŭttallin ŭi kyosi nŭn uri rŭl sŭngni ero komu handa" [The teachings of Lenin and Stalin incite us onward to victory]. *Cho-Sso Ch'insŏn* [Korean-Soviet friendship], April 1953, 2-6.

"Kim Ch'ang-man tongji ŭi t'oron" [Remarks by Comrade Kim Ch'ang-man]. In *Chosŏn nodongdang taehoe charyojip* 2. Kukt'o t'ongirwŏn. Seoul [sic], 1980. 181-197.

Kim Chin-t'aek. "'Chuch'e' e taehan olbarŭn rihae rŭl wihayŏ" [For a proper understanding of 'the subject']. *Rodong Sinmun*, 21 July 1956.

Kim Chŏng-il chidoja [Kim Jong Il, leader]. Tongbangsa. Tokyo, 1984.

Kim Chŏng-ja. "Kim Il-sŏng tongji ŭi chuch'e sasang ŭn maksŭ–reninjuŭi paltchŏn e kiyŏhan sasang'imyŏ chegukchuŭi wa sin'gu singminjuŭi rŭl pandaehanŭn t'ujaeng ŭi sŭngni rŭl tambo hanŭn widaehan sasang" [Comrade Kim Il Sung's Subject Thought is thought that has developed and contributed to Marxism-Leninism, and great thought that guarantees victory in the struggle against imperialism and new and old forms of colonialism]. *Kŭlloja*, April 1970, 4-7.

Kim Hyŏn-hwan. *Na wa chuch'e sasang kwa ŭi taehwa: chirŭi ŭngdap ŭl t'onghae arabon chuch'e sasang ŭi olbarŭn ihae* [My conversation with Subject Thought: Understanding Subject Thought correctly through a question and answer approach]. Chaju ch'ŏrhak hakhoe. Pyongyang, 1998.

Kim Hyŏn-suk. *Pulmyŏl ŭi chuch'e sasang* [Immortal Subject Thought]. Sahoe kwahak ch'ulp'ansa. Pyongyang, 1985.

Kim Il Sung (Kim Il-sŏng). "Cho-Jung ryangguk inmin ŭi chŏnt'ujŏk uŭi: Chunghwa inmin konghwaguk ch'anggŏn 10 chunyŏn e che hayŏ chipp'ilhan nonsŏl: 1959-nyŏn 9-wŏl 26-il, <Inmin ilbo>e balpyo" [The comradeship-in-arms of the Korean and Chinese masses: Essay written to mark the 10th anniversary of the establishment of the People's Republic of China: Announcement in the *Renmin ribao* on September 26, 1959]. In *Kim Il-sŏng sŏnjip* 4. Chosŏn rodongdang ch'ulp'ansa. Pyongyang, 1960. 441-442.

———. "Chŏnch'e chakka yesulgadŭl ege: 1951-nyŏn 6-wŏl 30-il chunggyŏn chakkadŭl kwa ŭi chŏpkyŏn sŏksang esŏ ŭi tamhwa" [To all writers and artists: Remarks made on the occasion of a reception with leading writers on 30 June 1951]. In *Kim Il-sŏng sŏnjip* 3. Chosŏn rodongdang ch'ulp'ansa. Pyongyang, 1953. 287-302.

REFERENCES

_____. *Chosŏn hyŏngmyŏng ŭi chillo: K'aryun esŏ chinhaeng toen kongch'ŏng mit' panje ch'ŏngnyŏn tongmaeng chido kanbu hoeŭi esŏ han pogo 1930-nyŏn 6-wŏl 30-il* [The Way Ahead for the Korean Revolution: Report to the meeting in Kalun of the leading members of the Young Communist League and the Anti-Imperialist Youth League, 30 June 1930]. Rodongdang ch'ulp'ansa. Pyongyang, 1978.

_____. "Chosŏn minjujuŭi inmin konghwaguk ch'anggŏn 10-chunyŏn ki'nyŏm kyŏngch'uk taehoe esŏ han pogo" [Report made at the commemorative meeting in honor of the 10th anniversary of the founding of the Democratic People's Republic of Korea]. *Kŭlloja*, 15 September 1958, 3-23.

_____. "Chosŏn minjujuŭi inmin konghwaguk esŏ ŭi kŏnsŏl kwa nam Chosŏn hyŏngmyŏng e taehayŏ" [On construction in the Democratic People's Republic of Korea and the revolution in south Korea]. *Kŭlloja*, 20 April 1965, 2-31.

_____. "Chosŏn rodongdang ch'anggŏn 20-chunyŏn e chehayŏ: kyŏngch'uk taehoe esŏ han Chosŏn rodongdang chungang wiwŏnhoe wiwŏnjang Kim Il-sŏng tongji ŭi pogo" [On the occasion of the 20th anniversary of the founding of the Workers' Party of Korea: Report made by Comrade Kim Il Sung, chairman of the Central Committee of the Workers' Party of Korea, at the commemorative conference]. *Kŭlloja*, 20 October 1965, 2-24.

_____. "Chosŏn rodongdang che 3-ch'a taehoe esŏ han chungang wiwŏnhoe saŏp ch'onggyŏl pogo: 1956-nyŏn 4-wŏl 23-il" [Concluding report on the Central Committee's activities made at the Korean Workers' Party's 3rd congress, 23 April 1956]. In *Kim Il-sŏng sŏnjip* 4. Chosŏn rodongdang ch'ulp'ansa. Pyongyang, 1960. 433-571.

_____. "Chosŏn rodongdang che 5-ch'a taehoe esŏ han chungang wiwŏnhoe saŏp ch'onghwa pogo" [Summing-up report at the fifth congress of the Korean Workers' Party on the work of the Central Committee, 1971-nyŏn 11-wŏl 2-il]. In *Kim Il-sŏng chŏjak sŏnjip* 5. Chosŏn rodongdang ch'ulp'ansa. Pyongyang, 1972. 416-529.

_____. "Chosŏn rodongdang che 6-ch'a taehoe esŏ han chungang wiwŏnhoe ch'onghwa pogo" [Comprehensive report of the Central Committee given at the sixth congress of the Workers' Party of Korea]. In *Kim Il-sŏng chŏjakchip* 35. Chosŏn rodongdang ch'ulp'ansa. Pyongyang, 1987. 290-387.

_____. "Chosŏn rodongdang chungang wiwŏnhoe che 5-ch'a chŏnwŏn hoeŭi esŏ chinsul han pogo" [Report at the fifth plenum of the Central Committee of the Korean Workers Party]. In *Chosŏn chungang nyŏn'gam*. Chosŏn chung'ang t'ongsinsa. Pyongyang, 1953. 55-71.

_____. *Chuch'e sasang e taehayŏ* [On Subject Thought]. Chosŏn rodongdang ch'ulp'ansa. Pyongyang, 1977.

_____. "Kangsŏgun tang saŏp chido esŏ ŏdŭn kyohun e taehayŏ: Chosŏn rodongdang chungang wiwŏnhoe sangmu wiwŏnhoe hwaktae hoeŭi esŏ han yŏnsŏl, 1960-nyŏn 2-wŏl 23-il" [On lessons learned from leading Kangsŏ County party work: Speech made at an extended conference of the Standing Committee of the Korean Workers' Party's Central Committee, 23 February 1960]. In *Kim Il-sŏng chŏjak sŏnjip* 2. Chosŏn rodongdang ch'ulp'ansa. Pyongyang, 1968. 505-542.

_____. "Munhwaindŭl ŭn munhwa chŏnsŏn ŭi t'usa ro toeŏya handa: Puk Chosŏn kak to inmin wiwŏnhoe, chŏngdang, sahoe tanch'e sŏnjŏnwŏn, munhwain, yesurin taehoe esŏ han yŏnsŏl 1946-nyŏn 5-wŏl 24-il" [Cultural workers must become fighters on the cultural front: Speech given at a conference of artists, cultural workers and propagandists from each province, people's committee, party and social group in North Korea, 24 May 1946]. In *Kim Il-sŏng sŏnjip* 4. Chosŏn rodongdang ch'ulp'ansa. Pyongyang, 1960. 96-101.

_____. "Osŭt'ŭrallia kijadŭl i chegi han chilmun e taehan taedap (1974-nyŏn 11-wŏl 4-il)" [Answers to questions raised by Australian journalists (4 November 1974)]. In *Chuch'e sasang e taehayŏ*. Chosŏn rodongdang ch'ulp'ansa. Pyongyang, 1977. 564-567.

_____. "Renin ŭi haksŏl ŭn uri ŭi chich'im ida: Renin t'ansaeng 85-chunyŏn e chehayŏ chipp'ilhan ronsŏl 1955-nyŏn 4-wŏl 15-il pu <kyŏnggohan p'yŏnghwa rŭl wihayŏ inmin minjujuŭi rŭl wihayŏ> e

REFERENCES

balp'yo." [Lenin's theory is our guide: Essay written for the 85th anniversary of Lenin's birth, made public on April 15, 1955 in "For a lasting peace and for people's democracy"]. In *Kim Il-sŏng sŏnjip* 4. Chosŏn rodongdang ch'ulp'ansa. Pyongyang, 1960. 287-299.

_____. "Sae minjujuŭi kukka kŏnsŏl ŭl wihan uri ŭi kwaŏp: p'yŏng'an namdo inmin chŏngch'i wiwŏnhoe esŏ bep'un hwanyŏngyŏn esŏ han yŏnsŏl 1945-nyŏn 10-wŏl 18-il" [Our task for the construction of a new democratic state: Speech given at the South Pyong'an Province Committee's welcome banquet, 18 October 1945]. *Kim Il-sŏng sŏnjip* 4. Chosŏn rodongdang ch'ulp'ansa. Pyongyang, 1960. 11-14.

_____. "Sahoejuŭi hyŏngmyŏng ŭi hyŏn tangye e issŏsŏ tang mit' kukka saŏp ŭi myŏt kaji munje dŭl e taehayŏ: Chosŏn rodongdang chungang wiwŏnhoe chŏnwŏn hoeŭi esŏ han kyŏllon, 1955-nyŏn 4-wŏl 4-il" [On a few problems of party and state work at the current stage of the socialist revolution: Conclusion presented at a plenum of the Korean Workers' Party Central Committee, 4 April 1955]. In *Kim Il-sŏng chŏjak sŏnjip* 1. Chosŏn rodongdang ch'ulp'ansa. Pyongyang, 1960. 532-559.

_____. "Sasang saŏp esŏ kyojojuŭi wa hyŏngsikchuŭi rŭl toech'i hago chuch'e rŭl hwangnip halde taehayŏ" [On Eliminating Dogmatism and Formalism and Establishing the Subject in Ideological Work]. In *Kim Il-sŏng sŏnjip* 4. Pyongyang, 1960. 325-354. Reference was also made to the slightly different yet identically-titled version in *Kim Il-sŏng sŏnjip* 9. Chosŏn rodongdang ch'ulp'ansa. Pyongyang, 1980. 467-495.

_____. *Segi wa tŏburŏ* [With the century]. In 8 volumes. Chosŏn rodongdang ch'ulp'ansa. Pyongyang, 1992-1998.

_____. "Ssoryŏn inmin kwa ŭi ch'insŏn kwa ryŏndaesŏng ŭn uri ŭi sŭngni ŭi hwakkohan tambo ida" [Friendship and connectedness with the Soviet masses is the firm guarantor of our victory]. *Kŭlloja*, 15 April 1959, 30-33.

_____. "Tang saŏp pangbŏp e taehayŏ: saengsan kiŏpso tang chojikwŏn mit' tang wiwŏnjangdŭl, to, si, kun dang wiwŏnjangdŭl ŭi kangsŭphoe esŏ han yŏnsŏl, 1959-nyŏn 2-wŏl 26-il" [On methods of Party work:

Speech given at a study meeting of provincial, municipal and county Party chairmen and Party organizers and chairmen at places of production, 26 February 1959]. In *Chŏsŏn chung'ang nyŏn'gam*. Chosŏn chung'ang t'ongsinsa. Pyongyang, 1960. 30-39.

_____. "Tangsaŏp ŭl kaesŏn hamyŏ tang taep'yojahoe kyŏljŏng ŭl kwanch'al halde taehayŏ: To, si, kun mit' kongjang tang ch'aegim pisŏ hyŏpŭihoe esŏ han yŏnsŏl, 1967-nyŏn 3-wŏl 17-24-il" [On improving Party work and implementing the decisions of the Party conference: Speech at a conference of provincial, municipal, county and factory Party secretaries, 17-24 March 1967]. In *Kim Il-sŏng chŏjakchip* 21. Chosŏn rodongdang ch'ulp'ansa. Pyongyang, 1983. 135-257.

_____. "Tangwŏndŭl sok esŏ kyegŭp kyoyang saŏp ŭl tŏuk kanghwa halte taehayŏ, 1955-nyŏn 4-wŏl 1-il" [On further strengthening class education among cadres, 1 April 1955]. In *Kim Il-sŏng chŏjak sŏnjip* 1. Choson rodongdang ch'ulp'ansa. Pyongyang, 1967. 497-517.

_____. "Uri tang ŭi chuch'e sasang kwa konghwaguk chŏngbu ŭi taenaewoe chŏngchaek ŭi myŏt' kaji munje e taehayŏ" [On our party's Subject Thought and a few issues in the domestic and foreign policy of the government of the republic]. *Kŭlloja*, October 1972, 2-18.

_____. "Widaehan ssobet'ŭ kundae e ŭihan 8.15 haebang 10-chu'nyŏn kyŏngch'uk taehoe esŏ han pogo, 1955-nyŏn 8-wŏl 14-il" [Report given at the conference held to commemorate the tenth anniversary of liberation by the great Soviet Army]. In *Kim Il-sŏng sŏnjip* 4. Chosŏn rodongdang ch'ulp'ansa. Pyongyang, 1960. 300-324.

"Kimilsŏng-kimjŏngiljuŭi nŭn Chosŏn hyŏngmyŏng ŭi yŏngwŏnhan paeksŭng ŭi kich'i" [Kimilsung-Kimjongilism is the eternal banner of our Korean revolution's invincibility]. Korean Central News Agency, 15 May 2012.

"Kim Il-sŏng tongji rŭl pirot han tang kwa chŏngbu chidojadŭl i chaeil tongp'o'dŭl i mandŭn ch'ŏnyŏnsaek changp'yŏn kirok yŏnghwa <choguk ŭi haepit' arae> rŭl posiyŏtta" [Comrade Kim Il Sung and other party and government leaders saw the color documentary film,

Under the Homeland's Sunshine, which had been made by Koreans in Japan]. *Rodong Sinmun*, 23 March 1967.

"Kim Il-sŏng ŭi ronmun <Panje panmi t'ujaeng ŭl kanghwa haja> nŭn segye ŭi ssaunŭn hyŏngmyŏnggadŭl ege nŭn muhan han yonggi-wa sinsim ŭl an'gyŏjunŭn kyogwasŏ ro toemyŏ wŏnssudŭrin chegukchuŭijadŭl egenŭn pokt'an ŭro toenda" [Kim Il Sung's thesis 'Let us strengthen the anti-American, anti-imperialist struggle' is becoming a textbook that instills unlimited courage and conviction in the world's fighting revolutionaries, and becoming a bomb for the imperialist enemy]. *Rodong Sinmun*, 10 December 1967.

Kim Jong Il (Kim Chŏng-il). "Chuch'e ch'ŏrhak ŭi rihae esŏ chegi toenŭn myŏt' kaji munje e taehayŏ: tang riron sŏnjŏn il'gun'dŭl kwa han tamhwa: 1974-nyŏn 4-wŏl 2-il" [On a few problems in understanding Juche Philosophy: A talk with party theoretical propaganda workers, April 2, 1974]. *Kŭlloja*, 1 April 1984, 2-6.

———. "Chuch'e ch'ŏrhak ŭn tokch'angjŏgin hyŏngmyŏng ch'ŏrhagida: Chosŏn rodongdang chungangwiwŏnhoe riron chapchi <Kŭlloja> e chun tamha, 1996-nyŏn 7-wŏl 26-il" [Subject Philosophy is an original revolutionary philosophy: Talk given to *Kŭlloja*, the theoretical journal of the Korean Workers' Party Central Committee]. In *Kim Chŏng-il sŏnjip* 14. Chosŏn rodongdang ch'ulp'ansa. Pyongyang, 2000. 189-202.

———. *Chuch'e sasang e taehayŏ: Widaehan suryŏng Kim Il-sŏng tongji t'ansaeng 70 tol ki'nyŏm chŏnguk chuch'e sasang t'oronhoe e ponaen ronmun 1982-nyŏn 3-wŏl 31-il* [On Subject Thought: Treatise sent to the National Subject Thought Discussion Meeting in honor of the 70th birthday of the Great Leader, Comrade Kim Il Sung, March 31, 1982]. Chosŏn rodongdang ch'ulp'ansa. Pyongyang, 1982.

———. "Chuch'e sasang kyoyang esŏ chegi toenŭn myŏt' kaji munje e taehayŏ: Chosŏn rodongdang chungang wiwŏnhoe ch'aegim il'gundŭl kwa han tamhwa, 1986-nyŏn 7-wŏl 15-il" [On some problems arising in Subject Thought instruction: a talk with the responsible officials in the Central Committee of the Workers' Party of Korea, June 15, 1986]. *Kŭlloja*, July 1987, 3-20.

_____. "Chuch'e sasang ŭn illyu ŭi chinbojŏk sasang ŭl kyesŭng hago paltchŏn sik'in sasangida" [Subject Thought is a body of thought which has inherited and developed mankind's progressive thought]. In *Kim Chŏng-il sŏnjip* 8. Chosŏn rodongdang ch'ulp'ansa. Pyongyang, 1992. 429-431.

_____. "Inmin kundae rŭl tŏuk kanghwa hamyŏ ch'ongdae ro hyŏngmyŏng ŭi chonggukchŏk sŭngni-rŭl irukhae nagaja" [Let us strengthen the People's Army more and bring about the final victory of revolutionary through the barrels of our guns]. In *Kim Chŏng-il sŏnjip* 18. Chosŏn rodongdang ch'ulp'ansa. Pyongyang, 2012. 175-183.

_____. "Kimilsŏngjuŭi ŭi tokch'angsŏng ŭl olk'e insik halde taehayŏ" [On properly grasping the originality of Kimilsungism]. In *Kim Chŏng-il sŏnjip* 7. Chosŏn rodongdang ch'ulp'ansa. Pyongyang, 2011. 475-482.

_____. "Maksŭ-reninjuŭi wa chuch'e sasang ŭi kich'i rŭl nop'i tŭlgo naagaja: K'al Maksŭ t'ansaeng 165-tol mit' sŏgŏ 100-tol e chŭŭm hayŏ" [Let us go forth holding high the banner of Marxism-Leninism and Subject Thought: In commemoration of the 165th anniversary of Karl Marx's birth and the 100th anniversary of his passing]. *Kŭlloja*, May 1983, 2-22.

_____. "Rodong haengjŏng saŏp ŭl tŏuk kaesŏn kanghwa halde e taehayŏ" [On further improving and strengthening the work of labor administration]. *Kŭlloja*, December 1989, 3-25.

_____. "On sahoe rŭl Kimilsŏngjuŭihwa hagi wihan tang sasang saŏp ŭi tangmyŏn han myŏt' kaji kwaŏp e taehayŏ: Chŏn'guk tang sŏnjŏn il'gun kangsŭphoe esŏ han kyŏllon, 1974-nyŏn 2-wŏl 19-il" [On some tasks facing the Party's ideological endeavor to permeate all of society in Kimilsungism: Conclusion given at a training course for Party propaganda officials from the whole country, February 19, 1974]. In *Kim Chŏng-il sŏnjip* 4. Rodongdang ch'ulp'ansa. Pyongyang, 1994. 7-66.

REFERENCES

———. "Sahoejuŭi kŏnsŏl ŭi ryŏksajŏk kyohun kwa uri tang ŭi ch'ongnosŏn: Chosŏn rodongdang chungang wiwŏnhoe ch'aegim il'gun'dŭl kwa han tamha, 1992-nyŏn 1-wŏl 3-il" [Our party's general line and the historical lessons of socialist construction: A talk with the responsible officials in the Korean Workers' Party Central Committee, January 3, 1992]. In *Kim Chŏng-il sŏnjip* 12. Chosŏn rodongdang ch'ulp'ansa. Pyongyang, 1997. 275-310.

———. "Sahoejuŭi sasangjŏk kich'o e kwanhan myŏt' kaji munje e taehayŏ: Chosŏn rodongdang chungangwiwŏnhoe ch'aegim il'gundŭl ap' esŏ han yŏnsŏl, 1990-nyŏn 5-wŏl 30-il" [On some problems regarding the ideological basis of socialism: A speech before responsible officials of the Korean Workers' Party Central Committee, May 30, 1990]. In *Kim Chŏng-il sŏnjip* 10. Chosŏn rodongdang ch'ulp'ansa. Pyongyang, 1997. 88-115.

Kim Pong-hŭi. "Chuch'ehyŏng ŭi p'i ga kkŭllŭn simjangdŭl" [Hearts boiling with Subject-type blood]. *Ch'ŏllima*, July 1974, 33-37.

Kim Sang-hyŏn, Kim Kwang-hŏn. *Taejung chŏngch'i yong'ŏ sajŏn* [Dictionary of common political terms]. Chosŏn rodongdang ch'ulp'ansa. Pyongyang, 1957.

Kim Ŭl-ch'ŏn. "Changbaek kŭn'gŏji e issŏsŏ choguk kwangbokhoe chojik ŭi hwaktaehwa wa kŭ ŭi yŏkhal" [The expansion of the Homeland Liberation Association in the Changbaek base area and its role]. *Kŭlloja*, June 1960, 51-56.

Kim Yang-sŏn. "Ch'ŏrhak ŭi kibon munje" [Fundamental philosophical problems]. *Kŭlloja*, July 1962, 43-45.

Kim Yŏng-nam. "Kyŏngae hanŭn suryŏng Kim Il-sŏng tongji ŭi yŏngsaeng pulmyŏl ŭi chuch'e sasang ŭn uri sidae ŭi widaehan segyejŏk sajo" [The beloved leader Comrade Kim Il Sung's eternal and immortal Subject Thought is a great global trend of our time]. *Kŭlloja*, April 1974, 26-33.

"Kyŏngae hanŭn suryŏng Kim Il-sŏng tongji kkesŏ chesi hasin widaehan 10-dae chŏnggang ŭl chŏljŏhi kwanch'ŏl haja" [Let us thoroughly implement the great 10 principles which the beloved Leader

Comrade Kim Il Sung has presented to us]. *Rodong Sinmun*, 10 December 1967.

"Kyŏngae hanŭn suryŏng Kim Il-sŏng tongji ŭi hyŏngmyŏng sasang ŭn chuch'e sidae ŭi yogu rŭl panyŏng hayŏ naon saeropko tokch'angjŏgin widaehan sasang" [The beloved leader Comrade Kim Il Sung's revolutionary thought is a new, original and great body of thought that reflects the demands of the Era of the Subject]. *Kŭlloja*, July 1974, 9-16.

Kyŏngje sajŏn [Economic dictionary]. Sahoe kwahak ch'ulp'ansa. Pyongyang, 1970.

"Maksŭ-reninjuŭi riron ŭi ch'angjojŏk sŭpdŭk ŭl wihayŏ" [For the creative acquisition of Marxist-Leninist theory]. *Kŭlloja*, October 1955, 3-10.

"Munhak esŏ ŭi chuch'e hwangnip kwa sahoejuŭi aegukchuŭi kyoyang ŭi kanghwa rŭl wihayŏ" [For the establishment of the subject in literature and the strengthening of socialist-patriotic education]. *Chosŏn Munhak*, July 1966, 2-3.

O Chin-u. "Uri tang ŭn widaehan chuch'e sasang e ŭi hayŏ chido toenŭn hyŏngmyŏngjŏgin tang ida" [Our party is a revolutionary party guided by the great Subject Thought]. *Kŭlloja*, October 1975, 22-40.

O Hyŏn-ch'ŏl. *Sŏn'gun kwa minjok ŭi unmyŏng* [Military-first and the nation's fate]. P'yŏngyang ch'ulp'ansa. Pyongyang, 2007.

Paek Kyu-hwan. "Kyosu saŏp esŏ ŭi hyŏngsikchuŭi t'oech'i haja!" [Let's eliminate formalism in instruction!] *Kyowŏn Sinmun*, 24 September 1955.

Paek Pong. *Illyu haebang ŭi kusŏng Kim Il-sŏng wŏnsu* [Marshal Kim Il Sung, liberator of mankind]. Inmun kwahaksa. Tokyo, 1972.

_____. *Minjok ŭi t'aeyang Kim Il-sŏng changgun* [The sun of the nation, General Kim Il Sung]. In 2 volumes. Inmunkwahaksa. Pyongyang, 1968-1969.

Pak Chong-sik. "Pak Yŏn-am ŭi sasiljuŭi munhak" [Pak Yŏn-am's realistic literature]. *Chosŏn Munhak*, December 1955, 140-158.

REFERENCES

_____. "Uri munhak esŏ chuch'e ŭi hwangnip kwa minjokchŏk t'ŭksŏng" [On national characteristics and the establishment of the subject in our literature]. *Chosŏn Munhak*, February 1961, 97-111.

Pak Chong-t'aek. "Tangsaenghwal e chuindapge ch'amga hara" [Participate in party life like a master]. *Rodong Sinmun*, 5 February 1954.

Pak T'ae-hwa. "Yi. Bŭ. Ssŭttallin" [J. V. Stalin]. *Cho-Sso Ch'insŏn*, April 1953, 7-13.

Ra Tong-sik. "Widaehan suryŏngnim ŭi hyŏngmyŏng sasang ŭn kajang chŏnghwakhan kwahakchŏk-kongsanjuŭi riron" [The Great Leader's revolutionary thought is the most accurate theory of scientific communism]. *Ch'ŏllima*, November-December 1974, 17-19.

Ri Chŏng-gu. "Uri simunhak ŭi che munje" [Problems in our poetry]. *Chosŏn Munhak*, August 1955, 128-148.

Ri Ho-il. "Chuch'e ŭi choguk, manse!" [Long live the homeland of the subject!] *Chosŏn Munhak*, August-September 1971, 11-13.

Ri Ki-yŏng. "Widaehan Ssŭttallin ŭn inmin-ŭi simjang-sok-e yŏngwŏnhi sara issŭl gŏsida" [The great Stalin will live on forever in the hearts of the masses]. *Cho-Sso Ch'insŏn* [Korean-Soviet friendship]. April 1953, 14-19.

Ri Sang-gŏn. "Chuch'e-ŭi saesidae-ga yŏllyŏtta!" [A new era of the subject has dawned!]. *Chosŏn Munhak*. April 1974, 36-39.

"Ro-nong tongmaeng ŭi kanghwa nŭn sahoejuŭi sŭngni ŭi chungyohan cho'gŏn" [The strengthening of the alliance between workers and farmers is an important condition for the victory of socialism]. *Rodong Sinmun*, 16 November 1955.

"Sahoejuŭi chinyŏng ŭi t'ongil ŭl suho hamyŏ kukche kongsanjuŭi undong ŭi tan'gyŏl ŭl kanghwa haja" [Let us protect the unity of the socialist camp while strengthening the solidarity of the international communist movement]. *Kŭlloja*, February 1963, 3-7.

"Sahoejuŭijŏk aegukchuŭi wa ryŏksa kyoyang" [Socialist patriotism and history education]. *Kŭlloja*, 20 November 1964, 2-8.

"Sasangjŏn ŭi p'osŏng ŭl himch'age ullimyŏ ch'oehu sŭngni rŭl wihan t'ujaeng e taejung ŭl chŏkkŭk pullŏ irŭk'yŏ nagaja" [Let the opening shots of ideological war ring out strongly, and let us aggressively call the masses to start the struggle for final victory]. *Chosŏn Nyŏsŏng*, June 2014, 50-51.

"Siljŏng e matke handanŭn kŏs ŭn muŏs ŭl ŭimi hanŭn'ga?" [What does it mean to do things in accordance with actual circumstances?]. *Ch'ŏllima*, December 2012, 38.

Sin Chin-gyun. "Chuch'e sasang ŭn kongsanjuŭijŏk chaju, charip ŭi sasang ida" [Subject thought is a practical ideology of communist autonomy and independence]. *Kŭlloja*, 5 October 1965, 7-21.

Sin Ku-hyŏn. "Yŏn-am Pak Chi-wŏn e taehayŏ" [On Pak Yŏn-am]. *Chosŏn Munhak*, January 1956, 177-183.

Sŏk In-hae. "Chuch'e-e taehan saenggak" [Thoughts on the Subject]. *Chosŏn Munhak*, June 1961, 78-81.

Song Jŏng-u. "Kyogwasŏ ŭi chil ŭl nop'igi wihayŏ" [For raising the quality of textbooks]. *Kŭlloja*, June 1962, 38-42.

"Suryŏngnim kke kkŭt' ŏpsi ch'ungsŏng tahanŭn kŏs ŭn chuch'ehyŏng ŭi kongsanjuŭi hyŏngmyŏngga ŭi kajang kibonjŏgin p'umsŏng" [Showing endless loyalty to the Leader is the most basic character of the Subject-type communist]. *Kŭlloja*, May-June 1974, 8-12.

"Tang ŭi yuil sasang ŭro tŏuk ch'ŏljŏhi mujang haja" [Let us arm ourselves more thoroughly with the party's unitary ideology]. *Kŭlloja*, April 1968, 2-12.

"Uri tang ŭi chojik sasangjŏk kanghwa paltchŏn esŏ ryŏksajŏk ŭiŭi rŭl kajinŭn chŏnwŏn hoeŭi" [A joint plenum of historical significance for the development of the organizational and ideological consolidation of our party]. *Kŭlloja*, 20 December 1962, 2-25.

"Uri tang ŭi chuch'e sasang kwa kŭ widaehan saenghwallyŏk" [Our party's Subject Thought and its great life force]. *Kŭlloja*, June 1968, 2-11.

"Uri tang ŭi widaehan chuch'e sasang kwa chaju, charip, chawi ŭi hyŏngmyŏngjŏk rosŏn" [Our party's great Subject Thought and the revolutionary line of autonomy, independence and self-defense]. *Rodong Sinmun*, 18 April 1968.

Wiedaehan chuch'e sasang ch'ongsŏ [Great Subject Thought series]. In 10 volumes. Sahoe kwahak ch'ulp'ansa. Pyongyang, 1985.

"Widaehan Renin ŭi hyŏngmyŏng sasang ŭn sŭngni hago itta" [The great Lenin's revolutionary thought is winning]. *Rodong Sinmun*, 22 April 1968.

Widaehan suryŏng Kim Il-sŏng taewŏnsunim hyŏngmyŏng ryŏksa: chung-4 [The Revolutionary History of the Great Leader Marshal Kim Il Sung: Middle 4]. Kyoyuk tosŏ ch'ulp'ansa. Pyongyang, 2003.

Wŏn Hyŏng-guk. "Tang ŭi kunjung rosŏn ŭi kwanch'ŏl kwa il'gun'dŭl ŭi kunjung kwanjŏm" [The implementation of the party's mass line and the cadres' view of the masses]. *Kŭlloja*, 1 February 1958. 33-42.

SOURCES IN KOREAN (ROK)

Cho Kap-che. *Pak Chŏng-hŭi ŭi kyŏljŏngjŏk sungandŭl* [Park Chung Hee's decisive moments]. Guiparang. Seoul, 2009.

Han Ki-hong. *Chinbo ŭi kŭnŭl* [In the shadow of progressiveness]. Sidae chŏngsin. Seoul, 2012.

Hwang Jang Yop (Hwang Chang-yŏp). *Hoegorok: Na nŭn yŏksa ŭi chilli rŭl poatta* [Memoirs: I saw the true principles of history]. Sidae chŏngsin. Seoul, 2006.

———. *Ŏdum ŭi p'yŏn i toen haetbyŏt' ŭn ŏdum ŭl palkhil su ŏpta* [Sunshine which has allied itself with darkness cannot shed light on it]. Wŏlgan Chosŏn sa. Seoul, 2001.

———. *Pukhan ŭi chinsil kwa hŏwi* [North Korea's truth and untruth]. Institute of National Unification Policy. Seoul, 1998.

Hwang Sun-wŏn. *K'ain ŭi huye* [The Descendants of Cain, 1954]. Munhakkwachisŏngsa. Seoul, 2014.

Hyŏn Su. *Chŏkchi'i yungnyŏn Pukhanŭi mundan* [North Korea's literary scene under six years of red rule]. Kungmin sasang chidowŏn. Seoul, 1952.

Kim Tae-ryŏng. *Yŏksa rosŏ ŭi 5.18* [May 18 as history]. In 5 volumes. B-Bong Books. Seoul, 2013.

Kim Yŏng-hwan. *Kim Yŏng-hwan, Sidae chŏngsin ŭl malhada* [Kim Younghwan discusses the spirit of the age]. Sidae chŏngsin. Seoul, 2012.

Kim Yŏng-su et al. *Kim Chŏng-il sidae ŭi pukhan* [North Korea in the Kim Jong Il era]. Samsŏng kyŏngje yŏn'guso. Seoul, 1997.

Lee Myung Bak (Yi Myŏng-bak). *Taet'ongnyŏng ŭi sigan, 2008-2013* [Time spent as president, 2008-2013]. Random House Korea. Seoul, 2015.

O Il-hwan. "Pukhan ŭi sŏn'gun chŏngch'i ŭi hyŏnhwang kwa chaengjŏm punsŏk" [An analysis of the present state and problems of North Korea's military-first politics]. *At'ae chaengjŏm-kwa yŏn'gu*, Spring 2006, 95-118.

Pak Chi-hyang et al. *Haebang chŏnhusa ŭi chaeinsik* [A new appraisal of the time before and after liberation]. In 2 volumes. Ch'aek sesang. Seoul, 2006.

Paek Hak-sun. *Pukhan kwŏllyŏk ŭi yŏksa: sasang, chŏngch'esŏng, kujo* [The history of power in North Korea: ideology, legitimacy, structure]. Hanul. Seoul, 2010.

Pak Hong. *Redŭ bairŏsŭ* [Red virus]. Kŏmok. Seoul, 1997.

Pak Kap-dong. *Pak Hŏn-yŏng*. In'gangsa. Seoul, 1983.

Park Chung Hee (Pak Chŏng-hŭi). *Chungdan hanŭn cha nŭn sŭngni haji mot handa: Pak Chŏng-hŭi taet'ongnyŏng yŏnsŏljip* [He who does not finish cannot taste victory: a collection of President Park Chung Hee's speeches]. Hallim. Seoul, 1968.

———. "Sŏngsŏ-rŭl ingnŭndanŭn myŏngmok arae ch'otbul ŭl humch'inŭn haengwi ka chŏngdang hal su ŏpta" [The theft of a candle cannot be justified in the name of reading a sacred book]. In *Pak Chŏng-hŭi taet'ongnyŏng sŏnjip* [The Selected Works of President Park Chung Hee] 4. Jimungak. Seoul, 1969. 13-22.

REFERENCES

"Pukhan Kim Chŏng-ŭn 2014-nyŏn sinnyŏnsa chŏnmun" [The full text of North Korea's Kim Jong Un's new year's message of 2014]. *YTN*, 2 January 2014.

Ryu Gŭn-il, Hong Chin-p'yo. *Chisŏng kwa pan chisŏng* [Intellect and anti-intellect]. Guiparang. Seoul, 2005.

Sin Il-ch'ŏl. *Pukhan 'chuch'e ch'ŏrhak' pip'anj'ŏk punsŏk* [A critical analysis of North Korea's 'Subject Philosophy']. Sahoe paltchŏn yŏn'guso. Seoul, 1987.

———. *Pukhan chuch'e sasang ŭi hyŏngsŏng kwa soet'oe* [Formation and decline of North Korea's Subject Thought]. Saenggak ŭi namu. Seoul, 2004.

Sŏ Chae-jin. "Chuch'e sasang ŭi hyŏngsŏng gwa pyŏnhwa e taehan saeroun punsŏk" [A new analysis of the formation and change of Subject Thought]. Korean Institute of National Unification. Seoul, 2001.

Yi Myŏng-jun. *Kŭ dŭl ŭn ŏttŏk'e chusap'a ga toeŏtnŭnga: han NL undongga ŭi hoego wa sŏngch'al* [How they became Subject Thought Group members: Memoir and self-reflection of a member of the NL movement]. Bao Books. Seoul, 2012.

Yi Pŏm-sŏk. *Minjok-kwa ch'ŏngnyŏn* [Nation and youth]. Koryŏ munhwasa. Seoul, 1948.

Yi Yŏng-hun. *Taehan minguk yŏksa* [History of the Republic of Korea]. Guiparang. Seoul, 2013.

Yim Ŭn. *Kim Il-sŏng chŏngjŏn* [The true story of Kim Il Sung]. Okch'ŏn ch'ulp'ansa. Seoul, 1989.

SOURCES IN OTHER LANGUAGES

Ali, Tariq. "Diary." *London Review of Books*, 26 January 2012.

Armstrong, Charles K. *The North Korean Revolution, 1945-1950*. Cornell University Press. Ithaca, 2003.

―――――. "The Role and Influence of Ideology." In *North Korea in Transition*. Edited by Kyung-ae Park and Scott Snyder. Rowman & Littlefield. Plymouth, UK, 2013. 3-18.

―――――. *Tyranny of the Weak: North Korea and the World, 1950-1992*. Cornell University Press. Ithaca, 2013.

Aron, Raymond. "The End of the Ideological Age?" In *The End of Ideology Debate*. Edited by Chaim I. Weizman. Simon & Schuster. New York, 1968. 27-48.

―――――. *The Opium of the Intellectuals*. Translated by Terence Kilmartin. Norton & Co. New York, 1962.

Atkins, Everett Taylor. *Primitive Selves: Koreana in the Japanese Colonial Gaze, 1910-1945*. University of California Press. Berkelely, 2010.

Barner-Barry, Carol and Hody, Cynthia. "Soviet Marxism-Leninism as Mythology." *Political Psychology* 15, No. 4 (December 1994), 609-630.

Belke, Thomas, J. *Juche: A Christian Study of North Korea's State Religion*. Living Sacrifice Book Company. Bartlesville, OK, 2002.

Bell, Daniel and Aiken, Conrad. "Ideology — a Debate." In *The End of Ideology Debate*. Edited by Chaim I. Waxman. Simon & Schuster. New York, 1969. 259-280.

Borhi, László. *Hungary in the Cold War, 1945-1956*. Central European University Press. Budapest, 2004.

Brugger, Bill. *China: Liberation and Transformation, 1942-1962*. Rowman & Littlefield. Lanham, MD, 1981.

Brzezinski, Zbigniew K. *Ideology and Power in Soviet Politics*. Frederick A. Praeger. New York, 1962.

―――――. *The Soviet Bloc: Unity and Conflict*. Harvard University Press. Cambridge, Mass. 1970.

Buchheim, Hans. *Totalitäre Herrschaft: Wesen und Merkmale* [Totalitarian rule: Nature and characteristics]. Kösel Verlag. Munich, 1962.

Buzo, Adrian. *The Guerrilla Dynasty: Politics and Leadership in North Korea*. I.B. Tauris & Co. London, 1999.

Calkins, Laura M. *China and the First Vietnam War, 1947-54*. Routledge. New York, 2013.

REFERENCES

Cassel, Pär Kristoffer. *Grounds of Judgment: Extraterritoriality and Imperial Power in Nineteenth-Century China and Japan.* Oxford University Press. Oxford, 2012.

Cha, Victor. *The Impossible State: North Korea, Past and Future.* HarperCollins. New York, 2012.

Chen, Chen and Lee, Ji-Yong. "Making sense of North Korea: 'National Stalinism' in comparative-historical perspective." *Communist and Post-Communist Studies*, Vol. 40 (2007), 459-475.

Cohen, Jerome B. *Japan's Economy in War and Construction.* University of Minnesota Press. Minneapolis, 1949.

Complete Text of the Declaration of the Twelve Communist and Workers Parties, Meeting in Moscow, USSR, Nov. 14-16, 1957, on the Occasion of the Fortieth Anniversary of the Great October Socialist Revolution. New Century Publishers. New York, 1957.

Connor, Walker. *Ethnonationalism: The Quest for Understanding.* Princeton University Press. Princeton, 1994.

Cumings, Bruce. "The Corporate State." In *State and Society in Contemporary Korea.* Edited by Hagen Koo. The New Press. New York, 2004.

———. "Corporatism in North Korea." *The Journal of Korean Studies*, Vol. 4 (1982-1983), 269-294.

———. *Korea's Place in the Sun: A Modern History.* Updated. W.W. Norton & Co. New York, 2005.

———. *North Korea: Another Country.* The New Press. New York, 2004.

———. *Origins of the Korean War.* In 2 volumes. Princeton University Press. Princeton, 1990.

Daniels, Robert V. *Trotsky, Stalin and Socialism.* Westview Press. Boulder, CO, 1996.

"Die Entlarvung des Dogmatismus als einer Waffe der Parteifeinde" [The unmasking of dogmatism as a weapon of the Party's enemies]. *Neues Deutschland*, 8 August 1953.

Dittmer, Lowell. *Liu Shao-ch'i and the Chinese Cultural Revolution: The Politics of Mass Criticism.* University of California Press. Berkeley, California. 1974.

Drixler, Fabian. *Mabiki: Infanticide and Population Growth in Eastern Japan, 1660-1950.* University of California Press. Berkeley, 2013.

Eberstadt, Nicholas. "Western Aid: The Missing Link for North Korea's Economic Revival?" In *North Korea in Transition.* Edited by Kyung-Ae Park and Scott Snyder. Rowman & Littlefield. Plymouth, UK. 119-152.

Eckert, Carter *et al. Korea Old and New: A History.* Iljokak. Seoul, 1991.

Everard, John. *Only Beautiful, Please: A British Diplomat in North Korea.* The Brookings Institution. Baltimore, 2012.

Fletcher, William Miles. *Search for a New Order: Intellectuals and Fascism in Prewar Japan.* University of North Carolina Press. Chapel Hill, NC, 1982.

Frank, Rüdiger. "North Korea's Autonomy 1965-2015." *Pacific Affairs,* Vol. 87, No. 4 (December 2014), 790-799.

———. *Nordkorea: Innenansichten eines totalen Staates* [North Korea: A total state seen from the inside]. Deutsche Verlags-Anstalt. Munich, 2014.

Gabroussenko, Tatiana. *Soldiers on the Cultural Front: Developments in the Early History of North Korean Literature and Literary Policy.* University of Hawai'i Press. Honolulu, 2010.

Gauthier, Brandon. "'Bring All the Troops Home Now!' The American-Korean Friendship and Information Center and North Korean Public Diplomacy, 1971-1976." Unpublished manuscript, 2014.

Germino, Dante. "Der italienische Faschismus in vergleichender Perspektive" [Italian fascism in comparative perspective]. In *Theorien über den Faschismus* [Theories about fascism]. Edited by Ernst Nolte. Kiepenheuer & Witsch. Cologne, 1967. 426-448.

Gourevitch, Philip. "Letter From North Korea: Alone in the Dark." *The New Yorker,* 8 September 2003.

Graham, Loren R. *Science and Philosophy in the Soviet Union.* Knopf. New York, 1972.

Gregor, A. James. *Italian Fascism and Developmental Dictatorship.* Princeton University Press. Princeton, 1979.

Groys, Boris. *Gesamtkunstwerk Stalin: Die gespaltene Kultur in der Sowjetunion* [Total artwork Stalin: the divided culture in the Soviet Union]. Carl Hanser Verlag. Munich, 1988.

———. *Das kommunistische Postskriptum* [The communist post-script]. Suhrkamp. Frankfurt am Main, 2006.

Haggard, Stephan and Noland, Marcus. *Famine in North Korea: Markets, Aid and Reform.* Columbia University Press. New York, 2007.

Han Hongkoo. "Colonial Origins of *Juche*: The Minsaengdan Incident of the 1930s and the Birth of the North Korea-China Relationship." In *Origins of North Korea's Juche.* Edited by Jae-Jung Suh. Lexington Books. Lanham, MD, 2013. 33-62.

Heffer, Simon. *Like the Roman: The Life of Enoch Powell.* Weidenfeld & Nicolson. London, 1998.

Hinton, Harold C. *An Introduction to Chinese Politics.* Holt, Rinehart and Winston/Praeger. New York, 1978.

Hsiung, James Chieh. *Ideology and Practice: The Evolution of Chinese Communism.* Frederick A. Praeger. New York, 1970.

Ienaga, Saburo. *Pacific War, 1931-1945.* Pantheon Books. New York, 1979.

Jacobs, Norman. *The Korean Road to Modernization and Development.* University of Illinois Press. Urbana, IL, 1985.

Jäger, Herbert. *Verbrechen unter totalitärer Herrschaft: Studien zur nationalsozialistischer Kriminalität* [Crime under totalitarian rule: Studies on national socialist criminality]. Suhrkamp. Frankfurt am Main, 1982.

Jameson, Sam. "Key is Self-Reliance: Korea Launches 'Purification' Drive." *Los Angeles Times*, 20 July 1976.

Kang, Allan. "The Lens of Juche: Understanding the Reality of North Korean Policymakers." *Review of International Affairs*, Autumn 2003, Vol. 3, Issue 1, 41-63.

Kim, Hakjoon. *The Domestic Politics of Korean Unification: Debates on the North in the South, 1948-2008.* Jimoondang. Seoul, 2010.

Kim Hyung-A. "The Eve of Park's Military Rule: The Intellectual Debate on National Reconstruction, 1960-61." *East Asian History*, Number 25/26 (June/December 2003), 113-140.

Kim, Hyung-A and Sorenson, Clark W. *Reassessing the Park Chung Hee Era, 1961-1979*. University of Washington. Seattle, 2011.

Kim Il Sung. *On Juche in Our Revolution*. Vol. 1. Foreign Languages Publishing House. Pyongyang, 1975.

"Kim Il Sung shushō 'tōitsu' de kataru" [Premier Kim Il Sung talks 'unification']. *Mainichi Shimbun*, 19 September 1972.

Kim, Suk-Young. *Illusive Utopia: Theater, Film, and Everyday Performance in North Korea*. University of Michigan Press. Ann Arbor, 2010.

Kim, Sung Chull. *North Korea under Kim Jong Il: From Consolidation to Systemic Dissonance*. State University of New York Press. Albany, 2006.

Kim, Suzy. *Everyday Life in the North Korean Revolution, 1945-1950*. Cornell University Press. Ithaca, NY, 2013.

Knight, Nick. "The Form of Mao Zedong's 'Sinification' of Communism." *The Australian Journal of Chinese Affairs* 9 (January 1983), 17-33.

_____. *Mao Zedong on Dialectical Materialism*. M.E. Sharpe. Armonk, 1990.

Kobayashi Toshiaki. *"Shutai" no yukue: Nihon kindai shisōshi e no ichi shikaku* [The course of the word *shutai*: A perspective on the modern history of Japanese thought]. Kodansha. Tokyo, 2010.

Koh, B(yung) C(hul). "An Elusive Quest with Mixed Results." *Pacific Affairs* 87, No. 4 (December 2014), 809-814.

_____. "North Korea and its Quest for Autonomy." *Pacific Affairs*, Vol. 38, No. 3/4 (Autumn 1965-Winter 1965-1966), 294-306.

_____. "The North Korean Political System Under Kim Jong Il: A Comparative Perspective." In *North Korea in Transition and Policy Choices: Domestic Structure and External Relations*. Kyungnam University Press. Seoul, 1999.

Koschmann, J. Victor. *Revolution and Subjectivity in Postwar Japan*. University of Chicago Press. Chicago, 1996.

Kovrig, Bennett. "Hungary." In *Communism in Eastern Europe*. Edited by Teresa Rakowska-Harmstone. Indiana University Press. Bloomington, 1979. 86-114.

Kronenberg, Clive. "Manifestations of Humanism in Revolutionary Cuba: Che and the Principle of Universality." *Latin American Perspectives* 36, No. 2 (March 2009), 66-80.

Kuark, Yoon T. "North Korea's Industrial Development during the Post-War Period." In *North Korea Today*. Edited by Robert Scalapino. Frederick A. Praeger. New York, 1963. 51-64.

Lankov, Andrei. *Crisis in North Korea: The Failure of Destalinization, 1956*. University of Hawai'i Press. Honolulu, 2007.

_____. *From Stalin to Kim Il Sung: The Formation of North Korea 1945-1960*. Rutgers University Press. New Brunswick, 2002.

Large, David Clay. *Nazi Games: The Olympics of 1936*. W.W. Norton & Co. New York, 2007.

Lee, Chong-sik. *Japan and Korea: The Political Dimension*. Hoover Institution Press. Stanford, 1985.

_____. *Korean Workers' Party: A Short History*. Hoover Institution Press. Stanford, 1978.

Lee, Chong-sik, Yoo Se-hee. *North Korea in Transition*. University of California Press. Berkeley, 1991.

Lenin, V.I. *"'Left-wing' Communism, an Infantile Disorder"* (1920). Foreign Languages Publishing House. Beijing, 1970.

Li Yuk-sa. *Juche! The Speeches and Writings of Kim Il Sung*. Foreword by Eldridge Cleaver. Grossman. New York, 1972.

Lie, John. *Zainichi (Koreans in Japan): Diasporic Nationalism and Post-Colonial Identity*. University of California Press. Berkeley, 2008.

McEachern, Patrick. *Inside the Red Box: North Korea's Post-Totalitarian Politics*. Columbia University Press. New York, NY, 2010.

McKenna, Joseph C. *Finding a Social Voice: The Church and Marxism in Africa*. Fordham University Press. New York, 1997.

Mao Zedong. "Rectify the Party's Style of Work" (1 February 1942). Marxists' International Archive.

Maretzki, Hans. *Kim-ismus in Nordkorea: Analyse des letzten DDR-Botschafters in Pjöngjang* [Kimism in North Korea: Analysis by the

GDR's last ambassador to Pyongyang]. Anita Tykve Verlag. Berlin, 2003.

Martin, Helmut. *Cult and Canon: The Origins and Development of State Maoism.* M.E. Sharpe. Armonk, NY. 1982.

März, Markus. *Nationale Sozialisten in der NSDAP: Strukturen, Ideologie, Publizistik und Biographien des nationalsozialistischen Straßer-Kreises von der AG Nordwest bis zum Kampf-Verlag 1925-1930* [National Socialists in the NSDAP: Structures, Ideology, Public Writings and Biographies of the National Socialist Strasser-Circle from the AG Nordwest to the Kampf Publishing House 1925-1930]. Ares Verlag. Graz, 2010.

Miller, Frank J. *Folklore for Stalin: Russian Folklore and Pseudofolklore of the Stalin Era.* M.E. Sharpe. New York, 1990.

Mortimer, Rex. *Indonesian Communism Under Sukarno: Ideology and Politics, 1959-1965.* Equinox Publishing. Jakarta, 2006.

Mudde, Cas. *The Ideology of the Extreme Right.* Manchester University Press. Manchester, 2003.

Myers, B(rian) R. *The Cleanest Race: How North Koreans See Themselves and Why It Matters.* Melville House Books. New York, 2009.

_____. *Han Sŏrya and North Korean Literature.* Cornell East Asia Series. Ithaca, NY, 1994.

_____. "Ideology as Smokescreen: North Korea's Juche Thought." *Acta Koreana,* December 2008, 161-182.

_____. "Mother of all Mothers: The Leadership Secrets of Kim Jong Il." *The Atlantic Monthly,* September 2004.

_____. "The Personality Cult of Kim Jong Un: Continuity and Change." *Journal of Peace and Unification,* Vol. 3 Number 2 (Fall 2013), 75-96.

_____. "The Watershed that Wasn't: Re-Evaluating Kim Il Sung's 'Juche Speech' of 1955." *Acta Koreana,* January 2006, 89-115.

_____. "Western Academia and the Word *Juche.*" *Pacific Affairs,* Vol. 87, No. 4 (December 2014), 779-789.

REFERENCES

Natsios, Andrew S. *The Great North Korean Famine: Famine, Politics and Foreign Policy*. United States Institute of Peace. Washington, DC, 2001.

Nietzsche, Friedrich. *Morgenröte: Gedanken über die moralischen Vorurteile* [Daybreak: Reflections on moral prejudices]. Anaconda. Cologne, 2011.

Oberdorfer, Don. *The Two Koreas: A Contemporary History*. Revised and updated. Basic Books. New York, 2001.

Paige, Glenn D., and Lee, Dong Jun. "The Post-War Politics of Communist Korea." In *North Korea Today*. Edited by Robert Scalapino. Frederick A. Praeger. New York, 1963. 17-29.

Park Chung Hee. *Our Nation's Path: Ideology of Social Reconstruction*. Hollym. Seoul, 1970.

Park, Han S. *North Korea: Ideology, Politics, Economy*. Prentice Hall. Upper Saddle River, NJ, 1995.

———. *North Korea: The Politics of Unconventional Wisdom*. Lynne Rienner. Boulder, 2002.

Pätzold, Kurt and Weißbecker, Manfred. *Geschichte der NSDAP: 1920 bis 1945* [History of the NSDAP: 1920-1945]. PapyRossa Verlag. Cologne, 2009.

Pepper, Suzanne. *Radicalism and Education Reform in Twentieth Century China: The Search for an Ideal Development Model*. Cambridge University Press. Cambridge, 1996.

Person, James F. "New Evidence on North Korea in 1956." Cold War International History Project Bulletin, Issue 16 (Spring 2008), 447-454.

———. "We Need Help from Outside: The North Korean Opposition Movement of 1956." Working Paper #52 (August 2006), 2-50.

Petrov, Leonid. "Turning Scholars into Party Bureaucrats: North Korean Historiography in 1955-1958." *East Asian History*, No. 31 (June 2006), 101-124.

Pfabigan, Alfred. *Schlaflos in Pjöngjang: Vom gescheiterten Versuch, einen skeptischen Europäer zu einem Mitglied der Großen Roten Familie zu machen* [Sleepless in Pyongyang: On a failed effort to turn a skeptical European into a member of the Big Red Family]. Verlag Christian Brandstätter. Vienna, 1986.

Ree, Erik Van. *The Political Thought of Joseph Stalin: A Study in Twentieth Century Revolutionary Patriotism.* Routledge. Plymouth, UK, 2003.

Reed, Edward P. "Unlikely Partners in the Quest for Juche: Humanitarian Aid Agencies in North Korea." *Nautilus.* 2003.

Richter, Bernd Stevens. "Nature Mastered by Man: Ideology and Water in the Soviet Union," *Environment and History* 3, No. 1 (February 1997), 90.

Robinson, Joan. "Korean Miracle." *Monthly Review* 16, No. 8 (January 1965), 541-549.

Robinson, Michael. "National Identity and the Thought of Sin Ch'aeho: *Sadaejuuǔi* and *Chuch'e* in History and Politics." *The Journal of Korean Studies* 5 (1984). 121-142.

Saccone, Richard. *Negotiating with the North Koreans.* Hollym. Seoul, 2003.

Salisbury, Harrison. *A Time of Change: A Reporter's Tale of Our Time.* HarperCollins. New York, 1988.

Scalapino, Robert. (Ed.) *North Korea Today.* Frederick A. Praeger. New York, 1963.

Scalapino, Robert and Lee, Chong-sik. *Communism in Korea.* In 2 volumes. University of California Press. Berkeley, 1972.

Schaefer, Bernd. "North Korean 'Adventurism' and China's Long Shadow, 1967-1972." Working Paper #44. Cold War International History Project. Washington DC, 2004.

_____. "Weathering the Sino-Soviet Conflict: The GDR and North Korea, 1949-1989." *Cold War International History Project Bulletin,* Issue 14/15 (Winter 2003-Spring 2004). 25-38.

Schlette, Heinz Robert. *Sowjethumanismus: Prämissen und Maximen kommunistischer Pädagogik* [Soviet humanism: Premises and maxims of communist pedagogics]. Kösel Verlag. Munich, 1960.

REFERENCES

Schmitt, Carl. *Der Begriff des Politischen* [The Concept of the Political, 1932]. Duncker & Humblot. West Berlin, 1963.

Schram, Stuart R. *The Political Thought of Mao Tse-tung.* Frederick A. Praeger. New York, 1963.

Schüddekopf, Otto-Ernst. *Linke Leute von rechts: Die nationalrevolutionären Minderheiten und der Kommunismus in der Weimarer Republik* [Left-wingers of the right: The national-revolutionary minorities and communism in the Weimar Republic]. W. Kohlhammer Verlag. Stuttgart, 1960.

Schurmann, Franz. *Ideology and Organization in Communist China.* University of California Press. Berkeley, 1971.

Service, Robert. *A History of Modern Russia: from Nicholas II to Vladimir Putin.* Harvard University Press. Cambridge, MA, 2003.

Shimotomai, Nobuo. "Pyongyang in 1956." Cold War International History Project Bulletin. Issue 16 (2007/2008), 455-463.

Shin, Gi-wook. *Ethnic Nationalism in Korea: Genealogy, Politics and Legacy.* Stanford University Press. Stanford, California. 2006.

Sigal, Leon. *Disarming Strangers: Nuclear Diplomacy with North Korea.* Princeton University Press. Princeton, 1998.

Slezkine, Yuri. "The USSR as a Communal Apartment, or How a Socialist State Promoted Ethnic Particularism." *Slavic Review*, Vol. 53, No. 2 (Summer, 1994). 414-452.

Sloterdijk, Peter. *Du mußt dein Leben ändern: Über Anthropotechnik* [You must change your life: On anthropotechnics]. Surkamp. Frankfurt am Main, 2011.

Smith, Hazel. "Reconstituting Korean security dilemmas." In *Reconstituting Korean Security: A Policy Primer.* United Nations University Press. Tokyo, 2007.

Song, Jiyoung. *Human Rights Discourse in North Korea: Post-Colonial, Marxist and Confucian Perspectives.* Routledge. London, 2014.

Spengler, Oswald. *Jahre der Entscheidung: Deutschland und die weltgeschichtliche Entwicklung* [Years of decision: Germany and world-historical development] (1933). Ares Verlag. Munich, 2007.

Springer, Chris. *North Korea Caught in Time: Images of War and Reconstruction*. Garnet Publishing. Reading, 2010.

Staritz, Dietrich. *Die Gründung der DDR: Von der sowjetischen Besatzungsherrschaft zum sozialistischen Staat* [The founding of the GDR: From Soviet occupation to socialist state]. Deutscher Taschenbuch Verlag. Munich, 1995.

Suh, Dae-Sook. *Kim Il Sung: North Korean Leader*. Columbia University Press. New York, 1994.

_____. *Korean Communism, 1945-1980: A Reference Guide to the Political System*. University of Hawaii Press. Honolulu, 1981.

Suh, Jae-Jung. (Ed.) *Origins of North Korea's Juche. Colonialism, War and Development*. Lexington Books. Plymouth, UK. 2013.

Szalontai, Balazs. *Kim Il Sung in the Khrushchev Era: Soviet-DPRK Relations and the Roots of North Korean Despotism, 1953-1964*. Woodrow Wilson Center Press. Washington, DC, 2005.

_____. "'You Have No Political Line of Your Own': Kim Il Sung and the Soviets, 1953-1964." Cold War International History Project Bulletin, Issue 14/15 (2003). 87-103.

Tertitskiy, Fyodor. "Soviet Officer Reveals Secrets of Mangyongdae." Dailynk.com. 2 January 2014.

Tian Chih-sung. "The Masses are the Makers of History." *Peking Review* 29, 21 July 1972, 7-11.

Tsou, Tang. *The Cultural Revolution and Post-Mao Reforms: A Historical Perspective*. University of Chicago Press. Chicago, 1986.

Unger, Aryeh L. *The Totalitarian Party: Party and People in Nazi Germany and Soviet Russia*. Cambridge University Press. Cambridge, 1974.

Wada, Haruki. *Kita Chōsen: yūgekitai kokka no genzai* [North Korea: the guerrilla state today]. Iwanami Shoten. Tokyo, 1998.

Warhol, Andy. *The Philosophy of Andy Warhol: From A to B and Back Again*. Picador. New York, 1977.

Wich, Richard. *Sino-Soviet Crisis Politics: A Study of Political Change and Communication*. Harvard East Asian Monographs 96. Cambridge, 1980.

Wilson, Sandra. *The Manchurian Crisis and Japanese Society, 1931-1933.* Routledge. London, 2002.

Winstanley-Chesters, Robert. *Environment, Politics and Ideology in North Korea: Landscape as Political Project.* Lexington Books. Lanham, MD, 2014.

Wong Siu-lun. *Sociology and Socialism in Contemporary China* (1979). Routledge. Abingdon, UK, 2005.

The World Historic Significance of the Juche Idea: Essays and Articles. Foreign Languages Publishing House. Pyongyang, 1975.

Yang, Key P., and Chee, Chang-Boh. "North Korean Educational System: 1945-Present." In *North Korea Today.* Edited by Robert Scalapino. Frederick A. Praeger. New York, 1963. 125-140.

Zagoria, David S. "Some Comparisons Between the Russian and Chinese Models." In *Communist Strategies in Asia: A comparative analysis of governments and parties.* Edited by Arthur Doak Barnett. Pall Mall. London, 1963.

Made in the USA
Las Vegas, NV
08 May 2025